Introduction to Youth Ministry

Introduction to Youth Ministry

John M. Dettoni

ZondervanPublishingHouse
Academic and Professional Books
Grand Rapids, Michigan

A Division of HarperCollins*Publishers*

Introduction to Youth Ministry
Copyright © 1993 by John M. Dettoni

Requests for information should be addressed to:
Zondervan Publishing House
Academic and Professional Books
Grand Rapids, Michigan 49530

Library of Congress Cataloging-in-Publication Data

Dettoni, John.
    Introduction to youth ministry / John M. Dettoni.
       p. cm.
    Includes bibliographical references.
    ISBN 0-310-57740-3 (alk. paper)
    1. Church work with teenagers. 2. Christian education of teenagers. I. Title.
    BV4447.D448   1993
    268'.433—dc20   93-21564
                                                    CIP

Cover design: Jeff Sharpton
Cover photograph: © C. Loumakis/Sharpshooters
Edited by William Carey Moore and James E. Ruark

Printed in the United States of America

93 94 95 96 97 98 / ❖   / 10 9 8 7 6 5 4 3 2 1

This edition is printed on acid-free paper and meets the American National Standards Institute Z39.48 standard.

To my wife, Carol McClenny Dettoni,
without whom life would be dull
and lonely, but with whom I have joy,
     companionship, and love.

"A wife of noble character who can find?
She is worth far more than rubies. . . .
A woman who fears the LORD
     is to be praised.
Give her the reward she has earned,
     and let her works bring
     her praise at the city gate"
                    (Prov. 31:10, 30–31).

Contents

Acknowledgments

After almost forty years of ministry—over thirty-one of them with my wife—and having spent much of that time in various forms of youth work and teaching youth ministry, I would need a very long list of people to acknowledge who have contributed to my understanding of youth and church-based youth ministry. But I would still need to single out several individuals and groups of people.

The first is my wife Carol, who has taught me what it is to think of youth, their needs, and the development of leadership in youth. With her encouragement and support this book is finally seeing the light of day. The second is our daughter Elizabeth Ann, who has taken several of my courses in her seminary education, but more importantly, has been a sensitive, perceptive, and intuitive youth worker, picking up principles of youth ministry from the air in our home and from watching her parents in action. To her, special thanks for helping take approximately five hundred pages of syllabus on youth ministry and make a book out of it. The third is our son David Benjamin, who has ministered in various cultures around the world. He has been a stimulus to articulate clearly the basics of youth ministry.

Fourth are the junior-highers at Lake Avenue Congregational Church, Pasadena, California, who allowed me to be their Sunday school teacher and youth worker for two years while I was in seminary. It was while working with them, many years ago, that I began to develop my basic philosophical foundations for effective youth ministry.

I also thank the many adult youth workers with whom I have ministered and the many students with whom I have interacted over fifteen years of college, graduate school, and seminary teaching. They have allowed me to crystallize my experiences into meaningful thoughts and have provided input and questions that have helped to sharpen my concepts and clarify ideas.

Finally, I thank God for the opportunity to have been involved with youth and to be a teacher of teachers of youth both here in this country and in other parts of the world. To God be all the glory! And may he use this book to help others become ever more effective in the spiritual formation, nurture, and discipleship of youth through an incarnational, agapic, and developmental approach to youth ministry.

Introduction

Almost all youth workers—whether they are paid, professional church staff or so-called volunteers recruited to help—go through the dreaded interview process. They stand (or sit) before a church committee that will dissect every word and thought. This is supposed to be a time when youth workers make clear what they believe and how they will do youth ministry. But have the youth workers clearly thought out *why* they do youth ministry, and what is the purpose of each element, that is, one's philosophy of youth work? This book will attempt to answer the philosophical questions of youth ministry.

Few youth workers expected the grilling they received when I was a member of the selection committee of my local church. But I believed that the questions we asked were important. No one should be involved in youth ministry until he or she can adequately answer them. By the end of this book, the reader will be exposed to the major philosophical issues in youth ministry and should have thought through at least these questions:

1. Tell us about your philosophy of youth ministry. Include why you think youth ministry is important, what its general goals should be, what the role of the youth leader should be, how youth ministry relates to the whole of the local church, and the role of the laity in youth ministry.
2. What are the key elements of a youth program? How do they relate to each other?
3. Briefly describe the major components in your view of youth ministry.
4. What is effective teaching? How do you define teaching? How does the Holy Spirit enter into your concept of teaching and learning?

11

5. If youth don't learn and grow spiritually, whose fault is it? What can *you* do about helping youth to learn?
6. Describe your leadership style. Are you casual, intense, a director, coach, or something else?
7. How do you go about planning?
8. If you are married, what is your spouse's view on youth ministry and, in particular, your involvement in youth ministry? What does your spouse feel about becoming involved in youth ministry with you?
9. Describe briefly some of your best teaching experiences, for example, experiences in which you felt you did very well as a teacher. What made it a good experience for you and for the learners?
10. What do you feel are the important theological issues of youth and how would you address them?
11. Of what does good youth programing consist? What does a good youth ministry look like? Describe attitudes, activities, and behaviors.
12. What are the relationships between organization, administration, programing, and leadership in youth ministry?
13. What will you look for to determine if youth ministry is successful?

Lest some think that this book is only for the "beginning" professional youth worker, let me emphasize that all youth workers, regardless of age and experience, can become more effective by rethinking their philosophy of youth ministry. Much instruction regarding ministry begins and ends with "how-to's," never asking crucial questions pertaining to its foundation.

In this book you will find a basic philosophy of youth ministry spelled out in elementary principles. You will encounter the concept of systems models applied to youth ministry. And you will be exposed to four basic elements of effective youth ministry along with essential principles of leadership development, administration and organization, camps and retreats, and evaluation.

Appendix A contains a sample handbook of how one church actually organized its youth ministry using the principles presented in this book. Appendix B is a long but not exhaustive bibliography of books that deal with youth ministry.

For our purposes, youth ministry deals with adolescence as the years spanning ages twelve through twenty-five—junior high, high school, and post-high school/college youth. Some churches have tried to place post-high school people in the adult department, but most of them usually discover that these people are not typically ready to be included as "adults." While there are tremendous developmental differences between younger and older adolescents, all have experienced the very great changes of puberty. Thus we believe that a church's youth ministry should cover this fourteen-year span.

It is my hope that the readers of this book will be stimulated both to think about and to practice youth ministry in order to be effective youth workers.

PART

I

Foundations of Youth Ministry

Part I examines three crucial, foundational concerns of youth ministry. Chapter 1 seeks to provide major principles and guidelines essential not only to youth programs but to all other Christian ministries. Three words describe the basic youth ministry philosophy: *incarnational*, *agapic*, and *developmental*. All other key words and concepts are built upon these three elements.

Chapter 2 looks at social systems models and applies this thinking to youth ministry. The thesis presented is that a model of youth ministry is the outgrowth of an articulated philosophy and a necessary step in the development of a program. By developing a model before developing a program, or by asking the questions that systems model thinking suggests, we will be more likely to establish an effective youth ministry. This chapter concludes with a list of criteria for evaluating a youth ministry model.

Chapter 3 focuses on the youth worker. Although everything here is applicable to volunteer youth workers as well, the chapter is written primarily with the professional, full-time youth minister in mind. This chapter is intended as an encouragement and a stimulus for going further in becoming a person whom God has called to minister to the exciting age groups of adolescence.

1

Philosophy of Youth Ministry

Most often youth workers—and especially youth pastors—are very pragmatic and oriented to the program: fun and games, Bible studies, camps, retreats, social activities, and such things. It is a little difficult to talk about philosophy and theology with youth workers in the morning when they know they are taking care of fifteen junior highers that same evening. Further, youth workers have a reputation not of being "thinkers" but doers, being more interested in how to do youth ministry than in the reasons and basis of it.

But this is the problem. The tyranny of the immediate forces many to neglect the weightier matters of youth ministry. Probably the most crucial issue in youth ministry is *why* there should be a youth ministry. This basic question precedes which programs should be operated and the "how to's" of programming. The question of philosophy of youth ministry goes directly to the heart of youth ministry operations and asks the foundational questions.

The oft-repeated statement is, "I don't have a youth ministry philosophy and I don't need one." Wrong! Everyone in youth ministry has a philosophy of youth ministry. It just may not be articulated in so many words. Given a Socratic dialogue with a knowledgeable person, a youth worker would be able to state at least an embryonic rationale for what he or she does in youth work. Such being the case, youth workers need to consciously reflect upon what they do, asking the "why do I do

> *The tyranny of the immediate forces many to neglect the weightier matters of youth ministry. Probably the most crucial issue in youth ministry is why there should be a youth ministry.*

these things?" question. Second, they must articulate their rationale in a coherent, consistent, and unified manner so that some sense can be made of their reasoning. Third, they must critically evaluate their philosophy, accepting feedback for corrections that may be needed. Fourth, they need to operate it, that is, use it day by day. And last, they need to continually refine it through reflection on what has been put into operation, through feedback from evaluation, and through critical responses from youth (the end users), other adult youth workers, parents of youth involved, church boards and committees, and finally the pastoral staff.

The words *philosophy* and *philosopher* do not occur in the Old Testament and are each used only once in the New Testament (Col. 2:8; Acts 17:18). In 1 Corinthians 1:20, the New International Version uses the word *philosopher* to translate a Greek word that literally means "debater" or "one who argues or discusses,"

which by implication is what a philosopher does. All three of these references have negative connotations. Usage in our day, however, is not restricted to endless disputes, arguments, and debates. Rather, the word *philosophy* indicates a world-and-life view. One's philosophy is a cognitive, conscious commitment regarding how one is going to interpret reality. It asks questions about what reality is and of what it is composed. A philosophy also asks about knowledge and how one knows anything and puts forth the basic values questions: What is important? What is life for? Why do I do the things that I do?

What will a philosophy do for a person? For a youth worker? Does it have pragmatic value? Its value lies not in what it will do in youth ministry programing, but rather, what it will do for youth workers. They will be able to make better, more informed choices, and will be able to define what they are doing. They will set outcomes and goals that are driven by values and truly important things, rather than by the need to meet timetables. And they will be able to relate Scripture to how youth are to be taught, thus working with the Holy Spirit rather than against him. A philosophy of youth ministry is a personal "North Star," giving guidance to program implementation and development and help for evaluation.

Ultimately, a philosophy of youth ministry will answer the dual questions: What is worth dying for? and What is, therefore, worth teaching and leading? A philosophy of youth ministry goes for the passion and values that drive a youth ministry. It states unequivocally what the "gusto" is on which youth ministry is built.

Several portions of Scripture are suggestive of a basic philosophy or statement of foundational values. Read these over to uncover the essential elements in each portion: Acts 20:24; Romans 1:16–17; Ephesians 4:11–16; and Colossians 1:9–10, 28–29. What are the values inherent in each of these portions? What is the writer-speaker's view of God, view of people, goal or outcome of teaching and leading, and view of the role of the leader-teacher?

ELEMENTS OF A PHILOSOPHY

A philosophy of youth ministry should encompass at least several critical elements. Following is a list of questions to be answered concerning each element. These should be conceived as building blocks for the youth worker to develop his or her own philosophy of youth ministry. They are not separate items as such but integrated into the fundamental principles of a youth ministry philosophy.

1. *View of God.* Who is God? Is he the ultimate reality and not a part of creation? Do humans create God in their image or is God totally differentiated from nature and all of humanity? Is God like us or are we like God?

2. *View of Scripture.* Is Scripture viewed as the final, trustworthy, and utterly reliable revelation of God? Or is Scripture just another "holy book" similar to the Koran, the Tibetan Book of the Dead, or others? Or is it merely a human book that talks about God without ultimate authority over our lives?

3. *View of reality (metaphysics).* Of what is ultimate reality composed? Is reality just mental ideas (a form of rationalism or idealism)? What is real after we exhaust the empirical world of our senses? Does anything exist apart from our being able to perceive it with our five senses? Does God exist? If so, how does one come to know that reality that exists apart from the physical world, the world after physics that philosophers call appropriately *metaphysics?*

4. *View of knowledge (epistemology).* How does a person know anything? There are seven basic classical philosophies of knowledge: idealism, rationalism, empiricism, pragmaticism, existentialism, mysticism, and Christian realism. These ways of finding truth are described

in the box on page 20.

5. *View of person.* What is Man? In particular, what are adolescents? What does it mean to be human? What does it mean to be created in the image of God? What implications are there for youth ministry that Jesus was born as any other human being and grew and developed as any other child in his day? Of what value are adolescents? How is an adolescent to be received—as an inevitable pain to be endured or as a fully human being in his or her own right with prerogatives, privileges, and responsibilities? Or are they somewhat lesser humans because they are young and should be treated as less than mature people? Are they just little adults marking time until they fully develop?

6. *View of learning (psychology of learning).* How do people learn? One's answer to this philosophical issue is dependent on one's views of reality, knowledge, and humanity. Does one learn because one is created to do so? Or does one learn because someone external makes us learn? Is learning dependent on teaching or do we learn because God has created us to learn, grow, and develop? Is it "natural" to learn? Must humans be cajoled into learning by rewards (positive reinforcements) and punishments (negative reinforcements)? Are humans molded by society to conform to social dictates or are people free to learn, grow, and develop into what God wants them to be?

7. *View of ministry.* Is ministry viewed as a profession with a set of skills and attitudes that can be learned by anyone? Or is ministry servanthood, a selfless giving to others so that they can grow and develop into all that God is calling them to be? Is ministry something that we do or is it something that we do with God and through the Holy Spirit's empowerment? Is it our ministry or his? Are only certain persons called to ministry, to be servants to each other and to the world? What are the roles of "professional, ordained ministers"?

8. *Rationale for youth ministry.* Why should

Seven Views of Knowledge

Idealism

Objects of the mind are dependent on one's consciousness. Objects do not exist apart from the knower; they are dependent on the knower. What is known is what is real. Reality is what is within a person. Thus one knows only what one can think about.

Rationalism

Truth is derived independently of experience. Knowledge is gained a priori, that is, there are laws of thought, innate ideas, eternal-universal truth. These exist quite apart from the person and from experiences. Even if humans did not exist, this knowledge would because truth exists in a realm apart from experiences.

Empiricism

Knowledge comes only from sense data. Nonempirical experiences, such as attitudes, preferences, likes and dislikes, values, beliefs, feelings, or emotions have no real existence in themselves (no ontological or metaphysical reality); they cannot be verified. These are subjective, internal, nonrational, and emotive. They are not true knowledge because they are unverifiable to others. Only what is empirically verifiable is real, but even this is open to relative perception. Empiricism leads to probability, not to certain, absolute knowledge. Absolutes do not exist, absolutely.

Pragmaticism

Meaning is in the practical nature of things, in their usefulness. What works is true and exists (in some way). Scientific verification—empirical evidence—is the pragmatic test for truth.

Existentialism

Existence precedes essence. Existence or the actual being of the person takes precedence over the essence (laws of logic, formal proofs, definitions of truth, abstract and immutable and ultimate principles). Personal and individual existence is ultimate. Only what one experiences personally can be true and real. The person is the subject and never the object. Truth is experienced internally.

Mysticism

Ultimate reality is personal union with whatever one considers ultimate. This ultimate (God, for the Christian) is known immediately without any mediation. Reality is known noncognitively and is not describable cognitively; it is subjective. A person is swept up into complete and perfect unity with God, losing his or her own consciousness to be conscious only of God. The empirical world is secondary.

Christian Realism

God is ultimate reality and is not part of creation. God created the empirical world out of nothing (creation *ex nihilo*). Matter exists because God created it. What God created was very good and he revealed and continues to reveal himself in his creation. All of creation is under God's sovereign rule. He is the sustainer and judge of all matter and people. Humans know only in part because we are finite creatures. Only God can know fully and completely because he is infinite. Reason and faith go hand-in-hand. We are not asked to believe what is irrational or nonrational. Nor are we required to suspend our judgment in order to know. We are, rather, encouraged to bring every part of our minds to bear in order to know as fully as we can.

Truth as revealed in Scripture and in creation can be known by the inquiring minds of scientists whether they be scientists as theologians or scientists as empirical researchers. What we can detect with our senses is real in and of itself because God has created it and did not create untruth. But the real world is more than what we can perceive with our senses. God dwells outside that world in an existence that is beyond the world of creation. We can know this part of reality through reflection on the meaning of creation, through study of Scripture's revelation, and by the work of the Holy Spirit in us.

we have youth ministry? Why are youth important to the church and to society? What makes young people worth focusing upon and spending time, energy, and money on?

9. *Relationship of adolescent development to youth ministry.* How does what we know about adolescent development affect our thinking about youth and youth ministry? Can an effective youth ministry treat adolescents as children or adults, or must such a ministry be focused especially on adolescent needs and developmental characteristics?

10. *Purposes and outcomes of youth ministry.* What are the purposes of a local church's youth ministry? In particular, what outcomes are hoped for and planned for? How do these purposes and outcomes show themselves in the actual youth ministry model (the entire curriculum or plan) and program?

11. *Leadership roles.* What are the general leadership roles of lay adult leaders, teenage leaders from within the group (distinguishing between junior highers, senior highers, and post-high school youth) and pastoral staff youth workers? How do the adult leaders, church staff, and laity relate to the youth? Are the adults coaches or performers? Who is responsible for the planning, execution, and evaluation of the youth ministry? Is it youth leaders, adult leaders, or both?

12. *Program elements.* How do the four basic program elements of worship, instruction, fellowship, and expression-service relate to the various aspects of the program? That is, how does a youth ministry's program seek to integrate the elements into its total organization? For example, *where* do instruction, worship, fellowship, and expression occur? What are the roles of the various church agencies such as the Sunday school, week-night meetings, expression or service projects, retreats and camps, and any other program components in relationship to these four basic elements?

13. *Evaluation.* What is the place of evaluation? Is evaluation seen as a final test to determine success or failure of a particular program? Is it viewed as a means to determine whether desired outcomes have been achieved, and as a tool for obtaining information in order to revise and improve the program? Is evaluation used to give a "grade" to youth workers? Or to help the youth ministry be more effective?

PRINCIPLES OF A YOUTH MINISTRY PHILOSOPHY

The essential building blocks of a philosophy have been suggested above. When we turn to actually developing a philosophy of youth ministry, we need to incorporate in one way or another all of the above categories. What these categories look like is detailed in the basic principles of a youth ministry below and further explained in subsequent chapters.

Principle One— Incarnational

The basis of an incarnational approach to youth ministry is squarely grounded in the incarnation of the Lord Jesus Christ. The pattern is clearly described in Philippians 2:6–8. Christ did not consider his state of being God something to be held on to. His prerogatives of deity, his divine characteristics and attributes, and all the glory of being God were set aside in order to become like those to whom and *with* whom he ministered. He came like us, not like God. He totally identified with humanity from conception through normal child and adolescent development into adulthood, culminating in death, and then showing us the victory over death through resurrection.

Jesus came as an ordinary human being without superior airs nor with condescending gestures. He came enfleshing the love of God so that we might experience firsthand that "God so loved the world that he gave. . . ."

There would be no doubt that God was concerned with humanity, that God cared for us. He wanted to stop the alienation between us and him, to remake us into new creatures, and to empower us to serve in his name and for his sake to this world.

Incarnational youth ministry functions as Christ himself did: forgetting the prerogatives of adulthood and becoming identified with youth without actually becoming just like youth. This means taking the role of servant to youth, becoming an adult for youth without taking on all of their characteristics. It is so identifying with youth that one can feel their hurts, know their minds, and predict to a certain degree what they will think, feel, and do. It means enfleshing Christ to youth: showing in our very being (words, actions, and attitudes) what Christ continually shows to us of himself. We "put on" Christ—take on his charactertistics and intentions (see Rom. 13:14; Gal. 3:27; Eph. 4:24). It requires that we not judge youth on external appearances, but accept them as they are without exception. It means spending time with them on their "turf," talking with and listening to them. And it means being *for* them at all costs. Like Christ, we too can be for youth; we can be their advocates, helpers, encouragers and, on occasion, their disciplinarians.

Principle Two— Agape Love

One of the primary implications of an incarnational approach to ministry is agapic love. Such love is best defined as an unconditional acceptance of others regardless of their particular value to us. God so loved us that while we were yet in our sin, Christ died for us (John 3:16; Rom. 5:8). This type of love does not ask what the other person can give to us in return for our help. Reciprocity is not an issue. Nor does it ask what the relationship is between "me and thee," nor what one owes another

from a legal or just perspective. Rather, agapic love sees a need and also sees oneself as helping to fulfill that need. It then acts to do so regardless of relationship, payback, or legal or just requirements. Agape love is the motivation behind Christ's incarnation and must be the same for youth workers' incarnational approach.

Adolescents are loved because God loves them. He values them because they are part of his creation and made in his image, and need a Savior and Lord. We love youth because God has given them a "God-shaped vacuum" that only he can fill; yet we can help them find that fulfillment. This means that youth workers love adolescents regardless of their age, stage, maturity, fears, joys, antics, and problems. We love them unconditionally because God so loves us. We can do no less when we minister in his name.

Principle Three— Ministry

To minister is to function in Jesus' place, doing his ministry in this world in his name by the power of the Holy Spirit. Ministry is grounded in Christ's commission, "As the Father has sent me, I am sending you" (John 20:21). Jesus' mission was to be a servant, that is, to serve and to help people (Mark 10:45). To be a servant like Christ is to take up his cross daily and follow him in humble service of those who need help to grow, develop, and mature in him.

It is crucial that one's philosophy of youth ministry be built on a radical acceptance of the concept of servanthood. Servanthood, however, is built on the first two principles of one's philosophy of ministry stated above, namely, an incarnational approach and agapic love. When the world screams in a thousand ways to be the boss, one can be a true servant only if driven by an incarnational perspective and motivated by agapic love. Without the incarnation and agape, servanthood becomes another way of manipulating people to do what we want them to do. Servanthood is to take up "towel and wash basin" to "wash" the feet of adolescents. It is, therefore, a ministry that seeks to serve the needs of youth as they truly are, not as we hope they might be.

Principle Four— Developmental

Developmental youth ministry means that it is implemented on the stages and levels of development that are appropriate for the youth and that it exists for the growth, development, and maturation of the youth in all areas of life. Just as Jesus grew and developed as a whole person, so youth are growing and developing into whole people in six major domains: physical, cognitive (mental), social, affective (emotional), moral, and faith/spiritual (Luke 2:40, 52).

Effective youth ministry seeks to reach youth on their various developmental levels so that what is communicated is understandable and can be received by the youth. But it does not stop merely at communication of data, or even of feelings and behavior. Effective youth ministry centers on facilitating the continuous development of youth into whole, mature persons. It helps youth to move from less to more maturity in all areas of their lives just as Jesus did as a child and a young person. So youth workers help youth to grow up into Christ in all ways (Eph. 4:13).

Teaching for development helps youth to actively explore their experiences and thinking with the help of and facilitation by adult youth workers. These workers help youth actively engage in thinking, exploring, searching, and determining their own answers for their life situations. Such developmental teachers help, encourage, support, urge, exhort, prod, and wait patiently while youth grow. They also pray! (1 Thess. 2:11–12)

This developmental principle views learning as something which enables growth. It recognizes that learning depends on experience, and on the construction of one's own internal meaning out of experiences with the environment and one's own thoughts. It is not just committing authority-controlled data to memory for regurgitation when the authorities ask again for it. Learning depends on the teacher and the learner, not just on the teacher. This principle considers teaching as sharing, helping, facilitating, and encouraging learning. The learners themselves are actively involved in the learning processes and actually control the learning. The developmental principle recognizes that what is important is *doing* and *being* and not just *knowing*. Evaluation consists of observing behavior and practice, not just the recalling of memorized data.

Developmental youth ministry has as its ultimate outcomes youth who (1) own their own selves; (2) own their own faith in Christ; (3) are being led by the Spirit of God into his truth and holiness; (4) continue to feed their spiritual needs, growing more Christlike; (5) practice Christian morality and ethics in the power of the Holy Spirit; (6) seek, find, and follow the will of God for their lives; (7) bring Christian values and motivation to all of their life experiences; (8) function interdependently with family, peers, church, and society at large; (9) develop the means to feed their own cognitive capacities, social relationships, affective needs, and moral judgments; (10) develop a proper view of and care for their bodies as the temples of God; (11) determine effective and balanced relationships to authorities in their lives; (12) are developing their own Christian view of life and the world; (13) begin to narrow their understanding of what they are called to in vocation; (14) develop a biblical view of sex and their sex roles in society; and (15) continue to mature in cognitive, social, affective, and moral ways.

Principle Five— People-Oriented

This principle flows from the first four principles. Youth ministry must be committed to youth and their needs. A focus on people means that youth's concerns, interests, problems, questions, and developmental issues are first in our minds. Too often youth ministry starts with the logical approach that youth need to know Jesus, so we try to evangelize them from the first word onward. Or, if they are already believers, we seek to hurry them into spiritual maturity. In both cases, we forget that Jesus' approach was usually to begin with felt needs and then go to more basic ones, moving into the core areas of people's lives where he was able to meet their real, underlying needs. He knew what was in each person because he had made us (see John 2:24).

This principle also saves us from focusing just on programs and activities and filling up rooms at our churches—getting larger numbers to make us feel better and to help us look good on year-end reports to official boards. It also means that when youth ministry focuses on youth, it does not keep looking for various nods of approval from official boards and other elder types. This principle means that the most important group of people in the church for a youth worker are the youth of the church and those to whom the group is reaching out.

Finally, this principle means that youth workers must focus on knowing adolescents. In particular, this means knowing their developmental levels and understanding their subcultures as best as one can. There is more than one youth subculture in any country; a number of subcultures make up the twelve-to-twenty-five-year-old age group. There are those identified by geography, such as inner city, suburb, urban area, and rural area; the socioeconomic status or educational level of parents; school interests, such as sports or academics; race and ethnic background; or church

denomination, and others. All of these factors tend to cause youth of similar backgrounds to find one another and "run" together. Within any given secondary school, for example, are numerous subcultures, all of which relate to a larger youth subculture.

In order to become people-oriented, three things are required of youth workers. First, they must be dedicated and competent adults who communicate on the youths' developmental levels. It is important to remember that dedication does not make a person competent. Someone said long ago that a dedicated but incompetent person is still incompetent. As has been asked, "How can a team that is so dedicated lose so frequently?" Dedication does not automatically imply ability to be effective.

The reverse of this is also true. A competent but undedicated person is still not dedicated. One may have the technical skills for youth work, but without dedication it is youth *work*, not youth *ministry*. The call to working with youth is a call to competence and dedication. Not one without the other.

Competence means that youth workers spend time getting to know youth. They are involved in the daily life of their youth in the group. It also means that youth workers know adolescents' general developmental patterns and in particular the developmental patterns of their own youth. Competent youth workers communicate on the developmental stages and levels of youth in order to meet their needs and in order for the communication to be effective. Communication—whether by words or experiences provided—that is too far below or too high above the developmental functioning of the youth involved will be misunderstood or almost totally ignored. Dedication and competence means that youth workers spend time knowing their youth in order to communicate effectively with them.

Second, to become people-oriented means developing personal relationships. Even in Jesus' least "personal" healings, he talked with or touched the person in need. There was almost always some warmth of contact between the divine Son of God and the human being in need. His most intimate times were spent with the disciples. As Ted Ward has suggested numerous times, Jesus spent three years on a camping trip with his disciples. He developed lasting personal relationships with his disciples. To meet their needs and to effectively teach them, he developed the closest of personal relationships with them by being with them.

Third—and this leads directly from the last requirement—people-orientedness takes time. One cannot develop personal relationships with youth without spending a great deal of time with them. Jesus did not live in heaven and make occasional forays to earth to be with his disciples. Instead, he lived with them for three years. They saw him all day and all night.

Effective youth ministry cannot be done without a major time commitment—time to help people change, grow, and develop into Christ-likeness. Time must be allowed for people to get to know a caring adult worker who will show the way, help young people walk in that way, and be there to help them make corrections along the way. And time must be spent in getting to know youth developmentally and personally. This means going to where they are (incarnational youth ministry), observing them, being with them, talking with them, and sharing experiences with them, sharing one's own self with them. All of this takes *time*.

Principle Six— Spiritual Focus

Church youth ministry has as its ultimate focus the development of youth into the increasing likeness of Christ. Youth ministry begins with evangelism and continues on to Christian nurture by means of discipleship. Christian youth groups are not the local YMCA/YWCA or Junior Achievement organization, nor are they some adolescent form of the Kiwanis or Rotary Club. Youth ministry is not baby-sitting. It is not Christian entertainment. Nor is it a substitute for public school events; an alternative to TV, videotapes, MTV, or movies; a cloister to shelter Christian isolationists; more formalized schooling; another church service; a social service or youth club; or for Christians only.

All of youth ministry needs to focus on the spiritual. It has a singlemindedness; it must lead to Christ and flow from him. All activities must be viewed as ultimately spiritual whether they be a church basketball victory or celebrating the Lord's Supper together. The total program of a youth group must be viewed as contributing to the holistic spiritual development of the youth involved. The world outside of the church has more than enough activities for youth, so there is no need to compete with secular society's offerings.

A spiritual focus does not mean that all program and activities are limited to some narrow definition of what is "spiritual," such as Bible studies, prayer meetings and/or evangelistic meetings. It does not dictate that youth workers act piously and use God-language all of the time. It *does* mean that the leadership recognizes that everything the church produces is ultimately spiritual in nature. There is an integration of program with purpose and goals or outcomes that views all youth ministry as spiritual. This means that leaders are aware that all that is planned and executed in youth ministry is governed by an incarnational approach, agapic love, and concern for the youth involved, and that, ultimately, if youth do not know Christ and grow up in him, youth, youth workers, and youth programs have achieved nothing.

Principle Seven— Leadership Focus

The leadership focus has two aspects. First is the development of the youth themselves.

They need to be encouraged to identify and develop their leadership gifts and deploy them in ministry for Christ both in the church and in the world. Second is the leadership development of those adults working with the youth. Adults too should be helped to identify and develop their various leadership gifts. Then, in turn, these workers can do the same for youth. Adult leaders should consider themselves as coaches, not players or performers. The basic principle is that adults should not do anything that the youth could learn to do. Adult workers, therefore, are continually on the offense to help develop leadership in the youth, helping the young people to be leaders.

Keep in mind that leadership development must be commensurate with the developmental levels of the youth involved. Early adolescents will need considerably more direction and guidance than middle adolescents. Late adolescents, or post-high school youth, generally need the least direct guidance.

Youth ministry needs to be *to, for, with* and *by* youth. These four prepositions are crucial. *To youth* means that youth—not adults, not programs, not denominations, not even parents—are the center of the ministry. It is a ministry that centers on youth and their actual felt and real needs, not on what adults think youth ought to have.

At the heart of *for youth* is also the idea that the ministry is not for other age groups but for the youth. It is a ministry that has them as the center. Church politics, pastoral problems, denominational battles, and intrachurch conflicts notwithstanding, youth are the reason for the ministry and the youth program. Youth ministry belongs to the youth, not to the adults, and is for the beneficial development of youth.

With youth focuses on helping them to become actively engaged in the design and development of their own ministry and program. Programs are not done to and for them by adults. Rather, youth are helped to become actively involved in the whole planning processes that focus on their felt and real needs.

Finally, *by youth* heightens the level of involvement of youth in the ministry and program. Youth themselves do the work of the ministry. They are not just spectators watching some "hot shot" adult youth workers do their thing in front of the group. Rather, youth not only plan their own youth ministry but also help to execute that same ministry.

Of course, "to, for, with, and by youth" does not mean that adults just sit back and watch the ministry unfold. Instead, adults are actively involved as facilitators, coaches, "prodders," and helpers. Yet even in early adolescence, the young people can and should be involved to the degree that they are developmentally capable of designing, developing, and producing their own ministry.

Involvement in leadership to, for, and by youth will produce the following outcomes:

- Participation by youth themselves and not just adult leaders means that the young people are actively involved in the entire learning process. Since learning is an inner, active, and personal process, youth learn by being involved in leadership.
- Youth create their own programs. The needs of youth predominate and youth focus on their own known needs, being helped in the process by effective adult leaders. Such interactions provide for natural contact with adults who facilitate program planning and execution, thus enabling informal, meaningful contact time with youth.
- Participation by youth provides for contextualization of the program within a particular time, place, and history for particular youth. The focus is on "our program," not the denomination's, parachurch's, some other church's, or some

The quality of our youth ministry is a direct reflection of our view of God. The great God demands that our ministry be great.

publishing house's program.

- Leadership by youth provides feedback for improvement by those directly involved as both leaders and consumers of the programs. Evaluation of programs leads to feedback, which in turn leads to corrections and changes that are intended to make the ministry more effective.
- Involvement of youth in leadership provides for leadership development and leadership experience *now*. Youth learn leadership principles and practice them immediately, instead of waiting "until they get older."
- Youth leadership provides for leadership education and development of future adult church leaders. The dearth of effective adult leadership in many churches can be traceable to the lack of leadership development of youth during their adolescent years. If the future of local churches is dependent on youth who will be the leaders of the church, then it is necessary for churches to implement effective leadership development programs for those youth.

Principle Eight— Church Focus

Ministry with youth belongs to the whole church. A church without a youth ministry is a church without a future. Tragically, youth ministry is too often seen as an "add-on" ministry that could be dropped if the circumstances demanded it. Rather, youth ministry is an integral part of the total church's ministry. The senior pastor, business manager of the church, other nonyouth ministry staff, and other church employees need to be cognizant of and involved to some degree in youth ministry. This does not mean that business managers or senior pastors should be youth pastors, too. It does mean that these staff people are aware of and supportive of the youth ministry in their church. All pastors and staff of a local church have a stake in the ministry of the church with youth. If they recognize this, they can then function more effectively in their leadership and in the fulfillment of their call to minister.

Youth ministry that has a church focus helps adolescents recognize that they are part of a larger body of believers composed of others both younger and older than they. Youth are accepted as they are since Jesus has called them into his body and into the fellowship of believers. All believers belong to the body of Christ. "There is neither Jew nor Greek, slave nor free, male nor female, for you are all one in Christ Jesus" (Gal. 3:28), and we could easily add our own "neither older nor younger, youth, child nor adult" (see Mark 10:13–16).

Youth workers need to maximize the givens of a local church's environment, making the most of the geographic location of the particular church body. If they are in the inner city, they can take advantage of the numerous offerings of the city, such as concerts, plays, movies, recreation facilities, and museums. If the church is in a rural area, the youth ministry can take advantage of opportunities for hiking, biking, river rides, and such. And all church groups can find another group in a geographic setting different from their own and become involved in mutual fellowship.

Therefore, the local church is the focus of strength for any youth group. If this is not the case, then the local church has some sort of sickness that will eventually cause it to die. Youth need to belong, be accepted, and be ministered to from the local church. Christ said he would build his church, not his parachurch group! As much as possible, youth need to get their strength and encouragement from the entire church and not just from their youth workers. It is necessary, fitting, and proper for youth to become actively involved in their local churches, in the worship services and ministries to the congregation, and to the world. Parachurch groups began in response to the local churches' failure to effectively reach youth. Yet they can never substitute for the local church, which is transgenerational, where the Word is correctly preached and the Lord's Supper and baptism are celebrated and properly administered.

Parachurch groups such as Young Life and Campus Life continue to have a vital role in youth ministry around the world. In recent years many such groups have begun to work more closely with local churches. When parachurch groups help to strengthen churches' youth ministries, they contribute to a church focus that enfolds youth into the mainstream of the people of God.

Youth ministry is not something *the church* does to adolescents until they grow up; it is ministry now that is *to, for, with,* and *by youth.* Youth ministry is an integral, integrated part of the church's total ministry because the entire church needs youth, and youth need the entire church.

Principle Nine— Worthy Focus

God alone is worthy of all praise and adoration. Our labor, including our ministry to, for, with, and by youth, is a reflection of what we think of God. Our ministry either reflects that God is worthy of the greatest praise and worship or that he ought to be satisfied with whatever crumbs we give him. The quality of our

youth ministry is a direct reflection of our view of God. The great God demands that our ministry be great.

Worship is a part of our ministry. Part of the problem in much of Christianity is that we have relegated worship to something that only happens on Sunday mornings in the "worship service." The remainder of the week, including most of Sunday, is not considered to be oriented toward worship. We fail to recognize that worship of the Triune God is not limited to one hour or so each week. In fact, our reasonable worship goes on constantly, beginning with our wholehearted dedication of our lives to God, being continually transformed by God's Spirit, continually renewed in our personhood, and making all of this a part of our reasonable worship (see Rom. 12:1–2).

Our ministry should reflect the fact that God is the God of excellence. Each of us is precious to God. Why would we in our ministry not want also to reflect the excellence that is God's? It seems only proper and fitting that what we do in our ministry should bring praise, honor, and glory to God and that God sees this as part of our worship and extolling of him. If God is the God of excellence, beauty, and goodness, then our ministry should reflect his values, not our worldly values that allow us to "just get by." Instead, we should strive to be and do the best for God.

Some people may interpret this emphasis of a worthy focus as meaning that a youth ministry should be deluxe or represent an extravagant expenditure of resources—mainly finances. This would be a misinterpretation. It is not the amount that one spends, but the inner drive and commitment to mission and ministry that makes the difference. Recall the widow's extremely small offering; it was hardly worth anything. Yet Jesus commended her not for the size of her offering but for what she had done: she gave all that she had to God (Mark 12:42). So in youth ministry what is important is not how much one has spent on programming or on retreats or camps. It is rather how much we give of ourselves. Did we give our all to demonstrate to ourselves, to others who might be watching, and to God who is watching that we love God with our whole heart, mind, soul, and body? Or do we give just a little bit, hoping to get by with minimal enthusiasm and lackadaisical effort? If the latter is true, we demonstrate in our thinking and actions that we have a low view of God, that ministry in his name can be half-hearted and cheap. We rob God of his dignity and majesty and lower ourselves, our ministry, and God in the eyes of the entire world. Christians do not have to be extravagant in their expenditures, but they should do the most possible with the resources they have.

Thus our youth ministry programming from beginning to end should reflect the quality that signifies that we are ministering in God's name to the world. If God can expend his creative energies on flowers and dumb animals, making them beautiful (Matt. 6:26), how can we not expend our creative energies to develop a ministry and program that reflects glory to the only worthy God?

Principle Ten— Balanced Program

They devoted themselves to the apostles' teaching and to the fellowship, to the breaking of bread and to prayer. Everyone was filled with awe, and many wonders and miraculous signs were done by the apostles. All the believers were together and had everything in common. Selling their possessions and goods, they gave to anyone as he had need. Every day they continued to meet together in the temple courts. They broke bread in their homes and ate together with glad and sincere hearts, praising God and enjoying the favor of all the people. And the Lord added to their number daily those who were being saved. (Acts 2:42–47)

The four basic elements of a youth pro-

gram—*instruction, worship, fellowship,* and *service*—are all mentioned in this section of Scripture. Each is necessary and holds a unique position in balance with the others. Additional elements are possible, of course, but these form the backbones and structure of a program (see fig. 1, page 30).

Instruction

Instruction is the intentional teaching for holistic development of youth so that they will grow up in every way into the likeness of Christ (Eph. 4:13). It is effectively communicating with youth so that Christ is formed in them and so they can continue to grow (Gal. 4:19; Col. 1:28–29). Such outcomes require that instruction be not only for youth's whole development but that communication be on their levels of development so they can understand it. For example, teaching the concept of the Trinity to most early adolescents and to many middle adolescents is often a waste of time. They are not cognitively capable of understanding such an abstract concept. In fact, many adults have a difficult time comprehending the Trinity. Instruction, to be effective, must be understandable developmentally before it can be acted upon.

Instruction is found throughout a youth ministry's program: Bible studies, Sunday school (if one's church has one), youth group meetings, camps, retreats, one-on-one discipleship, and counseling.

Often evangelical churches are strong on instruction, using almost every meeting to formally instruct the youth in attendance. These churches are strong on Bible content. But content alone never saved anyone. Memorized Bible verses and countless hours in Bible study do not guarantee a holy life. To be sure, Bible study and Scripture secured in one's mind and heart are necessary ingredients to holy living. But they are not sufficient. Additional elements are necessary for a holistic approach

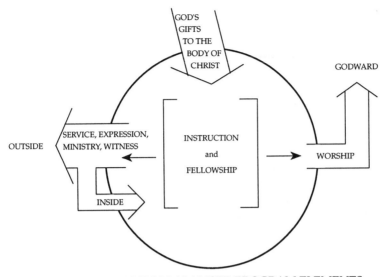

THE CHURCH'S BALANCED PROGRAM ELEMENTS

Figure 1

that provides for development of the youth. Instruction views knowledge as the first step that is then followed by accepting information for oneself, making initial behavior changes and, eventually, being a different person. Effective teaching is for transformation of the person, not just for delivery of information to the person.

Worship

Worship, the second element, is a focus on God. This is not the time to teach about God; it is the time to contemplate God and his actions and meaning in our lives. Our whole beings are focused on expressing worthiness to the one who alone is worthy to receive all glory and honor and praise and adoration (Rev. 4:11; 5:9–10, 12–14).

Few adult worship services truly are successful at focusing on God. More time is usually spent on announcements than on prayer. The preacher often conceives of the "worship time" as a preliminary or warm-up for the sermon. For most pastors and parishioners, the worship service is really the preaching service. But where is God's worthiness focused upon? In the race to finish in one hour, get all the announcements in, and the offering, special music, and perhaps a contemporary drama and message, God is practically left on the sidelines. He is not the focus of the worship. A balanced youth program will have a healthy focus on worship of God that is appropriate to youth's developmental capacities. (See chapter 5 on worship.)

Fellowship

Fellowship is the sharing of life with life. It is not just going to socials or socializing, or sitting next to someone in a movie or even in a church service or youth meeting. It is the opening of one's inner thoughts and feelings to another, finding acceptance and help to grow in Christ. Social activities often aid in

A curriculum consists of many components, while the entire course of a study is considered to be "curriculum." Beginning with the smallest component—a lesson, activity, meeting, or message—the following formula shows how a curriculum is built:

A Lesson	+ Lessons	=	A Unit *(a series of lessons, meetings, or activities)*
A Unit	+ Units	=	A Course
A Course	+ Courses	=	A Curriculum *(for a particular age group over a long period of time, usually a school year)*
A Curriculum	+ Curricula	=	The Curriculum *(the entire plan for a particular group of youth for three to four years, for example, for the secondary school youth*

Figure 2

breaking down resistance to fellowship, but such activities are not themselves fellowship.

Fellowship can occur in any venue of ministry, such as riding in a car from home to church or participating in a small group for Bible study, mutual help, and fellowship. Location and program are not the issues. The issue is that there are sufficient planned and informal occasions for fellowship. Are there opportunities for youth to share in common their selves and to receive each others' sharing?

Service

Lastly, expression, service, or ministry need to be part of the balanced youth ministry programing. Instruction, worship, and fellowship should result in ongoing service to God in the local church, in the local community, and around the world. A youth ministry that does not produce service is not really a youth ministry but some counterfeit program of religious entertainment for youth (Eph. 2:10).

Service, ministry, and witness are synonymous. These can be defined simply as the doing of good works. "To do good" is an act of testimony to God's gracious love in our lives and his desire to be received into the lives of others. Ephesians 2:10 and Galatians 6:10 make clear that good works are for the body of Christ and the world external: "For we are

God's workmanship, created in Christ Jesus to do good works, which God prepared in advance for us to do" (Eph. 2:10). "As we have opportunity, let us do good to all people, especially to those who belong to the family of believers" (Gal. 6:10).

What is most intriguing is that an effective ministry or service aspect of a youth ministry will enable youth to be instructed, will provide for deepening fellowship, and will encourage worship of God. This service/ministry element can be the key to effective youth ministry. (See chapter 7 on service.)

Principle Eleven— Curricular Focus

Youth ministry operates through a planned program, a curriculum (fig. 2). Curriculum is the planned interaction of youth with a variety of elements. Within this interaction, everything is ultimately pointed toward the development and growth of the youth involved. First, it is interaction with peers—learners together in a group. Second, curriculum takes place with teachers and other adult youth workers. Basically, these are authority figures with whom one has contact in the church.

Third, the learner interacts with other people who are not fellow learners or adult youth workers. These include administrators (such as the Sunday school superintendent), church staff members, or church elected leaders. Fourth, interaction occurs with instructional materials and media (books, papers, audiovisuals, and other things). Fifth, instructional activities and experiences provide interaction through courses, units of study, lessons, learner actions, teacher actions, programs, and activities. The adult youth workers' actions are made up of such things as lectures, discussions, and facilitating youth's leadership development. Finally, curriculum is the planned interaction of the learner with himself or herself through thinking, problem-solving, writing, and deliberate actions.

Design and Development

Curriculum is produced by the process of design and development. It includes, first, a number of philosophical foundations: one's understanding of the nature of reality, the nature of knowledge, the nature of learning, the nature of learner and teacher (roles), and the nature of the organization sponsoring the curriculum. These foundations will be determined according to the philosophy of ministry.

Second, a target group is necessary in order to effectively design and develop a curriculum. Third, the tasks that the learners will be expected to accomplish must be analyzed. Fourth, the basic content the learners will need to fulfill these tasks has to be determined. Fifth, a specific set of goals or outcomes needs to be determined.

Sixth, curriculum includes an instructional design consisting of the various educational components used in the development and implementation of curriculum. These are best expressed in the form of five questions:

1. *Who are the learners?* What are their needs, based on the philosophical foundation, on known psychological and social development characteristics, on life issues at each develop-

mental area, and on the particular needs of one's church within its sociocultural-political-geographic context?

2. *Why teach?* What are the purposes and anticipated outcomes for the curriculum, based on the established philosophy of youth ministry?

3. *What will be taught?* What is the content sequence—what content should be covered (biblical, theological, social)—and how does content relate to the needs, purposes, and outcomes of the ministry? How will the content be organized into courses, units, and lessons, for effective and efficient learning?

4. *How will the instruction occur (and with what)?* What will be the youth program? What instructional methods and materials will be developed?

5. *Who will teach the adult youth workers how to operate within the curriculum?* This is a program for teacher education. Such a program will explain educational philosophy and development as well as assist youth workers in implementing the planned curriculum. These workers should then be encouraged to continue their own development, continuing to learn how to be effective in their use of the curriculum.

6. *What procedures and production should be established for the implementation or teaching of the curriculum?*

7. *What happened when learners were taught?* This is evaluation for feedback and improvement—either of a curriculum, of several curricula, or of the overall program/curriculum—and the involvement of significant personnel in decisions.

Curriculum Summary

Curriculum is a *plan*, not materials per se. A curriculum plan includes thinking on the following: (1) Whom to teach—the target group or learners. (2) Why teach anything? What is the reason for teaching? (3) Desired outcomes for teaching. What should be accomplished in the areas of *Know, Feel, Do* and *Be?* (4) What to teach and (5) where to teach—what content, courses, agencies, and locations? (6) Who are the youth workers/teachers? (7) What methods will be used? (8) What materials are needed? (9) How successful is the program/curriculum? What is the evaluation? (10) What changes, according to evaluation and feedback, need to be made?

Principle Twelve— Dynamic Focus

Those who understand youth know that they are active, fun-seeking, adventurous people who look for thrills, action, and excitement. Few youth are willing to sit quietly while a speaker drones on incessantly about some esoteric aspect of God. In many cultures around the world, youth may politely look like they are sitting still, but their minds are probably off somewhere else. In the United States, youth will begin to talk and do their own thing, ignoring the speaker and often acting rude. To be sure, the youth in such a situation are discourteous, but the speaker who thus "ministers" shows that he or she does not understand youth's needs, interests, and concerns.

Youth need activity; they are still growing. Coursing through their bodies is a whole new set of hormones which are causing growth both internally and externally. They can hardly sit still because they are changing so rapidly.

Such dynamic and rapid changes stimulate the need for adventure, action, and excitement. Youth look for fun that challenges them, gives them some scares, and pumps up the adrenalin. A youth ministry must provide action that will challenge and channel the enthusiasm, energies, and drives of youth in a manner appropriate to their levels of development and to their cultural milieu. (See chapter 6 on fellowship.)

Principle Thirteen— Evaluation

This principle seeks to be a means of determining the degree to which the purposes and stated outcomes of a youth ministry have been achieved. Many people hear the word *evaluation* and immediately think of tests taken in school. They equate it with getting a grade. When most of us received our papers back, we looked at our grade and either agreed with the teacher or did not. We usually did not find out why we made certain mistakes and then seek to correct them.

Evaluation, properly understood in the church's youth ministry, is extremely helpful in determining whether or not the programming has been successful, why it has been so or why it was not as successful as planned. Evaluation is for feedback for improvement. It is not for a grade nor a promotion. Rather, it is for continually making the ministry more effective.

A youth ministry without evaluation and feedback for improvement is a ministry that has no idea how effective it is; it is blind activity. Without evaluation, a youth ministry can never know if what it is doing is worthwhile and working. With evaluation, a youth ministry can make corrections and improvements, and do reruns that will continue to help youth grow into more and more mature persons in Christ. (See chapter 11 on evaluation.)

Principle Fourteen— General Outcomes

It is crucial that youth workers know at what they are aiming, for what outcomes they minister. Below are seven general outcomes that seem to be extremely crucial for a youth ministry to achieve over the lifetime of early, middle, and later adolescents.

Outcome One: Spiritual Knowledge, Understanding, and Maturity. This is a lifelong quest to know God, and to internalize God's Word and work into the lives of youth. Youth need to know Christ as their own Savior and Lord, and to begin to learn how to walk in the Spirit. Scripture, by the work of the Holy Spirit, should be integrated into the lives of youth and continue to be so throughout the remainder of their lives. Youth need to know how and why to grow spiritually without someone else always feeding them and/or giving them spiritual highs. Young people need to be intentionally and continuously self-initiating in spiritual learning. They should be helped to measure their spiritual growth not in comparison with others but to the full measure of who Christ is.

Youth need to read and study Scripture for themselves, but even more importantly, Scripture needs to get into their lives. They need spiritual understanding and wisdom that all of life and substance are from God and belong to God; they are either good or bad stewards of all that God has given them. They need to act on the fact that the kingdom of God is not simply a part of their lives. Rather, it *is* their lives! They need to have a faith that is their own, not just one inherited from godly parents, other relatives, peers, pastoral staff, and older youth workers. Their faith is theirs because it has been internalized and they claim it as their own.

Outcome Two: Self-Acceptance. Youth need to know who they are, that is, to have a healthy self-identity. They need to know their capabilities, abilities, interests, and spiritual gifts. They need a proper self-image, thinking soberly neither too highly nor too lowly of themselves. They not only need to be aware of their spiritual gifts but to be developing those gifts and using them in appropriate manners. Youth also need to continually encourage others to acknowledge and use their spiritual gifts.

Outcome Three: Service. This is the active ministry to other believers and to the world

> *Youth need to act on the fact that the kingdom of God is not simply a part of their lives. Rather, it is their lives!*

outside of the church, regardless of the age of the recipients. Youth need to know how to give away their faith and help others in society to receive social justice. They also need to come into direct contact with missions, recognizing that they are the continuity of the Great Commission (Matt. 28:18–19; Acts 1:8). Youth need to know that missions are an option for their calling from God to service. Finally, and most importantly, they need to know that they are persons who are called to mission, they have a vocation from God to service in the name of Christ regardless of where they work and live; to serve is a requirement of being a Christian.

Outcome Four: Leadership. Youth need to be involved in direct planning, execution, and evaluation of their own programs. They should be given leadership development and supervised leadership experiences. They need to be leaders who experience the thrill of leading large and small groups. More mature youth need to be given the experience of helping peers and younger, less mature youth become prepared for leadership.

Outcome Five: Fellowship. Youth need to have a sense of spiritual unity—ever increasing—with all believers, not only in their own churches but also in the city, the nation, and around the world. They need to express friendliness, acceptance, and warmth to believers and nonbelievers. They need to know how to have a good time with both Christians and non-Christians without compromising their Christian values and beliefs. They need to be poised and comfortable in social situations and able to help others feel the same. Finally, they need to share comfortably and appropriately their own spiritual journeys and help others to do so, too. In a word, they need to fellowship with other believers.

Outcome Six: Worship. Youth need to truly worship God, focusing on his glory and worthiness. They need to so come into contact with God through worship that they, in their own way on their own developmental level, can sing, "Holy, holy, holy. . . ."

Outcome Seven: Church Men/Women. Youth need to identify with the local church, actively participating in its worship services as well as in the other activities of the church. They need to support the local church financially according to their means and be involved in appropriate leadership experiences commensurate with their developmental capabilities.

Outcome Eight: Holistic Integrated Development. Youth need to continue to develop as whole people in all six areas of development, namely, physical, cognitive, social, affective,

moral, and spiritual. They should be balanced people who continually look for avenues of continued growth and development. They need to view their bodies as temples of God, therefore to be taken care of for a lifetime. They need to continually expand their minds to encompass more and more complex ideas. They should never become lazy thinkers, but strive to give their minds and whole selves to Christ as part of their reasonable worship of the Triune God.

Youth need to guard their emotions, giving control of those new adolescent feelings to the God who created them in the first place. They need to become balanced, Spirit-controlled people who seek to help others. Youth need to move from making egocentric moral judgments, through socially oriented moral judgments, and into making moral judgments and forming behaviors based on God's perspective on justice and, ultimately, on his agapic love.

With these general outcomes in mind, youth workers can design and develop the beginnings of an effective youth ministry. They will also have the basics for effective evaluation for feedback for improvement.

2 | Understanding Models of Youth Ministry

In its general form, a social system model is a *basic, simplified* description and explanation of the components, organization, and interaction of a social system. On the more specific level, a youth ministry model describes the components and explains the operation and organization of a youth ministry. The model is often confused, however, with a philosophy or a program. Indeed, these three are interrelated but quite different. A philosophy comes prior to a model and a program.

A youth ministry *philosophy* is an abstract conceptualization, in written form, of the basic values upon which a youth ministry model and program are built. Basic values are the ideas, values, and commitments that shape and mold a youth ministry. They reflect what is important, including

- A theological perspective of ministry
- A view of what is real (metaphysics)
- A view of knowledge (epistemology)
- A theological and philosophical view of person
- A view of learning and the nature of teaching

- Leadership roles
- A rationale for youth ministry
- A delineation of basic components of ministry
- The basic interrelationship of components to each other
- The place of youth ministry in the whole church's ministry
- A commitment to proper evaluation.

In sum, a philosophy answers the questions, *"why* have a youth ministry?" and *"what* is youth ministry all about?" (See chapter 1.)

A *model,* as already mentioned, is a simplified description and explanation of what the outworking of a youth ministry philosophy should look like in real life. A model cannot exist without some sort of philosophy behind it, whether or not this philosophy is expressed. The philosophy is described in detail through a model's basic components. A model shows how these components relate both to each other and to the church's entire ministry. A model is still a verbal description, but it now talks about how the ideas and ideals of the youth ministry philosophy will be organized. A model answers the question: *"what* should a youth ministry look like?" But it is only plans—a conceptualization—at this stage, not yet a program.

A *program* is the detailed, planned activity of the model and philosophy applied to a particular youth ministry in a particular local church. It is the application of the model and philosophy to real life, becoming the actual "doing" of youth ministry. No two youth ministry programs are exactly the same. Programs consist of a wide variety of specific items such as the days and times of regular meetings, the activities, the personnel required, and necessary materials. Designed and developed out of the model and based on a particular philosophy, a program answers in detail the question, *"how* will our youth ministry operate?" No book, youth workers' conference, or "how to . . ." advice can indicate what a program should be. Only the

local youth worker, focusing on the local youth themselves in their context, can determine what the program will be.

PRESUPPOSITIONS OF A GENERAL SYSTEMS MODEL

First, a model will be made up of discernible parts and elements—a purpose and goals (or anticipated outcomes), people, content, and a program outline. Boundaries are set up to make clear what is in and what is not in of the youth ministry model. They serve as a sort of line that delineates between internal and external components, things that a youth ministry must do and what it will not do. The internal components will have discernible structures and organization of the parts and elements. In other words, the parts are placed in connection with each other in an organized way and are seen as clearly stating what belongs in the youth ministry.

The emphasis here is on the relationship of the parts to each other. They interact, the parts articulating with each other, and their activity being interdependent. Through integration of the elements, the model is a smooth, functioning, dynamic movement, each part having its place and a place existing for each part.

A second presupposition of a systems model is that the dynamic of *equilibration* and *disequilibration* will be present between parts as various internal and external forces affect the system. Disequilibration is the tension, mistakes and errors, the unsolved problems, and old and new issues of a particular youth ministry program.

Disequilibration in a youth ministry model particularly is caused by four things: (1) the less-than-perfect functioning of components in an imperfect world; (2) people changing in such areas as their needs, interests, concerns, and personal history; (3) a change in surroundings or societal history, and; (4) simply the growing up of adolescents as they continu-

Only the local youth worker, focusing on the youth themselves in their context, can determine what the program will be.

ally develop. Tension, stress, and strain occur between parts during disequilibration. In order for disequilibration to become positive, it needs to be viewed as a signal for adaptation to new realities through creativity, innovativeness, and positive change. A systems model is built with the expectation for—the planning for—change. In order to remain effective, the youth ministry model must be open to a changing world and to its own imperfections and shortcomings. Youth ministry in particular is full of disequilibration because of the nature of adolescence versus the nature of the generally stable and static church leadership and other adults. A youth ministry model is an open model, not closed to change.

Finally, a system model presupposes linkages to other subsystems within a common system, as well as to other systems external to its own. Each of these linkages will exert some sort of influence on the system of a particular model. A youth ministry model is one part of a local church's total ministry. It is connected to each other part in some manner as determined by the church's own overall philosophy. It is also connected to external systems, for example, public schools, local recreation programs, law enforcement systems, and others.

COMPONENTS IN A YOUTH MINISTRY MODEL

As has already been made clear, the model itself is made up of a number of components:

1. *Theological and philosophical foundations regarding what is believed, valued, and shared in mind and purpose.* A foundation must be laid concerning a view of God, a view of Scripture, a view of person (in particular, adolescents), a view of ministry, a purpose of youth ministry, a view of reality (metaphysics), a view of knowledge (epistemology), a view of learning (a psychology of learning), and a view of society and culture—how sociology and culture relate to and affect all of these.

2. *A description of the specific youth involved.* Where are they developmentally? What is their subculture? What are their characteristics and needs? And what implications do all these hold for the church's youth ministry?

3. *Intended outcomes.* What do we hope to accomplish? How will we know if a youth ministry is effective? What, specifically, should we look for in order to know we are on target?

4. *The elements of ministry and program: instruction, worship, fellowship, and service (or mission).* These basic four, along with any other features a local church may want to add, help to decide the content of the youth ministry program. To arrive at a basic program outline incorporating the four basic elements, ask the question, "What will we *do* in each element?" This outline will not constitute the actual details of a program, but will remain very broad. For instance, a specific model may call for a Bible study, recreation night, worship, and choir practice each week. Monthly, a one-and-a-half day retreat for fellowship, recreation, Bible study, and worship may be planned. These are part of the model, but the specifics concerning the events are left open for more in-depth program planning. The important thing is to have planned the general types of content and activities to be included under each main program element.

5. *The roles of both youth and adults.* It must be determined who the leaders are and what specific roles they will play. (Remember that all participants have some sort of role, whether or not they are in an official leadership position.) Adults involved in the youth ministry should be chosen carefully, based upon a set of established criteria. Decide how many adult workers will be needed as part of the model.

Both adults and youth in leadership will have particular ways of functioning within the group. Will they be active or passive, initiators or followers? Will the adults be "police," chaperons, coaches, or players? How much responsibility will be given to youth in leadership?

6. *Organization that is interrelated, interdependent, and well-articulated.* The parts need to be "joined and fitted together" into a whole. These are the internals of the system. At the same time, it must be determined what relation the youth ministry model (youth ministry in the local church) has to other external systems—other churches, denomination(s), schools, the general world of adolescents, parents and family. Are the relationships open or closed? Are they distant or close? Is it a two-way communication?

7. *Analysis, evaluation, and feedback for the purpose of correction, improvement, and change.* Why do we evaluate? And what are the basic items to be evaluated? A youth ministry model must be constantly sensitive to the need for improvement and change. This need is based on the imperfections to be found in any model or whole system or in people—no person or thing is perfect—and on the internal system's dynamics, which are open to change. Basically, the question that needs to be asked is, "How effective is our model, measured by the desired outcomes?"

8. *A means to participate, observe, analyze, introduce change, evaluate, lead others in the group, follow leaders of the group, help others to lead, and make improvements in the model.* A

youth ministry subsystem will, without question, have disequilibration and stresses within itself, with other subsystems within the larger church system, and with external systems and subsystems, such as schools, home, and workplaces. With this fact in mind, the model must leave room for the users to work through their disequilibration in a variety of ways.

CRITERIA FOR THE EVALUATION OF A YOUTH MINISTRY MODEL

The following comprise criteria to be used in evaluating a youth ministry model. Taking into account that each model will differ at least in some way from any other, these incorporate the basic necessities. Further discussion of many of the criteria will be integrated throughout the rest of this book.

- *All* components are adequately described.
- The model conforms to one's already established theological and philosophical positions.
- Theological and philosophical integrity are present.
- Jesus Christ the Lord is the ultimate focal point.
- Youth are encouraged and facilitated in their own total and holistic development in the Lord Jesus Christ.
- Adolescent characteristics and needs are adequately focused upon.
- All the basic elements of the program are present in sufficient quantity and quality to achieve the purposes and desired outcomes, and are in balance.
- The purpose and anticipated outcomes are *clearly stated*, and are *worthy* and *achievable* through the program. (Note that all three are necessary; one or two will not suffice.)
- The content flows *from* the needs of youth, *through* Scripture, and *to* programs.

- The program will likely accomplish the purpose and anticipated outcomes that have been established.
- Variety, creativity, innovativeness, and contemporaneity characterize the model.
- Youth are highly involved throughout the program.
- Leadership development and deployment are planned.
- The organization is simple but comprehensive and effective.
- Evaluation and feedback are planned for and useable.
- The program is developmental—both for the development of youth and on the developmental level of youth.

- Resources, materials, and methods are well done and readily available.
- There is balance and sequence to the program.
- The youth ministry model is affordable.
- Adult leadership roles are clearly stated and clearly acceptable to the local congregation, official boards and committees, adult leaders, pastoral staff, and youth.
- The model provides for flexibility and openness to change, and is changeable without major hassles.
- The model provides for the involvement and integration of nonbelievers into the youth ministry, recognizing the need for outreach and evangelism.

3

The Youth Worker

A youth worker is important in youth ministry. This statement seems obvious, but it may not be something that many youth workers have thought through. *Why* are youth workers important in youth ministry? The first reason is that what the youth worker *is* signifies what junior high, senior high and, to a lesser degree, post-high school youth will be for the next few years. The youth worker is an adult whom youth will choose to follow and emulate. Youth workers are, in fact, people who place themselves—and are placed by the church—in a position as models to youth of what it means to be a follower of Jesus Christ. On the flip side, youth workers are often copied blindly by youth, and they need to be aware of this fact. Unfortunately, many youth do not make the distinction between the youth worker as simply an example and as someone to duplicate.

Second, the expectations youth workers have for their youth will lead eventually to some sort of reality in the lives of the youth. It is the youth worker who challenges youth and sets the standards and goals to which they will aspire. Or, at the same time, it may be the lower standards or expectations of a youth worker which lull youth into complacency. A spiritually maturing youth worker more likely leads to spiritually maturing youth; a youth worker who is developing holistically leads to holistically developing youth. In other words, physical (to a limited extent), cognitive (mental), social, moral, affective (emotional), and spiritual development will occur in youth if the youth worker expects that growth, if the youth worker has a vision of what the youth are becoming, and if he or she works to help growth occur.

Third, the youth worker usually has the single most influence, apart from parents, on the spiritual development of young people involved. In a sense, the spiritual bonding between the youth worker and members of the youth group surpasses rational definition. It is a mutual bonding, a feeling of belonging to each other and loving each other through the multitude of changes and variableness of adolescence. This bonding is more emotionally laden for adolescents than it is for healthy adults because the adolescent has fewer deep relationships than adults. Through the bonding, however, adolescents learn about spiritual development, love and care for others and themselves, social relationships, and other significant things.

Fourth, youth need a "guarantor," someone "who is appropriately anchored in adulthood but who will walk with youth on their journey."[1] A guarantor will stand with youth and show them what it means to be a maturing adult, and that the journey is worth the effort. A guarantor stands up for youth as their spokesperson when other adults do not understand adolescent behavior, culture, and mannerisms. He or she does not pull and/or push youth, but shares with them and encourages them—helping them on the journey to adulthood. Youth need consistent emotional and moral support,[2] and it is natural for the youth worker to supply this, thus becoming a guarantor in their lives.

> *Many youth do not make the distinction between the youth worker as simply an example and as someone to duplicate.*

Youth desire deep and meaningful relationships with others. As guarantors, adult youth workers need to provide youth with a quasi-adult relationship, the kind of relationship in which the understanding adult can be an adult and at the same time be a kid. The youth worker should not mix the two, but should know when it is appropriate to be youthful and when to be adult. In a way, what I am describing is the incarnational approach: The youth worker comes to his or her youth, is with them—is one with them—and yet is not them. In other words, the adult youth worker is fully adult but also can participate with youth as one *with* them, though not *of* them. Youth are looking for this kind of adult with whom they can feel acceptance and security, with whom they can be themselves and with whom they can have serious adult-like conversations. This type of adult serves well as a guarantor for youth.

CHARACTERISTICS OF THE YOUTH WORKER

The following discussion of characteristics may prove discouraging for readers for they may be left wondering how anyone could be all of these things. But possessing all of the ideal characteristics is not the issue. It is impossible for any one person to have every one of these characteristics. One might as well expect someone to be a perfect combination of John, Paul, Moses, Abraham, Sarah, David,

Deborah, Esther, Priscilla, and Barnabas. The odds are that this will never occur. Rather, the point of reviewing the characteristics of a youth worker is to recognize what is required of youth workers, to determine one's weaknesses and begin to work on them, and to support and enhance one's strengths. It is necessary to "know thy self," to think soberly, examining oneself in prayer and asking for help from others. In doing this, we can recognize and count on God's power and strength: "But he said to me, 'My grace is sufficient for you, for my power is made perfect in weakness.' Therefore I will boast all the more gladly about my weaknesses, so that Christ's power may rest on me" (2 Cor. 12:9). (See also 1 Cor. 1:27–29, 31.) Recognizing our own weaknesses provides for humble reliance on the Lord for wisdom and strength.

What do youth want in a youth worker?

One survey done by Dr. Robert Laurent found that the top five characteristics desired by high school students in a youth worker were: availability, acceptance, authenticity, vulnerability, and sensitivity.[3] Another study applicable here, published in *Journal of Early Adolescence*, described the ideal teacher according to 2,490 twelve-to-fourteen-year-olds who were asked to describe in their own words an outstanding middleschool teacher. These are the characteristics they gave: *Nice*—"She's never grouchy." *A sense of humor*—"He jokes around with us." *Shows respect and understanding*—"She doesn't make me feel dumb." *Listens, easy to talk to*—"You can talk to her in confidence." *Patient and self-controlled*—"She doesn't get mad all the time." *Fair, does not show favoritism*—"He doesn't have a teacher's pet." *Explains things well, makes learning fun*—"When I don't understand, she explains it better."[4] All of the above would certainly be equally desired by young people of their youth worker, who is, in essence, a teacher.

At times, the church in general seems to want a youth worker who will be all things to all peo-ple—to parents, church leaders, the congregation, the senior pastor, other pastoral and church staff members, and the youth group. Yet a study done by the Episcopal Church found that the most desired qualities in a youth worker were a love for youth; a relationship with God and Christ; an openness to risk, learn, and grow; maturity; and a sense of being called and committed to youth work. The study also found that a good youth ministry is characterized by being rooted in the life of the church, being supported by the senior pastor and high quality, committed adults, and involving youth in many aspects of the church's life. Such a ministry has three goals: to help youth grow in their faith, to bring youth to a personal relationship with Jesus Christ, and to help youth discover themselves.[5]

What specifically are desirable characteristics of a youth worker?

Spiritual Characteristics

Obviously, it is desirous that a youth worker be a Christian, a follower of and believer in Jesus Christ as personal Savior and Lord. Without this as the core of the youth worker's very being, little or nothing of value to the church will follow from his or her ministry. The youth worker must set an example of Christian living—not in order to be copied, but to show how the Christian life can be lived out. This cannot be done unless the youth worker is an actively maturing believer who continues to acquire new knowledge of the Bible. Something must be happening in the youth worker's spiritual life, or he or she cannot be an example to youth of a growing Christian, with the goal to influence them to salvation and maturity in Christ. The youth worker must also be genuine; youth see quickly through sham, pretense, and hypocrisy, and they have no respect for those who evidence these things in their lives.

The youth worker must also show a personal devotion and unconditional commitment to

> *The youth worker should be someone who is seeking God's power, presence, and direction for his or her own life, as well as for the youth being served.*

the Lord. This will be manifested in his or her own high ideals and standards. These moral, spiritual, and ethical values are not just to be seen on the surface in the youth worker's behavior, but must be motivated and practiced from within as an integral part of the individual's being. As especially evidenced in recent years, those who purport to be Christian leaders may appear to say and do all the right things, while on the inside they are living in great sin. (No one should feel that he or she cannot ever fall into this trap.) "Not many of you should presume to be teachers, my brothers, because you know that we who teach will be judged more strictly" (James 3:1). This is an appropriate warning. We who lead are expected to lead and teach as living examples (1 Tim. 4:12) and we will be held accountable to a higher standard than others in the church.

Finally, the youth worker should be someone who is seeking God's power, presence, and direction for his or her own life, as well as for the youth being served. Such a worker should feel called to youth ministry as a result of God's direction; he or she will be serving Christ—not only in ministry, but in all areas of life—rather than serving self. The youth worker is someone who belongs to Christ, someone who would agree with Jim Elliot's words: "He is no fool who gives what he cannot keep to gain what he cannot lose."[6]

Psychological/Emotional/ Social Characteristics

The youth worker should be already at a certain adult level of maturity before working with young people, and he or she will want to continue maturing. The requisite level of maturity would include the ability to control his or her emotions, and psychological and emotional stability. Other characteristics necessary for daily, personal interaction include the ability to get along with people, sincerity, and warmth. Youth must feel that their youth worker is trustworthy, and can be relied upon. They must be able to entrust their feelings, their dreams, and their problems to their youth worker, receiving empathy and agapic love from this important adult. They must know that no matter what they may do, the youth worker will do everything possible to "be there" for them. Yet youth workers must prove themselves worthy of the trust placed in them.

Hand in hand with trustworthiness is the necessity of being someone youth can respect. The youth worker must be a person who holds firm convictions, who stands up for what he or she believes. At the same time, he or she must be willing and desirous to change if needed. Discerning when change is necessary, and being willing to admit that fact, is very important to the ministry of youth workers. They should ask for and accept criticism from youth, parents, and church leadership, heeding what is valid and discarding the invalid.

The youth worker should be a poised, dynamic individual with an ability to speak well in public. He or she must fit in with youth and be identifiable as an adult—yet not act or appear stuffy with youth. There must be an intrinsic honesty, an openness and sharing of the self; these things appear only in persons who are comfortable with themselves. And finally, youth workers should be socially adept; they should instinctively know which fork to use, and be able to avoid social errors such as putting drinks or feet on the furniture in the homes of youth or of the congregational members. They set an example for youth, and must function acceptably in the world of adults.

Mental/Intellectual Characteristics

As in the above characteristics, it is necessary also for youth workers to be maturing mentally, growing in knowledge, intellectual capabilities, and wisdom. They must be mentally alert; they must be continually learning—about youth, oneself, life. These qualities will be evidenced in part by someone who reads, studies, reflects, and thinks.

Youth workers must practice and improve on the most effective teaching techniques. Their goal is not just to impart facts; their teaching should be for the purpose of leading youth to change in *being*, which is manifested in changed behavior.

The worker should have a basic purpose in his or her own life and in youth work. Young people should be able to see this life's purpose demonstrated in an unswerving manner. The youth worker needs to be able to organize and plan, and then carry out a plan. And more importantly, he or she must be able to help youth organize and carry out their own plans.

A basic requirement of a youth worker is an ability to remember faces and names. The value of knowing each youth by name is immeasurable; it gives youth the message that they are cared for as individuals. Youth workers must also be able to see their own faults, to self-evaluate and self-regulate. Their own faults will be pointed out to them by youth, parents, and church board members, and they need to be ready to learn from these. Finally, they need to have contemporary attitudes and behavior in order to keep up with their youth.

This does not mean falling prey to every teenage fad that comes along. It requires an awareness of trends and attitudes, however, and a knowledgeable, active, positive, and critical interaction with them.

Physical/Temporal Characteristics

A youth worker's life is one of hard work and long hours. He or she needs to be able to keep up with and help plan myriad activities, studies, and events. Certainly, physical stamina is needed, as well as the ability to take the strain and stress of the position.

Also, it is necessary for the youth worker to be neat in appearance and to dress in contemporary style. Like it or not, appearance is of major importance to most youth. While seeing beyond appearance is something that every youth worker will want to teach, it is nevertheless true that youth may not listen to someone whom they have written off as "out of it" because of how he or she is dressed. At the same time, the youth worker should stay true to himself or herself. Youth are sure to see through anything fake.

Youth ministry requires vast amounts of informal as well as formal time with youth. They need time to talk with their guarantor and friend, so the youth worker will want to have time available. He or she doesn't have to live at the beck and call of the youth, however. When my wife and I were in youth ministry we kept an open house to youth. Not every youth worker can do this, however, and it is perfectly acceptable to declare one or two nights per week "off limits" to youth except in an emergency. Otherwise, young people should know they are welcome. In this way, youth workers can seek to maintain a balance of availability to the youth with whom they are ministering, as well as to their families and their personal lives.

Attitudes Toward Youth

First and foremost, the youth worker must have a love for youth. He or she must be interested in and concerned with youth, willing to accept all of them as they are. No youth can be rejected; this is without exception. All must be welcome and loved. And this love needs to be for youth as they are now, not for what they may become when they grow up or grow out of the current stage. Some youth are much easier to love than others, but youth workers are to be incarnations of the love of Christ.

This sort of love, agape, is not an emotion; it is a commitment requiring the power of the Holy Spirit. Agape in youth ministry embodies 1 Corinthians 13:4–8. Agape is patient with youth who do not always do things our way, according to our time schedule. Agape is kind even when youth behave like typical adolescents instead of like us "more mature" adults. Agape does not envy youth the things that youth have, nor their youthfulness and/or attractiveness. Agape does not boast about how much better we youth workers are than the immature youth. It is not proud of adult accomplishments. It is not rude to youth who are less sophisticated or less socially adept than adults. Agape is not selfish; rather it seeks to help youth instead of itself. Agape does not get angry very easily with youths' incessant provocations. Agape does not keep records of all the wrong things that youth do—and there are many. Agape does not delight when youth are found doing wrong things, but it does delight when it finds youth doing and acting truthfully and correctly. Agape always protects youth, always trusts them, always hopes that they will do the best and be the best, always keeps on persevering. Agapic love, like God's love for us, never fails—no matter what. Youth want and need to be loved with this sort of agapic love: love that sees that ultimate value resides in youth because God loves them. And because God loves them, so does the youth worker.

The youth worker needs to befriend, counsel, and listen to youth with an empathetic understanding. He or she cannot be easily shocked; an expression of shock can and will be easily misinterpreted by youth. For many youth, their self-esteem is fragile and they will easily feel unloved or unworthy. On the other hand, some youth will try to test the youth worker, to push for a reaction as a means of getting attention. Whatever the case, the youth worker must be someone who can remain calm and stable in all situations.

He or she should know youth both in general and personally. The worker should know each one in the youth group, spending time with as many as possible in smaller groups and one-on-one. He or she also attempts to build up group spirit, to foster unity among the youth. But the youth worker is not a chaperon, nor a chief, nor a director, nor the church bus driver. Instead, he or she acts as a coach, encouraging and building up youth personally and through other leaders, both adult and youth. Through everything, a sense of humor is invaluable to the youth worker.

Youth workers also need to be involved with their young people, to feel a part of their lives. Again, this includes being able to fit in with youth. Of course, youth workers are adults, but they need not stick out like sore thumbs. They should be willing to allow youth to take the initiative, treating them as if what they think and desire is important. They need to be impartial and neutral in dealings with youth, showing love, fairness, and justice, which helps youth feel free to come to them with problems. They then must both show confidence and keep confidences. Youth workers should realize that the right to be heard must be earned through how they deal with youth. Finally, they should express in attitude, behavior, and very being an incarnational approach to youth ministry: loving unreservedly, working with youth for their holistic development, and helping youth develop into leaders.

Relation to Church/Organization

It is necessary that youth workers be properly appointed by a church or organization. An official appointment gives them status and authority. They should have knowledge of the church or organization for which they are working. Who are the "opinion leaders" and "gatekeepers"? Whom must they see to make changes, to get permissions, to appoint other leaders? They also need a knowledge of the parents, because who the parents are has an immense effect on who the youth are.

The youth worker becomes a symbol of the youth program and guarantor of youth to the congregation. Attitudes toward the youth worker shape attitudes toward the youth ministry. Therefore, the youth worker should try to build the ministry's program with others so that the focus is not on one person. When he or she leaves the church or organization, a healthy ministry program will not collapse. The youth worker should work not only with his or her staff, but with committees, keeping them and the pastor(s) informed of the program's direction and progress.

Additional Assets

While certainly not necessary, it is very helpful for the youth worker to have a home which can be made available for youth who drop by and spend time. Youth want and need to get out of their own houses and see other adults functioning at home. In the same vein, a youth worker is one step ahead if he or she has finances available for the various odds and ends that come up with youth—treating one to a "Coke and fries," an informal trip to the bowling alley with a small group, or entertaining youth in the home. The funding for these things has to come from somewhere, whether supplied by the youth worker or, preferably, from the church youth budget.

Another asset to youth workers is to be skilled in some areas. These might include sports, computers, music, mechanical (automotive, woodworking, etc.), intellectual (for example, chess, stamp collecting), photography, painting, etc. Other hobbies such as camping, surfing, running, fishing, snow and water skiing, or acting also come in handy for the youth worker. All of these can be done with youth, and/or taught to them outside the formal youth program, and they provide opportunities to share life with life between youth workers and youth.

ROLES OF A YOUTH WORKER

When a person decides to become a youth worker, he or she takes on many roles with the ministry. First is the role of being a *model*—an example or demonstration—of spiritual, social, intellectual, moral, emotional, and physical development. He or she is not perfect but is "on the way," and already more mature than the youth. The youth worker is looked upon as a guide through these areas of development, as someone who has gone before and can reach back to encourage and coach youth.

The youth worker also fills the role of a *counselor*, someone who listens to and responds to youth and their problems or questions. And he or she is a *resource person*, someone to go to for information and help. But it is not merely facts or advice that is imparted. The worker is a *facilitator*, asking *why?* and taking on the role of catalyst and stimulator, or "disequilibrator."[7] The goal is to help youth think things through, to make their own decisions and not just passively receive someone else's answers.

A youth worker is an *authority figure* who knows when to say no and mean it. At the same time, he or she is a *friend*. Somehow, the youth worker must maintain a delicate balance between these two roles. Another prima-

> *The youth worker becomes a symbol of the youth program and guarantor of youth to the congregation or adults.*

ry role is that of *teacher-communicator*. This is where he or she will spend a great deal of time, both formally and informally.

Youth workers are *developers of leaders* (leadership educators) and *sharers* of leadership roles. They ask themselves, "Should I do this, or is a youth capable of doing it instead?" Youth workers are comfortable in either the leading position, or in observing youth leading. They don't always need to be up front with the group. But they help youth learn to be leaders; they do not thrust upon youth the leadership responsibilities that are inappropriate.

A youth worker places his or her trust and confidence in youth, and in return is trusted by youth. He or she is an *agapic-er* of youth, that is, one who loves agapically and believes in his or her young people, unconditionally. In the role of a *pastor*, the worker "cares for the souls" of youth. And finally, youth workers are *pray-ers*, lifting everyone and everything in prayer, including their work, personal life, and the youth with whom they are entrusted. This last role serves as the foundation for all the other roles of the youth worker.

Discipline in Youth Ministry

One of the roles listed above is that of an authority figure. Under the umbrella of authority falls an often disagreeable subject: discipline. Unpleasant though it may be, it is important for the youth worker to have a

grasp on discipline in the youth group. Even so, youth workers often experience the uncomfortable ambiguity of not wanting to act like policemen but having to insist that rules and laws be kept. Discipline is a difficult and stubborn issue in youth ministry. It is hard to balance the many variables that must be kept in mind when dealing with youth, variables that constantly change as youth develop and as the calendar moves on. Discipline that worked two months ago may not work now. What works now might not work in two months.

The disciplinary role is stubborn and never goes away. There is no respite from the continual need to help youth learn to discipline themselves. Youth workers and other adults need to enforce various disciplines to some small or large degree whenever and wherever the church's youth ministry operates. Discipline issues are not easily solved nor are they likely to go away if ignored. In fact, the issues and problems seem to become exacerbated when ignored.

How then is discipline to be handled in a local church's youth ministry? Several principles should be noted. Of course, these principles will be applied differently in each ministry, depending on the youth and the youth workers involved. Keep in mind that they are only *principles*—generalizations and fundamental rules that are to be applied contextually and not legalistically.

Principle One: Meet the needs of the youth.

Youth ministry must be developed to meet the needs of young people involved, and its program should be aimed squarely at the needs of today's youth. A program designed by well-meaning adults to meet adult needs will never keep the interest of the youth. And such an adult-driven ministry will surely encounter problems of discipline.

Often youth "act up" because they are bored to the point of misbehavior. They realize early on that the program is not for them and that the adult leaders do not understand them or know what to do with them. In such circumstances, youth may take charge by various means in order to clearly indicate their own assessment of the adults' program for them. The program must be changed in order to meet the felt and, ultimately, real needs of youth.

Principle Two: Foster a warm, positive, and knowledgeable relationship with the youth.

Youth workers need to know youth, both developmentally and individually. Relationships based on a knowledgeable understanding of youth will make discipline much easier. Young people most often want to please those adults who are significant in their lives. A warm, positive, and knowledgeable relationship will enable leaders to anticipate needs, and will provide feedback regarding whether or not the program is meeting the needs of youth. This kind of a relationship offers a forum in which to talk about discipline issues before they become a problem. If discipline does become a problem, the difficulty can then be addressed within a positive, caring environment where two or more people know and have mutual respect for each other.

Principle Three: Expect, anticipate, and plan for discipline problems.

As program plans are being formed, the youth worker needs to anticipate various scenarios in which discipline problems might arise and prepare ways to meet the challenge. One current problem is that of youth leaving the planned event to escape the eyes of the adult leadership. "Lock-ins" are one solution to keep this from happening. A program is announced as being a lock-in and no one may

> *A program designed by well-meaning adults to meet adult needs will never keep the interest of the youth.*

leave or come in once the program has begun.

Youth workers should think through the needs of their youth—especially when the youth program attracts "outside" young people. They must consider how individual youth might respond and then take steps to avert avoidable discipline problems.

Principle Four: Head off a problem before it becomes full-blown.

It may not be possible to plan sufficiently to avoid discipline problems totally, but it is possible to take action to alleviate them as they appear, before they become fully developed. It is normal for some kind of "horsing around" to occur when youth get together. It is also normal for some activity to get out of hand, making discipline necessary. The alert youth worker can usually see a problem developing. He or she can then act quickly and decisively to stop it in its infancy. A glance, a shaking of the head, a friendly but firm oral statement, or some other clear signal often will stop the problem before it matures.

Principle Five: Communicate rules and limits clearly.

It is the responsibility of the youth worker to communicate clearly the bounds within which a particular program is to be operated. A legitimate rationale, with consequences, should be stated. Youth should know up front what is expected of them, why that is so, and what will happen if they overstep the limits or intentionally break the rules. For example, most camps do not allow smoking on the grounds for fear of fire. If a youth worker knows that some attending camp are hooked on cigarettes, he or she has one of two choices: either (1) tell the smokers that they cannot do so and expect some of them not to attend; or (2) designate a place that is safe from the possibility of a fire, where youth can smoke. Youth should know the rules and expectations before they get to the program. It is when limits and rules are suddenly sprung upon them that they often rebel and act out their frustration in a negative manner.

It is wise to help the young people in the youth ministry develop their own set of rules and behavior. If they themselves determine the rules and the consequences of breaking them, they will be more likely to support and help enforce appropriate behavior. A youth worker must be careful to enforce behavior and rules that the youth have set.

Principle Six: Keep rules to a minimum; obey the law of the land.

Only those rules and limitations that are necessary for safety, enjoyment, mutual respect, and agapic love should be used. A ministry that is characterized by more than a few rules and limitations often is not a ministry but some sort of bureaucratic, religious jail. Consider the two great commandments that Jesus gave: Love God and love your neighbor. And Paul's commentary is that the law is fulfilled by love. The fewer the rules, the less adult workers will have to function as policemen and women; and the more relaxed everyone is. Then, leaders do not need to enforce a long list of do's and don'ts and youth do not have to be constantly concerned with what rule or limit they might be about to break.

Youth workers must be law-abiding citizens and expect that youth keep the law of the land. The workers show their own level of moral development by their responses to law and their expectations of youth to the law. At no time should youth workers encourage breaking the law, or "look the other way" while their charges engage in illegal activities (Rom. 13: 1–7).

Principle Seven: Uphold rules consistently.

Rules and limitations must be upheld consistently for all the youth and adults involved in a particular ministry; it is a form of love to do so. And all of the adult workers must be willing to uphold the rules. If one leader is soft on a certain rule or limitation, the youth will find out and oftentimes will maximize that softness to their own benefit.

Youth caught in violation of a rule or limit need to suffer the consequences that have been announced. It is absolutely wrong to speak of dire consequences befalling the breaking of a rule and then not follow through. On the other hand, the old common law principle that the "punishment should fit the crime" is applicable here. It is ridiculous to practically threaten eternal damnation for a minor infraction or for breaking a rule that was silly to begin with. Youth, parents, and church boards know the difference between necessary rules and limits and those that are merely petty. Therefore, when a meaningful, necessary, and worthwhile rule or limitation is broken, the consequences should fall justly on those involved.

Principle Eight: Discipline quietly, justly, lovingly, and swiftly.

If a boy or girl must be disciplined, it should be done quietly, justly, lovingly, and swiftly. A youth worker should not make a scene in front of the whole group. Nor is it loving to embarrass a young person for breaking a rule. Youth in the group will know who has been disciplined without the leader creating a public spectacle.

Principle Nine: Ensure that all leaders know, agree with, and uphold discipline.

All of the leaders and workers in a local church's youth ministry need to know and agree with the limits and rules, and be responsible to do so. Stated limitations and rules are as strong as the weakest leader who upholds them. If leaders cannot agree on the rules, then the rules should not be announced, or the leader or leaders who do not agree should be asked not to attend that particular program. As a last resort, if there is continual disagreement on proper rules and limitations, the leader(s) may have to drop out or be asked to drop out. Dissension should not be allowed to exist among the workers, nor can inconsistent maintenance of the rules be tolerated.

Principle Ten: Determine who will enforce discipline.

A youth worker needs to determine in advance who will enforce the rules and limitations. Should one adult leader be the "disciplinarian"? Or should all the leaders have equal authority?

The answer to these questions will vary from church to church, from leader to leader, and program to program. Normally, the adult leader nearest to the discipline problem should act first, quickly and decisively. If the problem persists or becomes a major issue, the official youth worker should be called upon. If a young person must be sent home or if some other drastic measure must be taken, only the official youth worker should take that responsibility. The person who has the ultimate responsibility for the youth program should be in charge of meting

out serious consequences for breakin the announced rules or limits.

Principle Eleven : Follow up on youth who are disciplined.

A day or two after youth have been disciplined, the adult who did the disciplining should contact the young people involved. They should be assured that the discipline they received was not a personal vendetta, and that the adult worker really cares for and loves them. It may be necessary to reiterate the reasons for the rules and why the consequences were meted out. Disciplined youth should be invited back, assuming that "banishment" was not the punishment. When they do return, a point should be made of talking to them personally in a spirit of love and acceptance, but not about the breaking of the rule. Youth should not be made to feel like spiritual or psychological lepers, nor punished repeatedly for one problem, nor should their return be made a spectacle.

Finally, discipline is never fun for youth workers or youth. But discipline is often the only loving action to take. All human beings need discipline at some time in their lives, adults as well as youth. No one is totally free—this is an illusion of the media and of shallow, egocentric thinking. Adult workers and youth themselves who are leaders must expect that the rest of the youth will know and willingly obey the rules and limitations for the good of the whole, as well as for the good of each individual. Youth need to know that the rules and limitations are not the result of some depraved adult mind that wants to dampen the fun. Rather, the rules come from those who care enough to set limits in a loving and just way. Youth need to be helped to recognize that the limits are not capricious but loving, and have been mutually agreed upon. Then they can be expected to follow them wisely in the spirit of love and not of law.

EDUCATION	TRAINING
inductive	deductive
tentative	firm
dynamic	static
understanding	memorizing
ideas	facts
broad	narrow
deep	surface
experiential	rote
active	passive
questions	answers
process	content
strategy	tactics
alternatives	goal
exploration	prediction
discovery	dogma
active	reactive
initiative	direction
whole brain	left brain
life	job
long-term	short-term
change	stability
content	form
flexible	rigid
risk	rules
synthesis	thesis
open	closed
imagination	common sense
This person is a LEADER	**This person is a MANAGER**

Youth Worker As Educator or Trainer?

Although the two are often confused with each other, education and training are not synonymous. Those who educate are leaders and developers, while those who train are managers and indoctrinators. It is desirable for the youth worker to lead youth rather than manage them, and to help youth themselves learn to lead. Warren Bennis, in *On Becoming a Leader,*[8] gives valuable insight into the difference between a person who educates and one who trains:

It is easy to realize that most of us would want to function as leaders in our ministries. It is also important for us to recognize that effective leaders need some management skills in order to be effective. The issue is, however, that many youth workers are given the role of leaders but only know how to function as managers. It is required of youth workers to become leaders and to help other adults and youth workers and youth themselves to develop into effective leaders, and not be mere managers. (See chapter 8.)

HOW TO BUILD RELATIONSHIPS AND EVENTUALLY PROGRAMS

A youth ministry is built on relationships between the youth leader, other adults working with the group, and the youth themselves. It is the place of the youth worker to take the lead in establishing relationships with the young people in a group, and from these to build the ministry program(s). The first step for the youth worker is to *observe* youth. He or she should spend time with youth on their own turf whenever possible. This can be done by attending school activities, visiting youth during their lunch periods (with the school's permission), hanging out at the mall, or chaperoning school dances—in general, going where the youth are. These times of observation are not for research alone; they are also opportunities to get to know youth and become their friend.

Ethnographic Principles

One effective method for observing youth comes from the field of ethnography. Ethnography is the intentional study of a culture or subculture by someone from outside that culture or subculture. The means by which this study is accomplished are personal observation, talking to informants, and participant-observation. Ethnographers seek to record mentally and/or in writing a given social group's behaviors and underlying cultural values, norms, social structures, economic structures, family-kinship structures, labor structures, and a host of other potential variables and variants of this list.

The ethnographer attempts to systematically gather data in an unbiased manner and to interpret those data accurately to reflect the reality of the culture being studied. Ethnographers usually deal with a social context that is in flux. At times they become a part of that social context and influence the behaviors that are under observation. They are a rather crucial part of the communication process, which involves both formal and informal interaction with others in the culture.

The work of the ethnographer is to be both an analyst and a participant-observer of a culture. Ethnographers constantly record in some fashion what people do and say, and also seek to get behind and below the content to the structures of the culture. By focusing on those structures and not merely on a culture's content, ethnographers are able to determine the meanings attributed to various actions, rituals, and work. This leads to the ability to predict the proper behavior of a culture's members in a given situation almost as well as the members themselves.

Ethnographers focus on the cultural-social dimensions of behaviors rather than on individual personalities or idiosyncratic dimensions of behaviors. Thus ethnographers look for cultural explanation rather than for behaviors that are associated strictly with personality. This means that there is a constant need to check sources and observations and to determine if information and observations are correct, rather than to rely on mere personal interpretation by the ethnographers or their informants.

The task of ethnographers is not to place value statements on cultural behaviors and values. Nor is it primarily to change the culture under study; rather, it is descriptive, interpretative, and predictive. Ethnography aims to understand a culture in order for the ethnographer or others to be better communicators within the culture. Ethnography is for description and prediction, not prescription.

Youth Workers as Ethnographers

Applied to youth ministry, the work of the ethnographer is to look for common patterns of sociocultural behavior, for expressions of such things as values and beliefs. Based on these findings, youth culture ethnographers seek for the meanings attributed directly or indirectly to what is observed and inferred. This leads to an understanding of how a given youth subculture functions both within its own subculture and in relation to the larger culture in which it is imbedded.

The net result is that the findings of the youth culture ethnographer are not for reports. Instead, they are for the benefit of the youth worker who functions within the particular youth subculture studied. Predicting how a given youth subculture functions and therefore how its members will act under given circumstances makes for more effective ministry and the meeting of needs of that subculture. Thus the youth worker is able to understand his or her youth in establishing relationships.

In summary, a youth worker ethnographic participant-observer does the following:

- *Describes* the culture/subculture, stating what it is;
- *Analyzes* it, showing how it works;
- *Interprets* it, stating its meaning to the culture's members;
- *Predicts* it, telling what will happen, and is able to live harmoniously within that culture.

Further Steps and Questions

Another way in which youth workers can understand youth in order to build relationships is by *reading* in a variety of sources. There are a number of psychological and sociological books and journals of adolescence. Current magazines for both adults and youth cover youth trends, as do daily newspapers. Sometimes denominational and religious periodicals are helpful.

While the youth worker is taking in what information is available about youth, he or she should be *reflecting* upon its significance: What meaning can be made for relationships with youth and their program based on participant-observation and current readings? The youth worker should also reflect on his or her own adolescence, applying that experience to the present in order to gain better understanding of the youth group.

Relationships with youth are a source of knowledge for the ongoing work of the youth program. The youth worker needs to use—in a good sense—his or her relationships with youth to plan with them and with other adults working with the group. Work together to set mutual goals.

Observing the Subculture

As a further aid to developing relationships with youth, the following is a list of questions to use in participant-observation of a youth subculture:

- How are status and prestige gained and maintained in the group?
- What is the composition of the group in terms of gender, ethnicity, sex, age, education, religion, etc.?
- How does one qualify for membership in this group?
- What are the main distinguishing features of this group?

- What sociopsychological needs seem to be met by participation in this group? Can you discern other sociological functions it performs?
- Describe the patterns of social interaction that you observed. Who does what, when, to whom, and how?
- What ethical and/or moral norms and values are emphasized?
- How does this group relate to others, both in the adolescent and nonadolescent worlds?
- What patterns of conflict and cooperation, with both internal and external forces or other groups, exist in this group?
- What type of identity can this group give its members which cannot be obtained outside of the subculture?
- Is there any sense in which the subculture is a counterculture?
- Describe the degree of association or identity of the youth with their subculture—is it full-time or part-time?
- Who are the leaders? Why are they leaders? Who made them leaders?
- Describe the kind of clothes they wear. Are there certain things which indicate that they are youth or a certain socio-economic class of youth?
- What do they believe in?
- How do they deal with deviations from their subculture's norms?
- Where do they get their money?
- How do they use their money? (Purchase what goods/services?)
- What do they consider their turf to be?
- How far do they travel from their own turf?
- How are outsiders who venture onto their turf treated?
- What does the group do that some of the individuals do not do? Vice versa?
- How large in numbers is their subculture?

- What peculiarities of language, speech, or gestures are part of the group's norms?
- How do they view the institutions of the larger society, for example, school, church, police, shopping mall, or recreational programs?
- What do they think about their parents?
- To whom do they turn for help?
- What do they see themselves doing and being in five years?
- Who are their idols? Least favorite person? Ask why.
- How do they communicate and with whom do they communicate outside their own culture?
- How do they get excitement?
- What do they think about _____ ? Fill in the word—sex, drinking, drugs, speaking in tongues, poverty, the President.

Investigating the Subculture

The following are some suggestions of questions for the youth worker to ask young people directly in order to discover more about their subculture:

- What do you think about? (both generally and specific items, people, ideas, or events)
- What is important?
- What are you afraid of? What is your greatest fear?
- Who is the most important person in your life? Why?
- Who are your heroes? Your idols?
- Who are the bad guys?
- What is God good for?
- What is the church good for?
- What do you think about: the church, Sunday school, the Bible, other spiritual matters, _____ ?
- What do you want from the church's youth program?
- How would you change your church?

- Do you want to be like either of your parents? Why/why not?
- What is your favorite TV program? Video? Song? Why?
- What is your least favorite TV program, video, etc.? Why?
- What does it take to be successful today?
- What do your friends talk about the most?
- If you could change three things in your world, what would they be? Why those three?

A SUCCESSFUL YOUTH WORKER

In summary, to be a successful youth worker one must love Christ, youth, and ministry—teaching, counseling, serving, and being with youth. The youth worker will demonstrate this love by showing concern for and interest in youth. He or she will talk *with* youth informally, treating them on an equal-to-equal basis and not focusing only on any adults present. He or she will *spend time* with youth on their "turf," wherever that may be—school, athletic events, the mall, and other places. And finally, the successful youth worker *wants* to spend time with youth and shows it clearly.

A BASIC SELF-EVALUATION FOR YOUTH WORKERS

Where do you think you stand as a youth worker? To find out, honestly rate the following statements on a scale of one to five, one being low and five being high. These statements are meant as a tool for evaluation—to discover in which areas you are weak and in which you are strong, and to use this knowledge for improvement. You may find it helpful to share your answers with your spouse, a trustworthy colleague, or a friend.

- I am truly committed to Christ as my Lord. I know this because. . . .

- I am truly committed to youth ministry and leadership *of* and *by* youth. I know this because. . . .
- I know what youth are like generally (developmental characteristics). I *know* the young people in my group, developmentally and personally.
- I have insightfully observed my youth's culture: values, behaviors, taboos, programs, etc.
- I know and respect youth as individuals.
- I am using my knowledge about my youth to help them develop goals and programs.
- I am involving youth in the decision-making process regarding programs that will affect them.
- My youth know that I love them.
- I have a sense of love from my youth.
- I spend *quality* time with my youth, both in large and small groups and one-on-one.
- We (adults, youth, and I) have developed a balanced program.
- We have evidence of the program's facilitating holistic and spiritual growth. I know this because . . .
- I have the support of pastoral staff, official boards, and committees.
- My spouse (if married) actively supports my ministry.
- I have someone or some group to whom I am regularly accountable, who asks tough questions, probes, is faithful to me, and prays for me regularly.
- I am replenishing my spiritual, physical and psychical strength.
- I have balanced time commitments.

HOW WILL YOU BE REMEMBERED?

Perhaps the final evaluation of a youth worker is some years in coming. The following piece from the *Campus Life* magazine Leader's Guide cuts to the heart of what ultimately is important in a youth worker:

You're working with a bunch of high school kids. What will they remember 15 years from now? I suspect they'll remember a *lot* about you as a person—and perhaps little else.

I recently had the opportunity to think back to when I was in high school. My former assistant pastor, John, and his wife, Carol, were in town visiting, and my wife and I invited them and six old high school friends over for an evening. One man even brought his guitar, the *sine qua non* of youth groups in the 60s. We reminisced about our youth group days. What did we remember?

We remembered a series of meetings on sex and sexuality. We remember playing *Sgt. Pepper's Lonely Hearts Club Band* and discussing the meanings of the songs. Forgotten was the content of about 245 other meetings.

But John and Carol influenced us significantly beyond the content of our meetings. They had an open-house policy; after school one or more kids would drop in to chat or just sit in the kitchen while Carol fixed dinner. We always felt welcome. They always had time for us. We spent many long evenings sitting around the fireplace, just talking.

We watched John and Carol interact with each other. They weren't perfect, and they didn't pretend to be. We noted how they treated each other and their young children, and if their lives were consistent with their teaching.

They helped us learn about ourselves and what we could do. We learned leadership skills because we were given large responsibilities. We were expected to plan and implement the Sunday programs, Wednesday Bible studies, service projects and retreats. John and Carol coached us, prayed for us, cried with us, encouraged us and rejoiced with us, but the major part of the program planning rested on our shoulders. On week-long service projects in the mountains of Kentucky we led the singing, we preached in church services, we even wrote our own music.

Were we the typical product of their ministry? During their years at the church, John and Carol worked with a couple hundred kids. They weren't all student leaders; some were the fringe kids. One girl, Sue, was overweight, from an unchurched home, unpopular. She called John a few months ago. She hasn't had an easy life. During their conversation she remembered the time (15 years ago!) when she was in the hospital and John sent her a card. It was the only card she received.

Sue probably doesn't remember much about the meetings she attended. But she sure remembers an adult friend who reached out and cared for her as a person.

I don't know where most of my old peers are today, or what they're doing. But I know we all learned a great deal about the Christian life from two youth leaders who reached out and loved us.[9]

PART II

Balanced Elements of a Youth Program

The next four chapters concern the four elements of a balanced youth program: teaching, worship, fellowship, and service (mission or ministry). These are a natural outgrowth of the basic philosophy and criteria for a youth ministry model advocated in part I.

Usually there is little or no argument regarding teaching, fellowship, and service. But some people look askance when told that adolescents should also be encouraged and helped to worship God at their respective levels of development. One clergyman in a liturgical denomination could not conceive how youth can worship God as meaningfully as adults can. It is our hope that chapter 5 will help adults to consider and promote effective worship experiences for youth.

A youth ministry may have additional elements, but these four are the minimum required for a successful, well-rounded ministry.

CHAPTER

4

Teaching Youth

The first steps to teaching the Bible to youth are the teacher's personal Bible study and lesson preparation. These require three things. First, *responsibility.* Study and lesson preparation should be undertaken only with the utmost seriousness. Responsibility requires teachers to recognize that they are dealing with the Word of God, not merely a Shakespearean sonnet or lyrics to some rock music. We must approach our teaching of the Word of God understanding that we teach the *powerful* Word of God. Scripture separates between the "bone and marrow"; it makes minute discriminations in our soul. (See Heb. 4:12–13.)

Second, an *understanding of the Bible* is necessary. Understanding the Bible requires us to diligently study Scripture and experience it in our lives so we may teach it from our own personal understanding and firsthand experience. We must explore and experience the truth of Scripture for ourselves before attempting to communicate truth to someone else.

Third, preparing to teach requires *time.* It has been said that the average teacher spends only twenty minutes in preparation of a lesson. This very small allotment of time should come under close scrutiny if we apply the words of James 3: "Not many of you should presume to be teachers, my brothers, because you know that we who teach will be judged more strictly" (v. 1). Read on through verse 12 and note the amount of attention given to the use of the tongue—a teacher's main means of communication. Before anyone should embark upon teaching youth, he or she should first consider carefully the implications of the undertaking. Keeping these things in mind, there is still more to know about teaching youth.

THE FIVE "KNOWS" OF TEACHING

1. Know the Purpose

One must know the *purposes* of Scripture. For this, we turn to Scripture itself. Understand that we teach the Word of God for three purposes, all of which reflect the purposes for which Scripture was given.

a. *We communicate effectively the Word of God in order to help people to change:*

Preach [or proclaim, communicate effectively] the Word; be prepared in season and out of season; correct, rebuke, and encourage—with great patience and careful instruction. (2 Tim. 4:2; cf. 1 Thess. 2:11–12)

The word of God is living and active. Sharper than any double-edged sword, it penetrates even to dividing soul and spirit, joints and marrow; it judges the thoughts and attitudes of the heart. (Heb. 4:12)

All Scripture is God-breathed and is useful for teaching, rebuking, correcting and training [instruction, understandingly using Scripture to teach for righteousness] in righteousness, so that the man of God may be thoroughly equipped for every good work. (2 Tim. 3:16–17)

I have hidden your word in my heart that I might not sin against you. (Ps. 119:11)

The entrance of your words gives light; it

gives understanding to the simple. (Ps. 119:130)

Direct my footsteps according to your word. (Ps. 119:133)

All of these passages focus upon a primary role of Scripture as helping us to change—to *be* different people because of our study of Scripture and our allowing Scripture to enter into us.

b. *We teach for development, for maturity, for equipping, and for the fruits of the Spirit:*

We proclaim him [Christ], admonishing and teaching everyone with all wisdom, so that we may present everyone perfect in Christ. To this end I labor, struggling with all his energy, which so powerfully works in me. (Col. 1:28–29)

It was he who gave some to be apostles, some to be prophets, some to be evangelists, and some to be pastors and teachers, to prepare God's people for works of service, so that the body of Christ may be built up until we all reach unity in the faith and in the knowledge of the Son of God and become mature, attaining to the whole measure of the fullness of Christ. (Eph. 4:11–13)

c. *Finally, we teach because we are called to teach.* Teaching is one of the spiritual gifts:

And in the church God has appointed first of all apostles, second prophets, third teachers . . . (1 Cor. 12:28)

It was he [Christ] who gave some to be apostles, some to be prophets, some to be evangelists, and some to be pastors and teachers. . . . (Eph. 4:11)

Not many of you should presume to be teachers, my brothers, because you know that we who teach will be judged more strictly. (James 3:1)

Be shepherds of God's flock that is under your care, serving as overseers—not because you must, but because you are willing, as God wants you to be; not greedy for money, but eager to serve. (1 Peter 5:2)

It is the job of the teacher to know what is appropriate and to teach it in an effective manner with the best methods.

And the Lord's servant must not quarrel; instead he must be kind to everyone, able to teach, not resentful. (2 Tim. 2:24)

2. Know the Learner

Know *whom* you are going to teach. First Corinthians 3:1–9 suggests that a teacher's job is to know the developmental level of the learners and to teach appropriately to that level (see also Heb. 5:11–14). Much spiritual food is inappropriate for immature Christians—children and youth especially, often because they could not possibly understand it; it is beyond their mental capacity. For example, the concept of "righteousness by faith" is hard enough for mature adults to grasp, let alone fourteen-year-olds. It is the job of the teacher to know what is appropriate and to teach it in an effective manner with the best methods. (Of course, there are many biologically older persons for whom much spiritual teaching is beyond their grasp.)

In order to know the learners being taught, a number of *characteristics* should be examined. First, there are the developmental characteristics—physical, cognitive, social, emotional/affective, moral, and spiritual/faith. Second, there are environmental surroundings, including people, cultures, cultural values, historic events, and geography. Is the environment supportive, hostile, or neutral? Also consider the educational environment—the teacher, learners, materials—and the location—a classroom, camp, etc.

Finally, there are the learners' motivations. What brings a person to learn? Are they being required to learn or experiencing social pres-

sure? Are they motivated by curiosity, anticipation, a desire to learn? Is disequilibration—that state of searching and uncertainty that leads to growth—taking place?

Motivation comes from within, but it is the teacher who stimulates it. Young people will want to know why the teaching is important and what value there is in studying. The bottom line for youth is: Why should I get involved in this? What good is in it for me? Why should this interest me?

Before a teacher can get the interest of the learners, he or she must first gain a hearing and obtain rapport so that youth will listen and follow their teacher's leading. To do this, speak on their developmental level of understanding. Find a point of contact, beginning with the personal. It also helps, if possible, to know the youth—particularly in a local church situation. In a church youth group, teachers have the opportunity to learn general characteristics of youth and get to know their own learners during the week.

The teacher should be friendly to youth. It is invaluable to become their friend and to show yourself as *for* them, as their advocate and guarantor. A friend is honest, and youth demand honesty from those with whom they have relationships. They see when the teacher messes up, whether or not it is in front of the group. This is one reason why it is best to be open and admit to mistakes.

Another way to gain a hearing from youth is to begin the teaching time differently from the usual. Use variety in getting their interest and in presenting material; for instance, tell a joke or anecdote, or create a dramatic beginning. Getting and holding their interest are two keys to motivating learners. These can be accomplished in a number of ways:

- Appeal to the known interests of the specific youth audience—hobbies, sports, socials, local, national, or international news.
- Appeal to their felt needs, such as to get rid of sin or to solve problems.
- Ask questions germane to the material, such as, "Who is your best friend?" Also, ask the kinds of questions you hear them asking.
- Tell a short story or recount an incident.
- Make a startling statement, such as, "God is dead," "Christ didn't come to make people good," or "Many of you are liars!"
- Pose "What would *you* do?" questions, allowing for a life problem study. For example, use the story of Joseph and Potiphar's wife, or ask a contemporary question found in a recent movie or popular song. One word of caution is that there must not be too many choices, and those must be clear, or it will become difficult to keep on track.

More ways to grab attention include:

- Paint a *vivid* picture of the life, character, and times of Bible events.
- Present a quotation from a famous person or a Bible character, such as Amos 5:21–24.
- Bring up a contemporary problem; for instance, what is a Christian answer to a particular social issue. For example, what is a Christian view of capital punishment?
- Distribute questionnaires to get learners' judgments and feelings. Then discuss conflicts in the group and introduce biblical material.
- Invite an adult to share how the passage to be studied helped him or her. (This person must be someone who can estab-

lish a rapport with the learners.)
- Present true-to-life dilemmas that youth commonly face.
- Use anything else that surprises, startles, or grabs the learners' wandering minds and helps them to listen and—especially—to think. Use these things to suggest that the Bible holds answers to whatever they encounter.

Another way to know who learners are is to *examine their expectations*. What does each person expect his or her experience will be? What type of role do they play in the learning setting? Two types of roles exist in the teaching experience—that of the learner and that of the teacher—each affecting the type of learning that will take place. The roles of the learner are either that of the active participant or the passive observer who will absorb content quietly. The roles of the teacher are more varied:

- "Policeman" or disciplinarian
- Authority
- Helper, facilitator
- Friend
- The "Enemy"

The teacher represents the content of the lesson as well.

The *abilities and capabilities of the learners* are further clues to "who they are." What are they capable of learning and doing? What do they already know? Using the above personal characteristics, ask the following questions:

- What are the learners' current behavior and knowledge?
- How long will they—can they—sit still?
- Do they learn best through talk, action, reflection, observation, or participation?
- What are their developmental stages?
- Can they think abstractly or are they limited to the concrete?
- What is their reading level?
- How long is their attention span?
- What spiritual and general knowledge do they have?

Finally, knowing who learners are requires that teachers *understand their learners' needs.* Teachers can develop an understanding of their learners' needs from both their characteristics and from personal knowledge. Needs are some lack or gap in development, growth, understanding, and application (to life) of information for use in life. Two types of needs exist—*real* needs, which can be recognized by outsiders as legitimate, and *felt* needs, which may or may not be legitimate to an outsider, but certainly feel real to those who have them.

3. Know the Intended Results

Know *why* you are going to teach. "Why" is built on two things: the Word of God or Scripture portion, and the learners—whom you will teach. (The latter includes an understanding of their developmental characteristics and needs, as mentioned above.) Within the "why," outcomes in four areas or domains are necessary. A lesson without outcomes or objectives in the four domains is like going on a trip without any destination in mind. The teacher will never know when and if he or she has arrived. To put it another way, *if you aim at nothing you'll be sure to hit it.*

The four areas of outcomes are (a) Cognitive—this answers the question, *What information, facts, ideas, etc., do I anticipate that the learners will receive as a result of my lesson?* The anticipated outcome is that knowledge is increased and/or changed. (b) Affective—*What do I anticipate that the learners will feel about the knowledge they gained from this lesson?* Here, feelings/emotions will be changed. (c) Behavioral—*What do I anticipate the learners will do as a result of my lesson?* The outcome expected is that some particular behavior is changed. (d) Existential—*What do I anticipate the learners will be as a result of my lesson?* The anticipated outcome is that learners' "being" or inner core of values and existence is changed.

Some key verbs for writing intended learner outcomes

The table on page 68 contains a long (but not exhaustive) list of verbs that may be helpful for expressing learner outcomes. You will certainly wish to add your own ideas.

4. Know the Subject Matter

Know *what* you are going to teach. A basic approach to Bible study and preparation for teaching will include *first* the reading through of the passage at least three times at one sitting. The outcome of this is to find the main idea(s) of the passage. *Second*, determine the theme of the whole book from which you are teaching. Read the book totally three times, each time at one sitting. Use different translations and other languages if possible. This will enable you, the teacher, to know the book's main thought(s).

Third, determine the context of the passage that you will teach: what went before and what is still ahead. The outcome is to know the particular passage's place in the book's thought. *Fourth*, analyze the passage by examining it in detail through the following questions:

- What are the actions in the verses? Look for verbs.
- Who is doing the actions? Look for nouns and pronouns.
- Who or what receives the actions? Search for direct and indirect objects.
- How are nouns, pronouns, verbs, etc., modified by adjectives and adverbs? Check out the colorful adjectives, adverbs, and phrases, such as "bountiful," or "greatly."
- Do word studies of important words. The anticipated outcome of these analyses is that the teacher will determine the author's meaning for the original readers.

Fifth, a basic approach to Bible study and

SOME KEY VERBS FOR WRITING INTENDED LEARNER OUTCOMES

COGNITIVE:
Learners
will:

adapt
add to
analyze
apply
arrange
assign
assess
categorize
change
chart
clarify
classify
combine
compare
compose
conclude
construct
contrast
convert
critique
decide
defend
define
demonstrate
describe
design
determine
develop
devise
diagnose
diagram
differentiate
discern
discover
discriminate
distinguish
divide
draw a conclusion
effect
employ
establish
evaluate
expand
explain
extend
find
form a new whole
formulate
generalize
give examples of
give reason(s) for
give the meaning of
harmonize
identify (cognitive)
indicate
infer
illustrate
interpret
justify
label
list
locate
make use of
master
match

memorize
modify
organize
outline
paraphrase
plan
predict
prepare
prioritize
produce
prove
provide evidence
put into one's own
    words
rank
rate
rearrange
rebut
recall
recommend
recognize
reconcile
reconsider
reconstruct
relate
remember
reorganize
rephrase
report
resolve
respond
restate
review
revise
reword
rewrite
select
separate
show
simplify
solve
sort
specify
state criteria/stan-
    dard/norm
state how/when to
    apply
state the implica-
    tions
substitute
suggest
summarize
support
synthesize
systematize
translate
unify

AFFECTIVE:
Learners
will:

abhor
accept
acknowledge
admit
affirm
agree
appreciate
appropriate

approve
aspire
assert
be adverse to
be assured
be comforted
be confident in
be content
be courageous
be determined
be dissatisfied
be enthusiastic
be joyful
be pleased
be sure of
be willing
believe
care for
cherish
choose
concur with
confess
confirm
consent
consider
cooperate
dare to
decide
delight
deny
depend on
desire
determine
devote oneself to
disapprove
embrace
enjoy
expect
express consistently
favor
feel obliged
feel persuaded
feel relief
feel sure
glorify
have courage
have no doubt
honor
hope
humble oneself
hunger for
identify (affective)
imagine
intend to
internalize
judge
love
mourn
object
praise
prize
promise
receive
reconcile oneself to
refuse
reject
rejoice
rely on/upon
renounce

repudiate
resolve
respect
rest
revere
select
set one's heart on
set one's mind on
sorrow
submit
support
surrender
treasure
trust
value
volunteer
yearn for
yield

BEHAVIORAL:
Learners
will:

abstain
accompany
act
alter
apologize
apply
ask
ask forgiveness
assemble
associate with
attempt
avoid
be a model of
be patient
be still
bear up
befriend
begin to
behave
bless
care for
carry out
change
channel
check up
comfort
conduct
contact
control
contribute
cooperate
create
defend
demonstrate
destroy
develop
direct
discard
discharge
discontinue
do
encourage
end
endure
engage in
enlist
examine

experiment
explain
fight against
follow
follow the plans to
forget
forgive
fulfill
fulfill responsibility
gather
get rid of
give
go
help
honor
improve
initiate
investigate
invite
join
keep
labor
lead
liberate
loose
make
make amends
make an effort to
make progress
    toward
make use of
minister
moderate
modify
obey
observe
operate
overcome
perform
practice
praise
pray
prepare
present
purify
put an end to
put into effect
refrain
refuse
reject
release
remain
renew
reorganize
request
resist
respond
restore
restrain
reestablish
separate from
serve
set an example of
set apart
show improvement
    in
speak the truth
stand firm
stand up against

stop
subdue
subject
submit
support
take
take advantage of
take charge of
take the first step
take the lead
take time for
tell
test
thank
try
turn to
volunteer
wait
witness
work
work for
work together
worship

EXISTENTIAL:
Learners
will:

abide
act consistently
be a _____
be alive with
be characterized
    by
be committed to
be confident in
be consistent with
be constant
be continually
    changed
be enlivened
be known as
be rooted
be spiritually dis-
    cerning
be transformed
become and con-
    tinue to
become alive to
become proficient
become strong
becoming
    more _____
conquer
continue
continue to be
    _____-minded
continue to grow
develop a habit
establish
keep on
maintain
make one's own
master
persevere
persist
remain
stand fast
sustain
transform

preparation for teaching includes determining the needs of the learners. To do this, the teacher must:

- Look at developmental characteristics, paying particular attention to cognitive, moral, and faith development.
- Examine the areas of developmental needs, interests, concerns, hurts, the socio-political context, family, and such things.
- Determine in the light of developmental characteristics and the needs of learners what *content* in the verses will be emphasized. Ask, what do I want to teach learners that will make a difference in their lives? How does the text relate to the learners' lives here and now?
- Develop intended outcomes based on what you have decided to teach. Ask yourself four questions: As a result of my teaching, what do I hope the learners will know? What do I hope the learners will feel? What do I hope the learners will do? What do I hope the learners will be?
- Remember that the weakness of many lessons lies with the outcome established from the beginning. If you aim at nothing, you will be sure to accomplish nothing. If you aim too broadly, you will try to cover so much in the time allotted that the learners will not be able to absorb it all. The center of the preparation and presentation battle is to work out a clear understanding of the outcomes. The whole lesson must be subservient to the stated outcomes.
- Use the following seven criteria for evaluating outcome statements. They are (a) *worthy,* on the developmental levels of the learners and for the development, growth, and maturity of learners. Outcome statements must be meaningfully related to the spiritual development of learners; (b) *clear,* focusing on relatively singular outcomes, as well as being easily

understood, free from doubt, and unmistakable; (c) *accomplishable* and attainable by the learners within the time frame of the lesson; (d) *suggested by the text*. This means they are determined through *exegesis*—read out of and agreeing with the text rather than through *eisegesis,* reading one's own biases and prejudices into the text.

They need to be (e) *stated operationally,* that is, the learners are told how they will know that they have achieved the outcomes; (f) *unified and not disjointed* in the four outcome areas of cognitive, affective, behavioral, and existential. That is, the cognitive outcome should lead to the affective outcome, then to the behavioral, and on through to the existential. The outcomes are, therefore, related to each other, building on each other and focusing on a change or transformation of the person—being, not just knowing; (g) *appropriate to each of the four domains.* Cognitive outcome statements must be cognitive, affective must be affective, and so forth. By accurately evaluating outcome statements, the teacher will be able to determine the desired outcomes and their relationship to learners' needs as well as the meaning of the text to learners' lives.

5. Know How to Teach

Know *how* you are going to teach. (Warning: Most teachers omit the first four "knows" and leap to this final one, which only causes calamity.) Determine how to teach your lesson in order to achieve the outcomes you hope to accomplish. Think of the following basic items: (1) What are the methods and materials that will be used in light of the learners, the content, the teacher, the current section of the lesson, the setting, and the outcomes desired? (2) Design and produce or procure

> *If you know the content, methods, and materials, and have a plan for what you are going to teach—determined in the light of the biblical text as well as the learners' needs and the outcomes desired—you are ready to teach.*

the desired materials. (3) Develop a lesson plan by asking: What will you as the teacher do? What will you expect the learners to do? Keep in mind that people learn when they are actively engaged in the learning process. Any good teacher will tell you that the person who learns most through a lesson is the one teaching. So plan to get the learners *actively* involved in the lesson. And plan in detail when you will use the various methods, materials, and teaching strategies. The intended outcome of the fifth "know" is to have in hand a plan, methods, and materials to teach the learners for each lesson.

How does a teacher know if he or she is prepared to teach? One way will be when he or she has definite, well-thought-out, logically related and integrated plans. If you know the content, methods, and materials, and have a plan for what you are going to teach—determined in the light of the biblical text as well as the learners' needs and the outcomes desired—you are ready to teach.

After the actual teaching of the lesson, evaluate the lesson. Do this first by listening to what the learners say following the lesson. Second, be your own critic. Third, ask your spouse, another close friend, or youth themselves to observe you and give you feedback. Or videotape your actual lesson and watch it with some helpful critics, including young people. Fourth, give the learners a feedback/evaluation instrument to help determine what is happening when you teach them. And fifth, actually use the evaluation to improve your future teaching. The desired

outcome is to determine how to improve your teaching, and to begin making plans for those changes.

The major criteria for evaluating the feedback gained from learners is whether or not the desired outcomes were achieved. If they were not, but some value was received, then the difficulty lies in the planning that was done. If the outcomes were not achieved, nor was there any value received, there probably was difficulty with the presentation, outcomes, and/or material. If the desired outcomes were achieved, but there was no value obtained, then the outcomes themselves were wrong. And, finally, if the outcomes were achieved, along with value received, then ask yourself: What was the best way to accomplish this? Did the learners follow the teacher all the way through the lesson, or was there a point where they seemed lost? And, might there be an even more effective method or style?

HOW TO STRUCTURE YOUR LESSONS

To review, we have learned the following from a developmental view of teaching and learning: (1) We teach for maturity, development, and growth, that Christ might be *formed* in the learner and that Christlikeness might be *developed* in the learner. (2) We do not teach for memorization, indoctrination, inculcation or manipulation. (3) In order for learning to occur, the learners must be *active* in the learning process. (4) Teaching must be done on the learners' stages of development in order for learning to be effective for Christian maturity. (5) People are whole beings. In the teaching/learning process, teachers need to be aware that the major areas of spiritual teaching addressed are cognitive, moral, and faith. (6) These three areas—cognitive, moral, faith—are integrated by the four outcome domains: to *know* the facts of the Christian faith (cognitive); to *feel* some kind of response to the facts of faith (affective); to *do* something with the facts and feelings of faith (behavioral); to *be* a different, transformed, changed person (existential).

Every learner—child, youth, and adult—is endowed with a genuine activity of his or her own.[1] We learn because we are active. If learners are not active in the teaching/learning process they will not learn effectively. If teaching is to be successful, it must use and direct that activity while providing adequate and good input or content.

Any lesson will have four basic parts: an introduction, main section, application, and conclusion. The first of these—the *introduction*—is the "hook," or launching pad, which grabs the attention of the audience. To know how best to use the introduction, begin by considering the needs of the learners. What are their interests, concerns, questions, and problems? The stages of human development will come into use here. What you know about your students will inform you concerning how to "grab" attention.

The introduction is a very crucial part of the lesson. If you do not manage to get the learners' attention here, you may never get it. Creative use of methods and materials will help. Ask yourself, "If I were one of my students, what would it take to get and hold my attention?" Then figure out how to do it. (See *2. Know the Learner* for ideas.) The outcomes of the lesson will also help determine what to emphasize in this opening section. Always keep in mind what you hope your learners will accomplish as a result of your teaching.

The *main section* looks at Scripture. The principles of how to prepare a lesson are employed to get at the meaning of the text. Outcome statements are also used here to determine what you will emphasize from your study of the scriptural text, and which methods and materials you will use throughout this section.

The third area of the lesson is *application*. This section brings the needs of the learners into focus along with the content of the biblical text. Here is where the "meddling" begins; the teacher intentionally intervenes into the lives of the learners by refocusing the lesson on their lives. If the teacher has prepared adequately with the learners in mind, has properly interpreted the Scripture, and has taught in the power of the Holy Spirit, the lesson will be effective when the application is attempted.

The *conclusion*, the final section of a lesson, is the wrap-up or summary. Be sure to give the students a chance, if appropriate, to talk about what changes might occur in their lives in the coming week as a result of what they learned in the lesson. You also may want to review the four major outcomes you hoped to achieve. Be sure to close in a prayer of commitment. This could be teacher-led, all could take turns praying, a few could pray out loud, or all could pray silently.

CHARACTERISTICS OF THE EFFECTIVE DEVELOPMENTAL TEACHER

In summary, an effective developmental teacher of youth is someone who teaches for the development of the whole person, with special emphasis on faith and spiritual development. He or she is committed to evangelization and Christian nurture. Second, the teacher teaches on the developmental levels of students, especially on the cognitive, moral, and faith development levels; he or she also teaches on the appropriate spiritual maturity level. Third, effective developmental teachers "scratch where learners itch." That is, they teach to the developmental and existential concerns and needs, and the personal interests, of learners. They teach as Jesus did.

Fourth, developmental teachers have definite but flexible goals for each lesson (outcomes in each category of know, feel, do, and be). Fifth, it is important that the teacher be maturing developmentally as a whole person, especially in the cognitive, moral, faith, and spiritual areas. The teacher is a learner, too! Sixth, the teacher must be person-oriented, with a concern for each individual learner and not just for communicating content.

Seventh, the effective developmental teacher is *able* to teach—not just know how—demonstrating the following:

- A proper exegesis of the biblical text
- Identification of the real needs of learners
- Identification of the appropriate outcomes for learners in light of their development and needs, and the biblical text.
- Effective planning of lessons

- The choice of appropriate methods and materials in light of the learners' development and needs, goals of the lessons, the particular parts of the lesson, the teacher's own personality, and the biblical text
- The execution of the lesson in a well-organized manner
- Preparation before arrival to teach—the lesson plans, methods, and materials are completed, the room is properly arranged, and the lesson plans are well in mind

Eighth, the developmental teacher constantly seeks to provide experiences and data for learners that will facilitate and enable learning to occur. Ninth, he or she evaluates the teaching-learning process and makes appropriate corrections as a result. Tenth, in conjunction with the youth of the church, the teacher designs and develops teaching-learning programs that are outcomes of the church's youth ministry philosophy and model. And, finally, effective teachers spend much time in prayer for both the learners and themselves.

5

Worship

Worship, the second of four program elements, is adoration (expression of love for God), praise (expression of his worthiness because of who he is), thanksgiving (expression of gratitude for who we are in Christ and God's blessings to us), and a feeling of awe in the presence of the Holy God; it is "seeing him who is invisible" and responding to him.

On a more technical level, worship is comprised of three basic principles. One is the personal, human side: persons involved and active. A second is the Godward side: God is active. And a third is the passive side: persons listen to God.

Originally, worship was defined as "the state of having worth." If something was worthy, it ought to be held in reverence and receive special honor. But worship has since come to have a deeper meaning, in the Christian sense. It is the communion of human beings with God—any act, thought, or feeling which brings one into close contact with God and through which the Triune God reaches into human life. Worship is a positive, warm, exciting, wonderful communion with God because of his greatness, majesty, power, mercy, grace, love, steadfastness, and faithfulness. Worship is the activity of Christians that most nearly approximates what occurs eternally in the very presence of God. Our worship, including that of young people, is a part of the awesome worship that a great multitude of the saints of all ages, the angels, and all of Creation offer to the Triune God. We join the angels and archangels and all the saints in the presence of God and express with them the worthiness of God. Like the hosts in Revelation 5, we proclaim, "Worthy is the Lamb, who was slain, to receive power and wealth and wisdom and strength and honor and glory and praise! . . .To him who sits on the throne and to the Lamb be praise and honor and glory and power, for ever and ever!"

Gerrit Verkuyl has identified nine steps to worship.[1] The worshiper (1) has positive feelings toward God, (2) has reverence toward God, (3) has a desire for communication with God, (4) has removed any hindrances from fellowship; in other words, his or her sins have been confessed and forgiveness has been accepted, (5) has a heart which opens itself to God, (6) finds him or herself with God and is glad, (7) speaks to God, (8) listens to God speak, and (9) acts on the knowledge of God's characteristics in his or her life.

In summary, not only does worship realize the presence of God, but it also practices his presence. In realizing his presence, worship is knowing that God is both "out there" and here; God out there is here with us! Practicing his presence consists of continuing throughout the day or night whatever is done in times of worship with God. The act of worship motivates us to be and live for God, and the feelings of worship lead to the actions of life.

An important element to keep in mind is that worship is God-centered, not believer-centered. It focuses on God rather than on Christian fellowship with other Christians, or on teaching or preaching. In worship, Scriptures, music, prayers, and spoken words all turn believers' minds and hearts to God.

> *Above all*, worship is not a spectator event. True worship is active, not passive.

What about emotions and worship? The affective state of "feeling" or emotions is basic to worship, for we are not talking just of an intellectual exercise; worship is a movement of the will, a stimulating of the emotions, and it involves the whole person's inner makeup. One cannot have worship without emotion:

- Worship makes a person feel something;
- Worship makes a person want to do something;
- Worship makes a person want to be something different because worshipers have come in contact with the living, Triune God.

But be careful not to confuse worship with emotional*ism* (focusing almost exclusively on emotions) or to focus only on an emotional high. The experience of worship is not merely some mindless emotion nor a cold, calculating mental exercise. Rather, it involves us as whole beings—our bodies, minds, spirits, and emotions—and a social group, a community of believers who gather together as part of the "called-together ones" to worship our God.

Above all, *worship is not a spectator event.* Worshipers actively worship God. Worship leaders, singers, instrumentalists, and others involved in directing worship plan to actively engage everyone present. True worship is active, not passive. Each must worship for himself or herself.

Since worship is central to the Christian devotional life, adolescents need to know how to worship. But this does not necessarily come naturally to them; they need instruction in what worship is and how to do it. Sunday school especially must provide for true worship or quit calling its "opening exercises" worship. At the same time, both youth and adults need to know how to worship in the main worship service of the church. Youth workers should know how to plan worship so they can help others to plan.

This chapter focuses on the planned worship experiences of a church's youth ministry. Much of what is said about corporate worship of youth can be applied to private worship by individuals, but private worship is not the focal point of the chapter. Youth should be encouraged to carry over to private worship what they have learned in corporate worship.

NEEDS AND NATURE OF ADOLESCENT WORSHIP

What makes worship important for adolescents? Many reasons could be given in answer to that question.

- Youth are now beginning habits that will last the rest of their lives.
- Youth are interested in the mind and in emotions, not just in physical life.
- Their sense of appreciation is developing.
- Their powers of reasoning are developing.
- Music reflects their feelings—adolescents can express feeling in hymns and contemporary songs.
- Their self-concept and self-esteem are developing in relation to God; they realize that God loves and accepts them and their worship of him.
- Youth desire to put knowledge to work; worship provides motivation.
- Adolescents enjoy the social contact of group worship.
- They respond, recognizing the authority of God.
- They are very conscious of God's existence and his revelation to humanity.

- Adolescents desire to respond to God who shows interest in them.
- They have a deep loyalty—both felt and expressed—to God.
- They feel the nearness of God and respond to him.
- They need to know that God is near them continually.
- Adolescents are looking to the future.
- They desire something almost martial, or challenging—a conflict with evil, or to fight to win over evil and wickedness.
- They are looking for personal experiences, wanting something for "me."
- They want to have their emotions and wills moved, as well as their minds.

Wisdom dictates that a youth worker at least begin by keeping worship within the framework of the local church tradition. Don't lead too far out too quickly. Remember that youth do need worship. It uniquely fills a need for them because it unifies by centering on one thing. It quiets a group, gives expression to their feelings, teaches an appreciation for church history, and offers a variety of experiences within a common framework.

Worship Outcomes

When planning for developmentally appropriate worship, the youth worker must have the outcomes of the worship experience clearly in mind. The following general outcomes are natural outgrowths of the needs of adolescents:

1. To recognize God's presence with us in the experience, and realized in our lives. He is available to receive our worship.
2. To express God's worthiness on the levels of, and in ways appropriate for, the youth involved.
3. To develop a holy mind. Youth are filled with the holiness and majesty of God. They "see" Him who is invisible and respond to him.

Worship music should be the best available to the youth involved. This music should not limit itself to the contemporary idiom, nor should it be relegated to the "old hymns of the faith."

4. To experience a sense of encouragement that God is with them now and that he never leaves them.
5. To enjoy a sense of fellowship with those in the group and a sense of fellowship with all believers who worship the Lord. They share the challenging task of finding and doing God's will.
6. To be continually transformed by their encounter with God in worship, developing a Christian character. Like Isaiah (Isa. 6), youth recognize the Lord's majesty and holiness and their own sinfulness; they confess their sins and receive forgiveness, and they receive a renewed call to service in the Lord's name.
7. To gain a right perspective to personal, social, national, and world issues.
8. To gain perspective on the relation of the self to God in body, mind, spirit, and service.
9. To develop a sense of courage to fight and win the battles of life, to overcome evil and unrighteousness.

ELEMENTS OF A WORSHIP SERVICE

Music

The importance of music to worship cannot be underestimated. It is a basic element in worship, for several reasons. First, it produces a proper atmosphere that is conducive to worship. It is also the element that provides most easily for the maximum group participation. And, through the media of words and music,

it is able to touch both the affective and cognitive that underlie both words and music.

Worship music should be the best available to the youth involved. This music should not limit itself to the contemporary idiom, nor should it be relegated to the "old hymns of the faith." The church has a variety of excellent worship music available that dates from the third or fourth century up to contemporary times. The issue is not the age of the music but its usefulness for and its appreciation by those singing it.

Some youth groups never sing a worship hymn. Youth who grow up without becoming familiar with "A Mighty Fortress Is Our God" and other hymns of high quality have been deprived of a rich Christian musical heritage. Other youth who do not come in contact with contemporary music such as "Thou Art Worthy" and "Majesty" are deprived of some of the best that contemporary composers and authors have to offer the church. It is thus fitting and proper to use a balanced approach in the choice of worship music, finding the best that is available and that the young people can sing. It is also important to teach high-quality music to youth so that they continue to grow and develop in their appreciation of the musical offerings of the church.

Many youth workers have grown up singing hymns that were meaningless to them, and therefore they avoid them completely. Others have had only contemporary music in their experiences. Some youth workers, having become Christians in their late teens or early twenties, are familiar only with contemporary music, period, and lack appreciation for anything that pre-dates the Beatles. When it comes to Christian music, they know mainly the contemporary idiom of short, repetitive, and sometimes musically inferior choruses.

To be able to help today's youth appreciate the breadth of church music and to avoid the limitations of a single idiom or genre, youth workers will have to become more knowledgeable themselves regarding excellent worship music. The church has always produced great music as well as inferior music. Because youth ministry seeks to help youth to develop holistically in all domains of their lives, so it must seek to help youth to appreciate and use the wide variety of superior worship music and the church's musical heritage.

Vocal

Numerous types of music can be used in worship, though of course not all should be used in a single worship experience. One is vocal music, which includes hymns, gospel songs, choruses, and contemporary music. Hymns are characterized by spiritual depth and a God-centeredness. Thought and emotion are united. In a hymn, music is servant to the words, which are doctrinally precise and deep.

Gospel songs are easily singable. They tend to be I-centered, or experiential and subjective in nature. Repetitiveness is also common, especially in the refrain or chorus. Another frequent factor is a testimonial, evangelistic bent—the songs are a method of seeking to convince the unconverted to become Christians. Accordingly, the conversion experience is also emphasized. Happiness is frequently expressed, and contemporary style and harmony are common to gospel music.

Choruses are enthusiastic and/or inspirational, rhythmic, and tuneful. Usually, they are light and repetitive and often devoid of spiritual strength and depth. A contemporary style and harmony is used. Choruses are simple and short—two to four lines, one stanza long.

Contemporary music is the musical idiom of the day according to style, harmony, beat, and tempo. Sometimes contemporary music combines the positive aspects of hymns, gospel songs, and choruses. It also tends to be balanced between objective praise and subjective praise. On the negative side, it can be simplistic and repetitive, experiencing little movement from one simple idea. In this way it can be more like a mantra than a hymn. At times it is nonrational and emotive, using frivolous words which are often theologically incorrect. Contemporary music can also be one dimensional, neither good music nor good poetry. Finally on the negative side, it too is often I-centered, not God-centered.

Gospel songs, choruses, and contemporary music are useful for opening a meeting enthusiastically, relieving tension, and complementing testimonial and informal meetings. They are *not* for a worship service, unless the songs have good, contemporary worship words and music.

Instrumental

Instrumental music is an ancient form that is also very modern and contemporary. A look at Psalm 150 reveals that worship in Old Testament times was not that different from what it is today. Instruments mentioned are the trumpet, lyre, harp, tambourine, strings, flute, and cymbals. Today, too, instruments are culturally oriented. We choose musical instruments that are acceptable within our particular culture and subculture. Their place is to lead people in singing and meditation, although sometimes they can drown people out and/or fail to keep the appropriate pace. Instruments provide a bright, rather than somber, background and/or accompaniment for singing.

A wide variety of instruments can be used in worship. The most common in youth ministry are still probably the guitar and electronic keyboard. Piano and organ are sometimes used. Other instruments include those in the brass, string, reed, and percussion families. A final option is prerecorded music on a sound system.

The Use of Music in a Worship Service

Each worship service allows for a variety of music. Yet those who plan the service should know what the purpose is of the two main uses: the *prelude* and *group singing*. The prelude is a time of quiet, and is intended to create an atmosphere for the participants. It will be determined by the theme for the service, for which it sets the tone.

The attitude of the accompanist and the song(s) chosen determine the effectiveness of the prelude. Types of preludes vary, from hymn tunes (not gospel songs) to classical or semiclassical. Often the instruments used for the prelude will be a piano, organ, guitar, and/or electronic keyboard. Or, the prelude may be a recorded tape. Both the choice of music and of instrument will depend on the musical sophistication of the youth involved.

Group singing is meant to direct the thoughts of participants to God, and to aid in reaching the planned goals of the service. A number of forms of congregational singing are used in a worship service. In singing the "Doxology," "Gloria," or other calls to worship, worshipers respond to God's presence with joy and praise, and remind themselves to praise God. The first hymn or opening group of God-centered contemporary songs provide the opportunity to express great Christian aspirations toward God, such as praise, adoration, or gratitude for blessings. These are still kept general, rather than being specific or relating to the theme, because the participants are usually not yet completely united to express truthfully as a group a definite commitment to God.

A hymn, or a series of worship-centered contemporary songs with a hymn midway in the service have an express purpose to relate to the theme, reflecting commitment and aspiration. These serve as a preparation for the message, or as a meditation, or both. The closing hymn or contemporary worship song expresses the group's purpose and response to worship, and to God's invitation to commitment. Interludes and offertory (if there is an offering) may be instrumental or vocal, bringing direct thoughts regarding the theme of the service. These are opportunities for participants to spend time quietly in meditation. Youth must be taught how to use these moments to think about God or talk to him, and not as a time to read or talk.

Choosing Worship Songs and Hymns

Since hymns and worship songs are crucial to worship, their selection is an important process. They must be culturally acceptable, and the words and music should go together in such a way that the music properly interprets the words. Further, those words must have spiritual depth and be God-centered, rather than focusing on *I, my, me, us,* or *our.* The subject of the hymn needs to be worth singing about. Just because a subject is mentioned in the Bible does not mean it should be sung. Music certainly must be a servant to the words, but the music is still very important; music in particular carries the affective or emotional part of worship. But it is important to have doctrinal precision and depth in the words.

The singing of a hymn should lead to a spiritual experience with God. "Redeemed, How I Love to Proclaim It" is okay for a new Christian, but he or she should mature to sing hymns with more substance, such as, "O, for a Thousand Tongues," or "Holy, Holy, Holy," or "I Love You, Lord." Good worship songs are idealistic and aspiring, stimulating the singer

Songs and hymns must be culturally acceptable, and the words and music should go together in such a way that the music properly interprets the words.

to greater commitment. Examples of such might be, "Take My Life," "Lead On, O King Eternal," "He Is Able," "Make Me a Servant," or "Seek Ye First." They give expression to discomfort with imperfections.

Hymns and worship songs must allow the singer to reflect sincerity. It is important not to make hypocrites out of youth by asking them to sing something that they cannot do wholeheartedly. The worship leader should try to reflect the actual possible feelings of a group. He or she may even ask what they are feeling. Also, the leader will want to consider the particular youth subculture involved. How "churched" are they? How do they respond to "churchy" things? And, finally, the musical literateness and experiences of the youth must be taken into account. Is MTV their only musical experience, or do they have a broad musical appreciation from classical to MTV?

How to Lead Music

The worship leader must be familiar with the words and music of the songs and hymns selected. This means having both a knowledge of the meaning of the words and being able to focus the singers on that meaning. An accompanist or musicians should give a simple, clear introduction and then back up the singers. Keep in mind that musical instruments are a support for the singing; the worship time is not meant to be a showcase opportunity for the musicians. The worship leader must begin with a clear, precise, strong note, and continue in a loud voice. Do not give leadership to the musicians or the group, but maintain leadership with the hands

and/or voice. Otherwise, the leader may lose control, and the purpose and meaning of the songs may be drowned out.

How to Teach a New Song

A worship service is not the best place for youth to learn a new song—at least not all at once. The best approach in teaching a new song is to use it as a prelude, interlude, or special number once or twice, and to be sure to choose music that the group will like, not just words that are good. The song will have greater impact if the leader and accompanist both know it well. The words could even be read as a poem in a service before the actual learning time.

When it comes time for youth to learn the song, hopefully they will already be somewhat familiar with it. The leader should give it a special introduction, showing its relevance to worship, and the Christian life, or emphasizing the doctrine in the song or hymn. At another time, the leader might comment on a concept or theme in the song that is relevant to a study being made, or he or she may talk about the life of the writer, explaining how the song was written or relating experiences people have had with the song. In other words, make the music and words come alive.

One final word: Make new songs a standard thing. Refuse to use the same old ones constantly without giving new life. Wise worship leaders maintain a record of group songs and special music used. Unfortunately, many worship leaders use the same 25 to 30 songs almost exclusively.

Musicians or Accompanist

The musicians or the accompanist need to know the musical text and to play well—for the support of singing. The worship leader must work with musicians to develop their accompanist skills. It is best to begin using youth as soon as possible, eventually giving them responsibility as leaders of worship.

Call to Worship

The call to worship is the appropriate time to relate the purpose and theme of a worship service. The leader directs the thoughts of participants to God and to the chosen theme. He or she announces that God is present and reminds everyone they are now entering into worship. Doing this helps in the transition from the all-too-prevalent cares of life to worship. Creative calls to worship might be choral, or they might come from Scripture such as Psalm 150 or Hebrews 13:15.

Prayer

The main purpose of worship-based prayer is to lead a person to a personal experience with God. This is expressed through reverent contemplation, through communion with God, through revelation from God, and through personal encounter with God. These will all be reflected in the following discussion of prayer and its uses and forms.

The Use of Prayer in a Worship Service

Prayer is used in a number of ways in the worship service, the first being the *invocation*. Its purpose is to unify the group by calling on the Name of the Lord with both aspiration and praise. An invocation serves to acquaint the worshiper with some of the great attributes of the God whom they are approaching. It asks for

God's presence in the service, although this is actually a reminder that God is already present.

The second use of prayer is as *confession*, an expression of the participants' sense of unworthiness. In this prayer, they express general and individual sins to God, preparing hearts and minds clear of sin in order to worship God in holiness.

Third is *praise*—adoration, joy, and true worship because of who God is. It is thanksgiving for his goodness and faithfulness. A fourth use of prayer is *intercession*, or praying for others, and a fifth is *petition*, asking for things one needs. This is done in fellowship with the Father. In the worship service, the leader centers the participants' thoughts around one or two attributes of God. Finally, there is the *benediction*, or the solemn request for divine blessing on all the participants, at the end of the service. The leader calls on the Spirit of God to go with people into their tasks of daily life. The raising of the hand is a symbolic gesture of bestowing the Holy Spirit upon the people. In the benediction, God's promise to be with the worshipers and to surround them with love and care is accepted by the worshipers.

Prayer Forms

At least six forms of prayer are available to use in corporate worship: (1) A leader's prayer, in which one person prays while the group is silent. (2) Sentence prayers, in which either several people are asked to pray ahead of time or several lead spontaneously in sentence prayers. (3) Scripture prayers, read from Psalms, or the Pauline letters, or other places. (4) Silent prayer or meditation, which leaders guide in line with certain themes or ideas. (5) The prayer hymn, such as "Breathe On Me, Breath of God," "Have Thine Own Way," "Come Thou Fount of Every Blessing," "Lord, Speak to Me" or "Draw Me Nearer." (6) Unison prayer, which may either be from a printed program or from memory (such as the Lord's Prayer).

The advantage of unison prayer is that it provides a place for common aspiration. A common experience unites the group, making reverence apparent. The disadvantage is that a group is not always sufficiently united in thought to respond reverently and sincerely, in which case the prayer can become merely an empty form. Another possible disadvantage is that though a prayer may be in good literary form, it is not well-suited to unison reading. Finally, the printed page could distract and therefore lessen the participants' sense of nearness to God. A group needs to be taught how to make a written prayer its own.

Planning Prayer and Prayer Material

Before planning any prayer for a worship service, it is wise to first analyze it. The progression of prayers in a worship experience should be praise, adoration, and thanksgiving; confession; petition and intercession; and aspiration. Prayer materials include hymns, Scripture (for example, Acts 4:24–30), Paul's prayers (such as in Phil. 1:4ff. or Eph. 1:16ff.), and Psalms—poems, printed prayers, and the leader's own written prayers.

Written prayers have both advantages and disadvantages. On the positive side, they help a worship leader keep thoughts centered on the theme of the service. And they help avoid rambling speech and vain repetition, such as, "Father, we just. . . ," and oral pauses such as ". . . just . . ." and ". . . uh. . . ." By using a written prayer, the leader can plan prayer time and hold it to a strict limit. He or she can also refer back to previous prayers to make sure that the same things are not being said over and over again. Further, a written prayer shows others the thought and concern that went into planning this aspect of worship. They are not merely extemporaneous

thoughts. Finally, it serves to get the leader in the appropriate mood for the service. Finally, planned prayers can always be discarded and replaced with extemporaneous ones. It certainly does no harm to be prepared.

The disadvantage of such a written prayer is that it may sound "canned," too formal, or stilted. If a church is very informal, some people may object to a prayer being written ahead of time. Finally, the leader may become dependent on written thought and not allow for the leading of the Holy Spirit.

Roles in Prayer

The worship leader has a feeling for the theme of the service and enters into it in a spirit of prayer. Because he or she has been thinking already about prayer, the leader is prepared to express thoughts for the group and provide for a common experience and language. Leaders must be aware, however, of the dangerous tendency to use vague and informal words, or to speak in cliches that lack group participation.

Above all, a group's role is to be active participants, not merely passive listeners. When prayers are being offered aloud, the group must actively listen—each person making the prayer his or her own in each heart. As the leader speaks, the group can think the leader's thoughts after they are uttered, and give the amen again in their own hearts.

Prayers in worship with youth should be brief and to the point, and true to the needs of adolescents. Prayers are always best formulated in terms of the interests and needs of those present. And finally, worship prayers are addressed to God the Father in the name of Jesus Christ. Reverence, praise, loyalty, obedience, and requests are all expressions in public prayer. But this is not a time for the leader's personal requests.

Scripture

Scripture is God's revelation. Through his Word he speaks to human beings. Not all Scripture is appropriate for worship of course (for instance, the imprecatory psalms), so the Bible reading must be chosen in harmony with the theme of the service and with the needs and developmental stages of learners clearly in view.

Methods of Reading

Many methods of reading Scripture are effective in a worship service; it is only a matter of choosing which is the most appropriate. One method is solo reading, which consists of one person reading a Scripture selection. A second is unison reading, everyone reading simultaneously. These should be kept to a reasonable length—ten to fifteen verses at most. In unison reading, a unity of thought is expressed. When using this method with youth, leaders should remember to prepare themselves and the youth beforehand. Sentences that are too complex, or that have strange words or names that might throw young people off should be avoided. In other words, avoid anything that might be confusing to some youth. And, important for our day, be sure all have the same translation of the Scriptures.

A third method, similar to unison reading, is responsive reading. These readings are often found in the back of a hymnal, or can be chosen from Psalms. In addition to these, the leader may want to prepare alternating Scripture sentences to be read between groups. Hymns or songs may be interspersed with Bible verses which have been written out ahead of time, or a compilation of verses that focus on a special topic may be read for a particular worship service. Further, Scripture may be paraphrased to meet the needs of youth. Finally, a whole group can repeat from memory familiar Scriptures, such as Psalm 23. Just make sure that the group does indeed know the Scripture to be recited together—and all in the same translation.

Yet another method is antiphonal reading from Psalms. In antiphonal reading, the leader reads a statement and is then answered. For example, in Psalm 136:

Give thanks unto the Lord, for He is Good,

His love endures forever.

This is not as easy as it appears, however, and takes some practice with a group.

Lastly, a prepared choral reading of the Bible ideally uses both heavy and light voices. Passages that work well with choral reading are Isaiah 52:7–12; 55; Matthew 5:1–11; 7:21–29; 23:1–12; Luke 15:1–12; John 1:1–14; and many of the psalms.

Preparing for Scripture Reading

When the Scripture portion of a worship service is beginning, it is wise to commence with an exhortation to listen. This can be done by using a verse that exalts the Word of God, such as: Psalm 119:15–16, 18; 43:3; Matthew 7:24–25; 1 Peter 1:24–25a; and 2 Peter 1:19–21. Or, the leader might begin by reading something about the passage, such as a quotation from a famous person or a poem. When appropriate, the historical setting for a passage, such as Psalm 51 or John 17, can be provided. Difficult words or meanings can be explained ahead of time, and the spiritual meaning of the passage to be read briefly summarized. This is not the time for a sermonette.

Although reading Scripture aloud may seem a very simple thing, in actuality the better prepared the reader is the more effective he or she will be. Before presenting a passage to a group, the leader should read it aloud several times. When finally in front of the group, one must remember to read slowly and with the expression appropriate for the passage.

Special Features (or Talk)

Special features might include a message or talk, a story, film, or simple dramatization. Their purpose is to provide an extension of the Scripture, the revelation from God through man. They can also lead to a new and deeper appreciation for God, giving insight into the participants' own Christian living.

A message or talk is positive, constructive, short, and relevant, and focuses on continuing the worship experience. When presenting it, get the attention of youth by starting with a need, asking a question, telling a short story or relating an incident, making a startling statement, or giving a quotation. Focus on one central thought in an organized manner, always keeping worship as the central thought. And, finally, make sure that the message applies to the lives of youth. Give them a challenge to apply it personally, and conclude your talk. Of course, a message does not have to be a "sermon"; it can come through as short talks or litanies spread throughout the service.

If you are telling a story, be sure to relate only one story. Stories are best kept brief while still providing a sense of action. Avoid moralizing, although a story should have a point which may often be a moral. Stories may come from a leader's own experience, from newspapers, from denominational publications and periodicals, from missionary biographies, and from general reading.

The principles of storytelling are these:

- Master the story and know the details,
- Practice by telling the whole story through three or four times,
- Speak with enthusiasm,
- Use direct dialogue,
- Live the story,
- And don't moralize.

A special event that may serve as the climax of the worship service is the Lord's Supper. It could come at the end of a message, a pastoral prayer, or a suitable hymn or special song.

Offering

The offering can be an essential aspect of praise and worship. Because God gave, we give. Giving is a reminder of how we have dedicated our lives to God. And when gifts are received by the church, they are from God's people for their Lord.

When in preparation for this part of a worship service, direct the thoughts of youth to giving by reminding them that God gave, and that he has commanded us to give. Tell them of their responsibilities as stewards, of participating in God's work, and sharing what God has given us. But do not leave them in the dark about where their money will be going. Tell them how much money has been coming in and how it will be spent. Announce any current needs.

A simple format for the actual offering time is to begin with a song, such as "Take My Life and Let It Be," v. 4, "When I Survey the Wondrous Cross," v. 4, or "We Give Thee But Thine Own," v. 1. After the offering has been collected, let prayer be offered and Scripture read, for example, Malachi 3:10, Matthew 6:17–21, Acts 20:35, or Colossians 3:17.

PHYSICAL ELEMENTS OF WORSHIP

The worship atmosphere is created through such things as the room, furnishings (pews, chairs, pulpit, worship center), and an environment free of distraction. Few places will be perfect, but for adolescents especially, the effort to provide the right physical elements is worth the trouble.

Room

A room used for worship would ideally be suggestive of worship. It must be of suitable size—just right for the group to sit comfortably with room for the guys especially to stretch their legs. If chairs are used, they should be of the right size, arranged in a logical order, whether a semicircle or formal rows. Adequate lighting and ventilation, and the proper room temperature, are also important; if youth are not comfortable, their focus will be on their discomfort rather than on worshiping God. Adolescent sweat glands are very active, so proper ventilation and room temperature will contribute greatly to their ease.

Make sure that the room and any materials such as hymnals, song sheets, transparencies and overhead projector/slide projector and screen are prepared before the first youth arrive. This will create the right atmosphere. It is best to hold worship services in a different room from the one used regularly for recreation and fun. But if this is not possible, then emphasize the distinction between worship and playtime. It would be well to actually set up a worship center (see below). Finally, make provision for latecomers so they will not distract from the service.

The Worship Center

A worship center can be valuable as a definite point of focus for the entire group. It has the ability to catch and hold attention for worship. Some possibilities for a center include a Bible, a cross, a picture, candles, and flowers. Be creative. A danger, however, is that the worship center can become too elaborate and call attention to itself and to the symbols rather than to worship and to God. Be sure that the worship center focuses youth's attention meaningfully on God. And the symbols used must be comprehensible to the participants.

Posture and Symbols

Various human postures reflect different aspects of worship. Kneeling with a bowed head shows reverence. Standing shows adoration and praise. Sitting readies a person for

> *A room used for worship would ideally be suggestive of worship Create the right atmosphere.*

receiving instruction and revelation. Use all three of these when appropriate.

Symbols—external trappings that speak of God, the Trinity, and worship—are visible signs that suggest something invisible, often abstract, that aid worshipers in their acts of worship. Symbols are necessary for several reasons. First, the pressures of daily life contribute to a lack of realization of the presence of God. Symbols fill this tangible need. Second, humans are suggestible, and relate well to symbolism. Third, symbols help create a proper setting for worship. And finally, we all employ symbols both consciously and unconsciously in our daily lives.

Good symbols are simple, for something that is complex only detracts from the purpose of the symbol. They are aids to worship, but not ends in themselves. They should lead to better worship of God. A helpful test of a symbol is to ask, "Does it make me think of God more?" Remember, though, that symbols are relative; not everyone has the same reaction to any particular one. And symbols, form, ritual, or artifacts should never take precedence over the divine presence and revelation. Better to use one meaningful symbol than many symbols that dilute the attention of the worshipers. Of the many symbols used in worship, it is important to make sure that youth understand those that are being presented to them. They need to know why a fish (ICHTHUS), a cross, candles, a Bible, vestments, a dove, and color changes have meaning.[2]

DIFFERENCES IN WORSHIP BETWEEN THE THREE ADOLESCENT AGE GROUPS

It seems obvious that junior highers, senior highers, and post-high school youth all can worship God effectively—but often they do not. Youth in an adult-oriented Sunday morning worship service are usually bored by a liturgy that is often not even meaningful to adults, let alone youth. Even so-called nonliturgical churches have their own formalized order. Yet, youth as well as children and adults all ought to be meaningfully involved in worship of God. Youth workers often seek to provide a meaningful worship experience on retreats and camps and at other youth-only activities. Sometimes these attempts are successful, sometimes not. They are successful only when the youth worship experience is congruent with the developmental maturity of those in the youth group. Incongruency is often caused by the imposition of an adult worship liturgy and elements on young people.

When youth workers help their youth plan a youth-oriented worship experience, they need to be aware of several crucial factors. One is the need to understand clearly what worship is: the expression of the worthiness of the Triune God by worshipers to each other and especially to God himself. As discussed earlier in this chapter, all who worship God are to be involved inwardly and outwardly in adoration, praise, and thanksgiving to the Triune God.

Youth workers too often fail to recognize the essential differences between junior high, senior high, and post-high youth. The three age groups *are* different from each other. These developmental differences, based on ages and stages, are crucial for youth workers to know and apply as they work with youth to design and develop worship experiences. Consider each of these age groups separately, using the following categories in each age group to determine the differences in their worship experiences.

Junior High

Needs

Junior highers need to take their minds off of themselves and focus on God. They need to experience God as the Solid Rock who is a steady, faithful, unchanging Friend and King. They also need to express loyalty to God and to perceive again that God has standards for them in their daily lives.

Music

Songs that emphasize loyalty to God, God's wonder, and his majesty make sense to junior highers. Gushy, sentimental, emotional, and slow-moving songs are inappropriate. One junior high director insisted on having the youth sing "Humble Thyself in the Sight of the Lord." The youth were not too sure what "humble thyself" meant, and not many of them were so proud as to need more humbling than they were already experiencing, nor did they particularly appreciate the slow-paced music.

Junior highers respond best to songs that are present-oriented, not tied to the past or looking toward the future. Singing about heaven is usually not too meaningful for junior highers. These youth can appreciate *good* contemporary songs, and with proper education, traditional hymns that are within their age/stage experiences.

One should not expect junior highers to willingly sing solos. For that matter, many youth workers will testify that getting these young people to sing out loud is a major effort in itself. This is understandable when we realize that junior highers are so very self-conscious to begin with. Add to that the fact that junior high boys' voices are changing. Few boys are willing to open their mouths to sing loudly, not knowing what pitch will come out, a squeak or a basso profundo.

Aesthetics

Junior highers do not understand nor appreciate the more typical adult-oriented atmospheres with candles and banners—or "smells and bells," as an Anglican rector friend called them. Most junior highers do not appreciate the abstract nature of symbols because their minds think concretely. They cannot usually see beyond the concrete object to the reality behind it. Symbols and "neat" aesthetic devices, such as altars, tables, a cross, candles, or various church calendar color changes do not speak to junior highers.

If you use symbols and aesthetic devices to enhance junior highers' worship experiences, then explain these worship aids before the youth worship together. They should understand the meaning of any symbols and other devices used and—even more importantly—they should appreciate them.

Prayer

Prayers that are meaningful for junior high worship are short, personal, relevant, and life-related. Short sentence prayers or directed silent prayers are good means for entire group participation. We should not expect much response if we tell youth to bow their heads in silent prayer but do not give them directions as they pray. Their minds usually will not remain focused on God for long; the world around them is too easily perceived and God is too remote for them to focus on him for even a minute in silent prayer. It is better for the worship leader to direct the prayers by saying things such as, "Think of God's great power. Thank him for that power. . . . Think of God's love for each of us. Thank him for his love." The more specific, the better.

If junior highers are expected to pray out

> *Effective Scripture is practical, life-related, and centered in the here and now.*

loud, it is wise to ask for short sentence prayers on topics already suggested above. Or a youth worker could direct the sentence prayers just as he or she would direct silent prayers.

Appropriate prayer hymns and scriptural prayers from Psalms or the Epistles could also be used. Youth could prepare ahead to read these prayers at the designated time.

Message

The talk, if there is one, should be short, eight to ten minutes, focused on the relationship of God to junior highers' lives. Effective messages are challenging, concrete, personal, and related to each individual present. Retelling biblical narratives or other stories is appropriate to the way many junior highers experience their realities. The speaker's excitement and sanctified imagination will bring the talk alive to the junior highers. Heroes, both contemporary and biblical, could be used. Personal Christian living in relation to God's revelation of himself to us is always appropriate.

Atmosphere

The best atmosphere is one that is informal, dynamic, light, bright, fast-paced, and full of variety. Junior highers will not tolerate boredom or irrelevancy. They need to feel God's presence with them as they worship him and recognize that he is involved in their lives daily.

Emotions

Junior highers' emotions are on the proverbial "roller coaster." It is easy to tweak their emotions and give them an emotional high or totally forget about their emotions and appeal mistakenly only to their minds. The "golden mean" is appropriate here: Youth need to feel God emotionally without emotionalism. They need to be able to respond to God's revelation of himself with both the mind and the emotions. They are able to feel love for God, praise and adoration for him, and a thankfulness for all that he is doing in their lives. These are healthy emotions and are part of effective worship.

Scripture

Whatever biblical text is used, it should be in a modern translation that junior highers can understand. The Living Bible is usually appropriate. Often the more formalized versions are too adult-oriented. Likewise, Shakespearean thee's and thou's are not part of junior highers' normal vocabulary and should not be used in their encounter with the Triune God.

Effective Scripture is practical, life-related, and centered in the here and now. It could be read in various creative ways and not only by the adult leaders. With proper preparation, these youth can do dialogue reading or even a relatively simple dramatic reading. Responsive reading might be appropriate if the group members are comfortable with each other and are not too self-conscious to read aloud.

Planning and Leadership

Junior highers are more than capable of being involved in planning their own worship experience. However, they need definite adult guidance and help in designing and developing the worship experience. Possessing little tolerance for mistakes, bloopers, or slip-ups, they will only laugh at these, and their laughter usually destroys any sense of worship,

focusing on the mistake rather than on God. Thus they need help to prepare well so as to avoid seemingly terminal embarrassment in front of their peers.

Planning can best be accomplished in small groups rather than with large groups of ten or more. By working in small groups more youth can become involved, different ideas can be examined, and everyone can contribute to the whole worship experience.

Focus

Junior high worship is most effective when it is informal, life-related, and dynamic. It should focus on what junior highers can receive now, not in the future, and should be practical and concrete. It should involve symbols that junior highers both understand and appreciate, remembering that, for the most part, this age group still thinks concretely and literally about any abstract symbols or metaphors.

Senior High

Needs

Senior highers are receptive to worship and can appreciate many of the things that junior highers cannot. Senior highers are idealistic and loyal, and feel the need to serve and want to do so. Most can understand more abstract concepts and symbols. These youth need to be addressed in accordance with their newly developed ability to think abstractly as well as with their ongoing need for a practical faith.

Music

Senior highers appreciate a variety of musical idioms. They can "get into" contemporary hymns and choruses as well as meaningful, traditional hymns of the church. In all cases, this age group needs to be taught the difference between God-centered worship songs and the I-centered music that characterizes so many contemporary songs and traditional gospel music. While junior highers are egocentric and music that is such would be appropriate to them, senior highers are moving away from egocentricity into other-centeredness. Songs that emphasize the solidarity of Christians and the community of believers in worship of God are appropriate at this point.

Senior highers want to express their own experiences with God. They look for songs that express where they are in their relationship with the Triune God. They are also open to new types of songs. Thus, if a youth group has been using mostly contemporary music, it would be suitable to gradually introduce the senior highers to some of the more traditional and/or classical church music that speaks to their particular life situations.

Senior highers are ready, especially the older ones, to understand both the words and the music and how the two form a whole message. Thus the choice of songs is rather crucial because senior highers are now sensitive to the total musical idiom. It is fitting for youth workers to teach new songs and to reteach old songs for more in-depth meaning to the senior highers.

Aesthetics

By senior high age, youth are beginning to respond to beauty and symbolism. Their aesthetic sense is developing and they feel the nuances of the ambience. Symbols, candles, colors, pictures, and other art can be used with senior highers, provided that the youth know the meanings attached to them. These youth are beginning to think abstractly and can appreciate the various deeper meanings of symbols and the realities behind the concrete symbol.

Prayer

Senior highers, like their junior high counterparts, look for personal, relevant, life-related prayer. This age group is not appreciative of long or short fancy prayers that climb the sublime heights of theological insights. They want down-to-earth prayers that connect with their lives. Like junior highers, senior highers need to be directed in silent prayer. Youth will usually respond to opportunities for them to pray short, meaningful, focused prayers. Prayer hymns and Scripture prayers are still very useful, but only if the youth know what the prayers mean experientially. Conversational prayers, short sentence prayers, directed praying, and prayers focused on their needs are all meaningful for this age group.

Message

Senior highers are able to learn by listening. They are more likely to remain focused for a longer period of time than junior highers. The youth themselves can often be helped to prepare and deliver the "message" or talk. This aspect of the worship experience, if used, needs to be centered on their relationship to God. Whatever the actual content of the message, it should relate to how senior highers view and respond to God.

Atmosphere

Like their younger friends, senior highers look for a fast-paced variety. They are more comfortable with MTV-paced events than the formal atmosphere of a cathedral setting. Contemporary, light, bright, and dynamic surroundings appeal to them.

Emotions

These young people are still characterized by easily swayed emotions. One can have these youth laughing uproariously one minute and about to cry the next. They shift easily and can be led by the use of emotions. Worship experiences need to capitalize on their emotional sensitivity, but this should obviously be

Junior high worship is most effective when it is informal, life-related, and dynamic. Worship for senior highers is personal and participative.

done carefully. It is not right to play on their emotions nor is it proper to totally ignore them. God's presence needs to be felt emotionally and not just mentally. A proper balance should be sought in the selection of music and Scripture and in the delivery of a message or talk. Emotionalism should be avoided.

Scripture

What is true for junior highers is also true for senior highers regarding Scripture. Senior highers need a contemporary translation or version. One short, focused idea works best. The youth should be involved in the reading of Scripture, but preparation is necessary for an effective oral reading. A youth worker would do well to help those who will be reading Scripture to understand the meaning and feeling that a particular Bible portion contains and how it relates to the planned worship experience.

Planning and Leadership

Senior highers want to participate if their involvement is to be meaningful. Worship experiences should rely heavily on their participation both in planning and in execution. Preparation is essential and youth workers will need to spend time working with the youth to achieve this. Adults will need to check up on the youth to make sure that they are preparing consistently.

A worship experience is often more meaningful if the youth have been actively involved in its planning and leading. All who care to

participate should be involved at some time during the year. Many senior highers have musical talents, and these talents, dedicated to the Lord and encouraged in their use, can become very effective tools in worship.

Focus

Senior highers are idealistic, and they want contact with God that appeals to that idealism. God needs to be seen as the Person who expects the best from us, his children. A senior higher's world view is expanding and encompasses more of the adult world than is true of junior highers. Most look for experiences that will help them fill the need for this broader view of the world.

Worship for senior highers is personal and participative. They seek worship experiences that will provide opportunities for them to plan and execute, and that focus on personal needs.

Post-High/College-Age

Needs

Post-high school, older adolescents (aged nineteen to twenty-five) are still youth developmentally. They constitute a crucial part of any comprehensive youth ministry in the church. Post-high youth are able to think for themselves. Most think abstractly and critically. They are still pragmatic, but in a more cerebral sense. Their minds look for answers to the issues and questions of life. They are concerned for their own future: vocation, marriage, security, social role, and so forth. They seek for a more mature faith which is expressed in their worship experiences. These youth will not be satisfied with a junior or senior high worship experience; they want an encounter with God in worship that is on their level of development and that meets their more mature needs.

These youth—particularly college students—tend to be aware of what is happening in the world. This generation of college students could be called "world people." And they seek a worship experience that speaks to their worldwide view. For God to be relevant, he must be seen as the God of the universe and not just a warm, personal friend.

Music

The post-high school group is ideal to use the doctrinal, timeless hymns and new, theologically deeper contemporary songs of the church. This group needs to go beyond more shallow music to that which speaks to their levels of development. This is a good time to break with much of the frivolous, shallow, experience-centered contemporary music and to experience the meaningfulness of some older hymns and deeper contemporary songs.

Aesthetics

These youth respond to various aesthetic atmospheres. Abstract symbols speak to them and help them focus on their worship of God. Art, music, and other worship aids are understandable—though it may be necessary at first to explain the meanings of these symbols. However, once explained, the meanings behind the concrete expression can be comprehended. Since post-high school youth still like change, a variety of symbols can be used with good response.

Prayer

Prayers can be longer, with a more encompassing scope. Periods of silent prayer can also be used without the need to structure them too tightly. It is still appropriate to use directed prayer, but they need not be highly directive. For instance, a mere suggestion to think about God's love for humanity should suffice. Just as with the younger ages, this group values personal participation and usually is willing to lead in prayer.

Message

Because of the higher cognitive development of these youth, messages or talks can be centered on abstract characteristics of God as well as on more concrete ideas. This age group does not look for experiences that satisfy an emotional need as much as for a total experience that addresses them as whole persons. They look for questions and doubts to be addressed in their contact with God through worship experiences.

Emotions

Emotional appeals need to be tightly controlled. While emotions are part of every human's total personhood, they are not an effective means to appeal to this age group. Emotional appeals usually are counterproductive with post-high school youth. They need a broader and deeper contact with God that is not oriented to emotions as much as to the mind and will.

Atmosphere

The atmosphere to which these older youth respond is one that uses meaningful symbols. This age group relates to an unpressured atmosphere that stimulates intellectually, as well as touches the feelings and will. They look for a time to reflect and meditate (something

> *The post-high age group does not look for experiences that satisfy an emotional need as much as for a total experience that addresses them as whole persons.*

one should probably never try with junior highers and only occasionally with senior highers). They respond well to a surrounding that touches their senses and causes their minds to dwell on the worthiness of God. The total atmosphere should speak of God's greatness and our continual response and commitment to him. In a sense, each worship experience needs to address this continual, on-going commitment of the post-high school group.

Scripture

A variety of contemporary translations and versions can be used with this age group. Whereas the Living Bible and other paraphrases were useful and perhaps even necessary with younger age groups, this group is capable of understanding the more formal translations such as the New International Version, the Revised English Bible, and the New Revised Standard Version.

Proof texts are not acceptable nor well-received uses of Scripture. These youth seek to know and experience the total meaning of a text and should be helped to do so.

Planning and Leadership

Post-high youth should plan and execute the whole worship experience with little or no direct help from adult youth workers. The adults' roles should be limited to continual stimulation of thinking and helping to focus. There is no place for a worship experience for these youth operated by older adults. They should be encouraged to do this on their own.

Focus

These youth want a personal, intellectually satisfying, God-centered worship experience. For the first time in their lives they can appreciate God as he has revealed himself rather than on a truncated lower level of development that characterized their earlier years. In this context, they seek experiences for themselves that help them to see him who is invisible, with deeper appreciation for all that God is to and for them. They can be appealed to intellectually and as whole persons—not forgetting but not centered on emotions. They seek to respond in worship to the whole being of God as whole persons.

PLANNING A WORSHIP SERVICE

Avoid last-minute planning. Get it done ahead of time. Begin by determining the needs to be met. Then look for variety, integrating all the parts to make a unified service. Do not be afraid to be progressive or to try new things. At the same time, avoid being so startling that the focus of the service is lost. Finally, make use of the best talent available so that the worship of God is real and of the highest quality.

Building a worship service involves a series of steps: (1) Decide on a theme. (2) Choose outcomes, wording them in the form of responses. What do you want participants to know, feel, acknowledge, do, and be? (3) Plan which elements of worship to include and in what order they will go. (4) Gather material. (5) Organize the group that you are working with, assigning parts and jobs. (6) Check and test the personnel doing the job, and the plans for proper length, coherence, purpose, and best use of materials. (7) Rehearse the service if many people are involved in doing different things. (8) Put on the service, no longer thinking about the mechanics involved. (9) Evaluate it afterward: Was it real worship? Did it magnify the Lord? Were the outcomes achieved? Did it meet particular needs? Did it take the group further in their Christian experience? Was the presence of God experienced? Was the atmosphere conducive to worship? How could all of it be improved?

TEACHING WORSHIP

Adult youth workers can learn about worship in a divisional or department workers' meeting, or in a small group of teachers, workers, or sponsors. They will learn best by demonstration, by participating in a worship service as it should be experienced. So it is important that the youth worker who is teaching help the learners really feel worship, not just know about worship. Try doing something unusual, something not in the routine church service and Sunday school opening exercises. Afterwards, discuss how the particular elements were used in the service. Analyze what you have done, teaching the essence and importance of each element. Let the learners express themselves, their doubts and questions. Then provide them with principles found herein to use in planning and building a worship service program.

Youth themselves could learn about worship in a youth group meeting, or in Sunday school from their teachers as they prepare a Sunday school or youth meeting worship service. The main thing to remember in teaching anyone about worship is that the worship experience itself is the wrong place to learn about worship. God, not a teaching about worship, is the focus of a worship experience.

The key word for adolescent leadership in worship is *involvement*. Youth need to be involved in worship on every level possible. Two basic ways this can be done stand out: They can be active participators in worship, and they can be active in both planning and executing worship. There is no reason to exclude them from the planning of their own worship services. Give them opportunity to actually lead in prayer, Scripture reading, accompanying on keyboards, piano, and guitar, presenting special music, and, if the youth are mature and respected, giving a message or talk.

USE OF WORSHIP IN THE PROGRAMS OF A YOUTH MINISTRY

Sunday School Department and Class

Assuming a Sunday school opening assembly, a full worship experience is best used once a quarter; this could be assigned to a different group each quarter. For the remainder of the quarter, a song time, announcements, and teaching time are enough. The primary role of Sunday school is instruction rather than worship, and the church as a whole has a worship service each Sunday. Worship can, however, be incorporated profitably into individual classes.

Some may consider scheduling worship time as a department at the end of Sunday school. This is not as feasible as the opening because it means coordinating all individual classes to finish at the same time. Depending on the church, many youth will be immediately attending a worship service after Sunday school. And it seems rather counterproductive to try to hold a youth worship service that is in competition with "adult" worship, anyway. There is a great need for intergenerational worship, rather than separatism by age in the worship of God. Youth need the contact with the fellowship of the community of believers of the

> *Youth need the contact with the fellowship of the community of believers of the entire local church in worship.*

entire local church in worship. This has ramifications for the main church worship services, but that is beyond the scope of this chapter.

At the end of class, worship might be used as a means of motivation to put into practice what youth have just learned. Such a time will be informal, because the group is likely to be small. Both the leader and youth can use knowledge gained in the class as a foundation on which to build the material of worship. Elements of worship may even be correlated with the lesson.

Other Meetings, Camps, Clubs

Worship is appropriate for a youth group meeting on special holidays, such as Thanksgiving, Christmas, New Year's Eve, and Easter. Or it would work nicely to teach about worship and then have an actual worship service. To begin or end every meeting with worship tends to be artificial. After a period of time, through mere repetition, it becomes an empty form devoid of meaning. And it would be wrong to lead youth to the assumption that worship is a mere repetitive duty.

Camp is a wonderful place to hold a worship service. Emphasis falls naturally on praise for God in nature. And youth are usually motivated by a camp experience to serve and to use the knowledge they have gained. Both formal and informal worship may take place with a larger group, using the camp setting as an enhancement. Informal worship happens everywhere—in cabin groups, on hikes, canoe trips, burro rides, a pack trip, or a nature walk. (See chapter 10.)

As with a Sunday school class worship, weekday clubs are conducive to informal worship time. When a strenuous activity comes first, as well as teaching, youth have more motivation to put into practice what they are learning by participating in worship. The purpose of youth retreats is usually motivation, appreciation, and revelation. As at camps, retreats and group outings provide informal opportunities to praise God for nature and his revelation through it.

WORSHIP VS. TEACHING

Worship and teaching seem often to become confused. Sometimes youth workers have trouble keeping one or the other in focus. As a help, the chart that follows compares the two experiences.

WORSHIP VERSUS TEACHING

Worship experience	Teaching experience

MUSIC

Worship experience	Teaching experience
Call to focus on the Lord	Less serious songs
God-centered songs sung to him: praise, worship, adoration, thanksgiving, to glorify God	Songs about God, about how we feel about our Christian life, etc.
Build around a familiar theme	Teach new songs, or about songs
Can include group singing, solo, duet, trio, choir, or other excellent lyrics and music to fit	For edification
	Group singing
Appreciated by singers	Understood by singers

PRAYER

Worship experience	Teaching experience
Worship expressed is "vertical," centering on praise and the worthiness of God	Emphasis on "horizontal"—"Help us, Lord" prayers
Worship prayers: adoration, praise worthiness of God, confession of sins, receiving forgiveness	Intercessory/Petition prayers

MESSAGE, TALK, "HOMILY"/LESSON

Worship experience	Teaching experience
Active focus on God	Focus on the learners
Purpose: to express feelings to God and to learn more of his worthiness	Purpose: to get new information for transformation
Goal: affective response, transformation from actively contemplating God	Goal: active response, application, transformation from knowledge
No discussion or questions	Allows for discussion, questions, and sharing
Sharing	

CHAPTER

6

Fellowship

A fter teaching and worship, we come to the third program element. Fellowship is often defined in terms of social interaction and activity—games, socials, sports, bull sessions, etc.—in which the social aspects are emphasized to the exclusion of any other aspects. For many American Christians, fellowship means coffee and doughnuts, or a Coke and a hamburger and talking about anything at all with other Christians. This *might* be fellowship, but it has nothing to do necessarily with Christ. It is not particular to or peculiar to Christianity. There is nothing "Christian" involved in it.

The New Testament concepts of fellowship are much deeper. Two Greek words define it: *koinōnia*—fellowship, or communion, and *metochē*—sharing. *Koinōnia* is related to the word *koinē*, which means "common," and *koinō,* meaning "to share," "make common." The fundamental idea is that of sharing in something with someone.

Fellowship ". . . designates that social relationship existing between Christians who are regenerate members of God's family and their cooperation in the work of the Lord. Fellowship posits as its prerequisite a likeness of nature that transcends external and temporary differences. True fellowship can exist only between believers."[1]

The basis of fellowship, according to 1 John 1:3, 6, 7, is a vital union with the Son to the Father effected by the Holy Spirit. It is the saving relationship we have with God by the power of the Holy Spirit, made possible by the redemptive act of Jesus Christ on the cross and won in triumph in his resurrection. This relationship that a Christian has with God bears a twofold direction: a vertical one from a person to God and a horizontal one from one Christian to other Christians. This second direction is where fellowship comes in, but it does not operate without the vertical relationship.

To put it another way, Dietrich Bonhoeffer said:

> We belong to one another only through Jesus Christ. What does this mean? It means, first, that a Christian needs others because of Jesus Christ. It means, second, that a Christian comes to others only through Jesus Christ. It means, third, that in Jesus Christ we have been chosen for eternity, accepted in time and united for eternity.[2]

Fellowship extends to all Christians, to each person in the family of God regardless of color, sex, age, race, or denomination. To quote Bonhoeffer again:

> My brother is rather that other person who has been redeemed by Christ, delivered from his sin, and called to faith and eternal life. Not what a man is in himself as a Christian, his spirituality and piety, constitutes the basis of our community. What determines our brotherhood is what that man is by reason of Christ. Our community with one another consists solely in what Christ has done to both of us.[3]

Our fellowship as Christians is manifested in action. An example given to us is found in Acts 2:42ff., where the believers' inner unity and spiritual participation in Christ led to an outward manifestation of fellowship. This is found in their care for each other, in their joint corporate worship, praise, and mutual edification, and in their "breaking bread," or taking the Lord's Supper, together. In other words, their daily contact with other Christians was centered in Jesus Christ. Bonhoeffer warns that this unity or fellowship—community—was not an ideal to which they ascribed, but a spiritual reality which the believers accepted and acted upon by faith. Unless this finds concrete expression in one's personal life, the concept of fellowship is useless.

A basic hindrance to fellowship is found when Christians hide their real selves behind facades. One cannot share the Christ he or she knows and the fellowship with Christ unless they can do so without hypocrisy. Many believers are afraid to show their real selves, and they develop an array of defense techniques to use as masks. Yet, to have fellowship demands openness and truthfulness. Believers must avoid espousing the false "I" of the Pharisees in favor of revealing the true "I" of the publican who said, "Lord, be merciful to me a sinner," or of Paul when he said, "I am the chief of sinners."

On a practical basis, therefore, fellowship is a mutual sharing of ourselves with someone else through a mutually experienced social activity. The social context affords the medium through which koinonia is effected. This is done by revealing of ourselves, giving of ourselves to another, removing the mask or facade for a little while, being "me," and receiving the other's self-revelation.

The social event includes talking, but not just small talk for its own sake; it includes activity, but not just for activity's sake. Talk and activity break down barriers to allow each to participate in the sharing of self (fellowship) with other(s). They are means to an end of personal encounter with two or more people who share or participate in the same Holy Spirit and Lord. In talking, we share our lives in that

> The church must treat the whole person and all his or her basic needs, for it is impossible to minister to the spiritual needs of youth without ministering to their other needs.

we express those things that Jesus Christ has been revealing to us that would be of benefit to others. We share our lives by helping others in their need—spiritually, psychologically and emotionally.

To summarize, fellowship consists of the sharing of life in Christ, which presupposes (1) personal salvation through Christ, (2) the work of the Holy Spirit in one's life revealing Christ to the individual, (3) a social context in which to share, and (4) the truthfulness of self in relationship with others. Judged by this standard, much of church "fellowship" is socializing but not fellowship at all. The following will suggest how to remedy this discrepancy.

HOW THE DEFINITION OF FELLOWSHIP WORKS IN YOUTH MINISTRY

Fellowship Needs

Adolescents' needs for fellowship can be found established in each of the six developmental domains. First, *physically*, youth need activity for their developing muscles; they are learning about coordination of these muscles. Learning and practicing good health habits are a necessity, as are new skills that will continue

to be helpful. A final consideration is to relieve excess energy.

Second, *cognitively* or *intellectually* they will grapple with problems in a discussion. Youth can use their intelligence to make judgments and decisions—and they can use their creativity and imagination—in planning and executing a fellowship program. They also make time to follow interests and hobbies.

Third, *socially*, youth would like to be part of a peer group. They should have contact with the opposite sex in a proper environment. In this context, they can learn and practice social poise and manners, as well as make friends.

Fourth, *affectively* or *emotionally*, adolescents are searching for a sense of belonging, security, and acceptance by others of their persons and of their revealed selves. They are working to gain self-confidence in social situations, to feel that they can do something of worth and accomplishment. They want freedom of expression and adventure—within bounds. And, especially, they want to have fun.

Fifth, *morally* youth want a moral universe—not an immoral or morally chaotic one—in which they can function as whole people. They want to be treated with justice, equality, and love, and to know that they can *be* themselves with others without fear of rejection, being mocked, and/or reprisals. Youth need to abide by rules, to practice justice, to learn noncompetitiveness, and to apply agape in their interpersonal relationships.

Sixth, *spiritually*, youth need to know that all of life is sacred for Christians. They should see no false bifurcation between the secular and the sacred. Adolescents also want to see the practicality of Christianity—how it applies to their lives in general. Filling these fellowship needs leads to ultimate fellowship—the sharing of what God is doing in others' lives, and strengthening each other spiritually by putting Christianity into practice.

The Church's Role in Meeting Fellowship Needs

Some may ask why the church should provide for these needs. Are not its major tasks evangelism and Christian nurture? But the fact is that all adolescents' needs will be met to some degree and through some means. The concern should be whether or not the meeting of these needs will be achieved in the best way; will the world meet these more intimate fellowship needs, or will the church? The church can provide youth with a wholesome environment in which to play and recreate, to develop socially and to share with one another. It must treat the whole person and all his or her basic needs, for it is impossible to minister to the spiritual needs of youth without ministering to their other needs.

Evangelism and Christian nurture are indeed the major tasks of the church, but we must gain a hearing with young people before we can reach and teach them. A proper program of fellowship will refute the idea that many adolescents have of Christianity, that it is a dry creed with all joy squeezed out of it. If correctly administered, fellowship will provide for meeting many of these needs and will consequently make the young people more Christ-like and loyal to their local and universal church.

"Proper" fellowship opportunities do not mean unsupervised play or chatter; rather, they mean activities and conversation designed to increase adolescents' knowledge of each other and of the Lord. The first step in fellowship activities is never as great as the final goal. Immediate goals may be only to provide for physical and social needs. But the ultimate goal of knowledge of each other and the Lord should be in mind even at the beginning and should be kept in view at all times. The final goal will serve as a measuring stick for the effectiveness of a fellowship program.

Dangers

Some dangers do lurk in a fellowship program for youth. One is that of *duplicating community programs* when these are already wholesome and good. (Of course, in some cases it is necessary to provide church programs because the community's are not satisfactory.) When the community has good programs and facilities, a fellowship program should offer something other than what the community does. For instance, say the community maintains a sports program that meets physical needs and also potentially can meet some "fellowship" needs. In this case, a church does not have to focus on meeting physical needs. Rather it could provide social-fellowship programs that would satisfy unmet needs rather than duplicating others and competing with the community. Not competing also better utilizes the limited resources of a church, enables it to be a good steward, and allows it to minister in the community.

Isolation is another danger in fellowship programs. Christian youth may withdraw from all activities in the community and from public school events and offerings. Attempting to supply all the needs of all youth creates too great a demand on the youth program, facilities, personnel, supervision, and organization. This should be attempted in only the most dire circumstances when local situations are so deplorable that the church must intervene.

A final danger is that of *encouraging weak Christians* and *discouraging strong Christians*. Having all activities centered in the church youth group tends to make weak Christians dependent on church for all initiative and fun, and makes strong Christians have to face a conflict between church (spiritual) and secular (unspiritual). Strong Christians may feel that they have to decide between living in the world or apart from the world—but we have been told to live *in* the world, while not being *of* it. In addition, if virtually all activity centers in the church, Christian youth end up being

Having all activities centered in the church youth group tends to make weak Christians dependent on church for all initiative and fun, and makes strong Christians have to face a conflict between church (spiritual) and secular (unspiritual).

taken out of contact with non-Christians. A solid fellowship program will bring in outsiders who need Christian contact and faith. Here a comprehensive, encompassing program will be an evangelistic tool as well as a fellowship tool.

The Purposes and Values of a Recreation Program

Traditionally, much of fellowship refers to recreation in one form or another. Therefore, it is necessary to think through recreation's purposes and values. A recreation/fellowship program begins with the premise that everything a youth group and other church organizations do teaches the basic values of the group, whether positive or negative.

Recreation is not in the church just to make youth happy, but also to help make them holy. It is, of course, fun, with the added benefits of spiritual enrichment, growth in Christ, personality growth, and the breaking down of barriers between people. Games and socials play a large role, but recreation also includes such things as reading, drama, music, art, hobbies, interests, bull sessions, and Bible studies.

Moral development occurs during recreation as youth learn consideration, kindness, friendliness, fair play, self-control, self-understanding, understanding of others, and social role-taking. Social integration is helped when youth learn to be with the opposite sex in a social situation, and how to handle themselves in such a situation.

A recreation program enlists on God's side the adolescent's natural desire for fun activities and socializing. It aids in winning individuals to Jesus Christ and to the local church, and keeps them within the church's sphere of influence. Also, tensions and emotions are both stimulated and reduced, providing better learning as a result. And recreation encourages a zest for new experiences and living in general.

By meeting some of youths' basic needs, recreation enables the church to find a point of contact from which to find and meet spiritual needs too. Christianity is vital to more than Sunday church, and recreation programs show that all of life involves Christian living and operates on Christian principles.

Recreation demonstrates that Christians, too, do have fun. It breaks down social barriers, providing a natural setting in which to share informally, helping to develop Christian friendship and fellowship. Finally, recreation helps to build unity and provides a chance to participate in unified action.

The Fellowship Program

All of the basic needs listed above are incorporated into objectives and actual activities of the fellowship program. Practically, these break down into two types of activities: sharing and recreational. Sharing activities assume that the natural walls between youth are broken down and they can communicate openly with each other. One of these is *Bible study.* When focused on fellowship, this will not be leader-centered. Youth might read a passage in order to find out what it says to the original readers, to each individual, and to the group. Learning activities should emphasize primarily self-disclosure rather than content. (See chapter 4 on teaching.)

Another activity is the *prayer meeting.* Have youth share what God is doing in their lives, making known their own needs as well as those of others. Then fellowship together in prayer. *Youth-planned worship services* and *sharing times* are further opportunities for youth to experience fellowship with each other. Any of the above could be separate activities, or part of larger events. (See chapter 5 on worship.)

Recreational activities tend to focus somewhat on breaking down barriers between people, although some spiritual needs are met along with physical and social needs. The following are suggested activities: team sports, such as basketball, baseball, volleyball, and football; socials; trips to a city museum, a planetarium, a car show, or sports show; a shopping trip; sporting events on various levels; concerts and parades; dinners, banquets, or breakfasts; day hikes and overnight hikes, camp-,outs, backpacking; canoe, bike, sailing, or ski trips; pool parties at the local "Y," school pool, local public or private swim facilities; picnics with a class or group; hobby and interest groups, such as chess, boating, snow or water skiing; go-carting and horseback riding; sleigh rides and hay rides; going to amusement parks; indoor games such as Ping-Pong, Foosball, pool, board games, air hockey, Nintendo, computer games, or more; crafts or reading programs; after-school sports activities and after-church activities; and unplanned, unstructured get-togethers.

Permeating all of the above ideas is the fact that they are not ends in themselves. The outcome of each is the breaking down of barriers and the sharing of oneself; this needs to be impressed both directly and indirectly upon youth *and* adult leaders. The absence of this

goal might create a deluge of social recreation but a dearth of fellowship.

Be creative and innovative in planning a recreation program. Don't do the same things repeatedly. Surprisingly, many youth will want to continue their traditional ways of doing things. Like adults, they can become mired in their own tradition. Help them break away from a rut! One way is not to use just standard games; modify them to fit your group and its location. Change locations and some of the parameters of the games; what is appropriate at camp may not be appropriate in the church parking lot. Use games and other activities that are noncompetitive or use competition to a minimum, stressing fun.

The Question of Competitive Activities

Competition carries with it both assets and liabilities. The question to ask is, should we even use it? And if so, how? Note the assets of competition:

- It is natural for youth to compare themselves with others.
- Both perception and conception of self come about through comparison with others.
- Competition adds excitement to activities.
- It provides a setting in which youth can react to new experiences and discover new potentialities within themselves.
- It is good when it occurs spontaneously, and when it is not destructive.
- Competition is productive; it gets results.
- If zest outweighs the bitterness of losing, and if a friendly attitude prevails and pervades, then it might be good.
- It is helpful when the goal is to improve, not to prove or beat.

The liabilities of competition occur when it fosters the following:

- Getting things for self and preventing others from having a chance.
- Getting attention for oneself.
- Seeking to vanquish and not just to vie; seeking to conquer others and not just to compare one's earlier self with the current self.
- Deriving satisfaction from making others look silly and not solely from mastering an activity.
- Driving people to shy away because they are afraid to compare themselves with others.
- Having little concern about the activity itself, but only with winning.
- Allowing competition to control a person.
- Requiring that some have to fail—in a church group, no less.
- Drawing attention to one person rather than to the whole group.

When making decisions about competition, keep in mind some basic principles:

- Most males in the American culture are competitive, as are quite a few females.
- Help kids to work as a team, using competition as a comparison, not a time to conquer.
- Each person on a team must contribute to the goal.
- Everyone should win something.
- The goal is fun and recreation, not winning.
- Don't make too much out of winning and losing.
- Use biblical principles of competition— "Carry each other's burdens, and in this way you will fulfill the law of Christ. If anyone thinks he is something when he is nothing, he deceives himself. Each one should test his own actions. Then he can take pride in himself, without comparing himself to somebody else, for each one should carry his own load" (Gal. 6:2–5; also see Mark 10:35–45.)
- See if competition is biblical. Many have looked for biblical support, but cannot find it as a part of being disciples of Christ.

The Distinctives of a Christian Fellowship Program—A Summary

A Christian fellowship program is set within the framework of a basic Christian philosophy of life. While not all the participants will have a Christian outlook, at least the leaders' viewpoints are Christ-centered. And probably many of the youth would share those same viewpoints.

The goal of the fellowship program is not just fun, activity, and/or conversation, but to deepen personal relationships with each other and with Jesus Christ. Wholesomeness and propriety are the rule rather than exception. An active fellowship program results in outreach to non-Christian youth. At the same time, Christian character is developed as youth learn to be fair and just—a justice based on agapic reasoning—and as they gain a desire for wholesome activities. Finally, competition is minimized.

LEADERSHIP IN A FELLOWSHIP PROGRAM

Adults serve mostly to supervise a fellowship program (more closely for junior high, less for senior high, and even less for post-high youth), allowing youth to participate fully. Adults may aid in planning by facilitating, helping, encouraging, and coaching. Because the adult has a good grasp of the overall goal and philosophy of the group, he or she may serve to suggest ideas, to spark interest and enthusiasm. Or an adult may be a resource person, obtaining books and ideas for fellowship, games, activities, skits, stunts, or inductive Bible study.

In addition, adults can help in executing

Stop an activity when youth are still enjoying it, not when they are bored with it.

---

socials and outings for early- and middle-adolescent groups by leading games and other events. It is easier for an adult to do this because he or she can more likely hold the attention of the group. Also, all of the adolescents then have a chance to participate in fun, even if they have been part of the planning team.

Youth may lead a fellowship program on many levels—planning, decorating, preparation of food, clean-up, or other things. Late adolescents will generally do best at directing their own social activities.

Following are eleven rules in recreational leadership:

1. Make definite and thorough plans for each occasion.
2. Consider the first opening activity or event as important; a social begins when the first person arrives.
3. Give directions clearly and simply.
4. Have only one designated leader during a social. This person should have a thorough knowledge of the entire social. He or she should: study the games—know what the rules are and how to explain them, make sure any necessary material is gathered, dress appropriately, and have a plan for such emergencies as an accident, fire, unruly participants, drugs, alcohol, or sexual harassment.
5. Capitalize on mistakes by being willing to laugh at oneself or to make a joke out of them.
6. Include each person in an activity.
7. Create a vacuum around the resident "wise guy" so that he or she cannot disrupt the event.
8. Secure discipline throughout the group.
9. Vary the play. When an activity has served its purpose, stop it. Use a variety of activity types.
10. Control activities through the mental alertness of the leader. It is impossible to erase every problem or to have a planned solution to every situation.
11. Stop an activity when youth are still enjoying it, not when they are bored with it.

Appropriate Fellowship Activities

While it is important that activities be planned by adolescents, they do not always have the perspective of over-all philosophy and purpose when they are making their choices. Sometimes, youth may see only the immediate "fun" which an activity will generate. The results of this may be hurt feelings, physical harm, a lack of good taste in the program, a questionable activity, or improper conversation, jokes, skits, or stunts.

Thus, it is necessary to lay out principles by which to judge the selection of activities.

1. Is it spiritually beneficial?
2. Is it a hazard?
3. Is it legal?
4. Does it stimulate the mind, not the passions?
5. Do people who engage in this recreation symbolize an ideal of Christian living?
6. Will it hurt anyone physically, psychologically, spiritually, or morally?
7. Is it in good taste?
8. Would Jesus willingly participate?

Planning Fellowship Activities

Before any planning is done, choose a theme and decide on a purpose for each activi-

---

CHARACTERISTICS OF A GOOD SOCIAL

A Good Social

- Is planned carefully and involves everyone who is present,
- Is fun for all,
- Begins and ends on time (measured from when the first person arrives to when the last person leaves),
- Builds Christian character and personality,
- Is consistent with Christian standards,
- Breaks down barriers and closed cliques,
- Is spiritually purposeful.

---

ty to go along with it. Next, the youth leader will want to organize, and then supervise, the events. A sample planning team might consist of a chairperson, activity leader, and a number of subcommittee chairpeople: facilities and decorations, food, entertainment, games, transportation, clean-up, and devotions. Once the initial planning is done, the specific jobs will be delegated out.

When pulling together all the pieces of fellowship activities, a number of issues must be decided. Fourteen areas are essential for discussion:

1. The choice of activities will depend on what facilities are available, the capacities of the group, the attitude of the group, and who is leading. Plan for more activities than will be needed, and plan for variety; for instance, alternate between active and quiet games. Decide what equipment and materials are needed and who will be in charge of obtaining them for the appropriate activities. Determine a schedule, including the timing (down to minutes) and ordering of all parts of the fellowship activity.

2. Decide who will lead the entire social. This will most likely be adults for junior highers, and usually for senior highers as well. The important characteristics of activity leaders are that they are fun loving, easy going, totally in control of themselves, able to exert control over the group by personal abilities, personality, and magnetism, and not authoritarian.

3. Decide on a time (start and finish), date, location, and transportation for each event.

4. Clear the date with the church office.

5. Decide on appropriate dress.

6. Determine the cost to each individual. Are subsidies or scholarships necessary?

7. Decide on the entertainment, if any.

8. Decide on decorations. What type will be used? What kind of access will there be to the location for set-up?

9. Decide on food—it should be plenteous and good. What materials and equipment might be needed for preparation?

10. Consider how to make devotions fit into the purpose and theme of the activity. If devotions are appropriate for a specific event decide who should lead them. Prepare youth for devotions by having them sit in a circle for the last game before devotions, or plan that game to be more quiet than the others. The devotional leader could also lead the last two games, and go naturally into devotions. Or, from the last game the group could move into informal singing and then into progressively deeper songs and devotions. Use variety in moving from fun time to the more serious time.

11. Notify the group's publicity chairperson of each activity, theme, dress, cost, etc., so that the process of letting people know about the event can begin. This process may include flyers, posters, phone calls, skits in meetings, personal contact by adolescents, adult leaders' notification, and a blurb in the church bulletin announcements.

12. Decide on how to welcome guests and introduce them to others comfortably.

13. Prepare for clean-up. Who will do it? How will it be organized? What needs to be done?

14. When it is all over, evaluate the activity for the following: Character—what did it do for youth's character development? Spiritual—did it help the spirit or the flesh to grow? Health—did it help the body? Also ask, was it too late at night, too strenuous, too dangerous? Did it break down social barriers, reduce cliques, make everyone feel "in"? Did everyone enjoy it? Was it in good taste? Could everyone afford it? And did it encourage fellowship?

An activity should be completed when its purpose is accomplished, for instance, when a mixer has "mixed." It should stop when the activity is still at its height, and people want more. But at the same time, youth should not have a sense of incompleteness or frustration; they should have enough time to enjoy the activity. In other words, it is wrong to stop too soon or to play too long. Of course, if an activity gets out of hand—beyond normal limits—it needs to end immediately.

7

Service

The fourth program element is service, or ministry. It is experience-oriented learning. Service activities are central to a youth program because for learning to be effective, one must be actively involved in the process of acquiring and using data. Service is the focal point, the place where learning can be formed on a cognitive-affective-social-spiritual-behavioral base. Thus, a developmental approach to learning is the foundation to a youth program and in particular to the element of service or ministry. Service projects are usually the central part of the expressions or ministry-service element in most youth ministries.

DEFINING THE CONCEPT

Service projects are youth activities that are centered around doing something for someone other than oneself. Experience-oriented learning is an integral part of service projects.

1. An experience-oriented learning project begins with the youth's interests, needs, and concerns.

2. From this point on it involves the youth in their thinking

activities as they grapple with various data provided by themselves or by others. This constitutes the inner, active phase of learning.

3. Throughout the learning process there is a continuing growth and maturity in interaction with the data, and a growing articulation of an increasing number of possible refined answers. These are the continuous and, in part, maturing aspects of learning.

4. The entire group—each individual and the youth worker—helps sustain the learning process and disciplines itself to achieve the set goals. Discipline is not authoritarianism. It is the mutual encouragement, exhortation, or even loving rebuke that the members of a group employ once they know, trust, and love each other. This is the real discipline of learning.

5. As the members internalize (comprehend) the data and begin to see how it works out in practical ways, they continue in the maturing process. As they put themselves to the task of working out the data in concrete terms, they maintain social, spiritual, intellectual, and psychological growth. This is the constant maturation phase within the context of learning.

6. Through this process of experience-oriented learning, group members come to personal answers—not ready-made ones. They find out for themselves which answers are most satisfactory according to their needs. These answers are internal and meaningful because of the direct involvement. The youth have done the intellectual work necessary to arrive at the answer at hand. If they are not satisfied, they can rethink the data and/or the experiences. If they still are not satisfied, they can test other responses in other situations.

WHY HAVE SERVICE PROJECTS?

Service projects have been in existence for quite some time, but their rationale has seldom been connected directly with learning.

> *Service projects are not merely accidental or even intentional activities connected with learning; they are learning.*

The first reason most often given for service projects within a traditional youth ministry is that they provide youth with expressional activity. Basic to this idea is the traditional view of learning that separates knowledge from experience. Christian education in the evangelical church has traditionally been compartmentalized into two meeting times—a Sunday school, and some sort of midweek group meeting. Within this mentality service projects are primarily outlets for a frustration built up from a constant reception of spiritual truth apart from real-life situations. The process of learning is broken down into neat, logical, and theoretical packages; one "learns" in the weekly Sunday school session and expresses what he or she has "learned" in the occasional service project. This fragmentation of the learning process reputedly produces better over-all learning for the pupils.

A second reason within the traditional Christian education program of the local church is a pragmatic one: "Use them or lose them." A characteristic need of youth is to be active. They have a seemingly unlimited amount of energy, idealism, creative talent, altruism, and time (or at least a willingness to make time). This second rationale for service projects can readily be seen in such statements as "hold their interest in your church," "give them a sense of belonging," and "develop their talents and leadership abilities."[1]

These two traditional reasons for service projects misplace the emphasis. Service projects are not expressional activities conceived of apart from the whole teaching-learning situation. They are the most profitable teaching-learning situations imaginable. They provide the setting in which experience-oriented learning occurs. They are the activity of learning, not the product or by-product. They are not merely accidental or even intentional activities *connected* with learning; they *are* learning. There is no learning without personal involvement in direct experience. It is possible to directly experience God in the classroom, but only an extremely limited amount of God's person can be encountered in isolation from everyday life. One does not learn about God and then try to find experiences to corroborate the learning; one learns about God as one experiences him. To have cognitive knowledge of God but not to have experienced him is not Christianity; it is religion with a Christian nomenclature.

Experience-oriented learning, or service projects, cannot become part of the teaching-learning process simply to balance out a program for youth. It cannot be tacked on as another "good" activity for youth. It *should be* the program. And instead of saying "use them or lose them," we should say "use them because that is the way in which they learn."

With the third reason for having service projects, the developmental and traditional viewpoints begin to coincide. Both believe that service to others is a necessary part of the Christian life. But even further, service is not an option; it is an obligation. One of the purposes of the Scripture is to fully equip Christians " . . . for every good work" (2 Tim. 3:17). Christ himself commanded it of his disciples: "Let your light shine before men, that they may see your good deeds and praise your Father in heaven" (Matt. 5:16). "Whoever wants to become great among you must be your servant, and whoever wants to be first must be slave of all" (Mark 10:43–44). Christ pointed to his own life as the outstanding example of service: "For even the Son of Man did not come to be served, but to serve . . ." (Mark 10:45).

Service is one of the purposes of the Christian's salvation: "For we are God's workmanship, created in Christ Jesus to do good works, which God prepared in advance for us to do" (Eph. 2:10). And, good works are the proof that we have truly developed a personal relationship with Jesus Christ through faith: "What good is it, my brothers, if a man claims to have faith but has no deeds?" (James 2:14). "Because of the service by which you have proved yourselves, men will praise God for the obedience that accompanies your confession of the gospel of Christ . . ." (2 Cor. 9:13). Service—good deeds toward others—is to be part of the warp and woof of the Christian's life in Jesus Christ. It is a necessity for a truly Christ-like life.

Closely associated with this obligation to serve is the method Christ used in teaching his disciples. He knew the value of learning by experience. He gathered disciples around himself, but he did not teach them in a pedantic manner. Instead of simply talking about the power to cast out demons, to heal, and to do signs, wonders, and other miracles, he gave them those powers and sent them out to do them (see Luke 10:1, 8–9, 17–19). He did not teach about the necessity of faith apart from instances of faith. Rather, when the disciples had less faith than necessary he taught them about it, but not before they brought up the subject as part of their experience-oriented learning (Matt. 17:14–21).

Another factor related to the obligation to serve is that God expects Christians to use the spiritual gifts he has given them both to serve and to upbuild the church. God has equipped each member of the body of Christ with one or more spiritual gifts to be used for "works of service" (Eph. 4:7–13). "Each one should use whatever gift he has received to serve others, faithfully administering God's grace in its var-

As the youth learn, they return to the world outside the church and become the light, salt, and leaven of the Gospel. Their personal knowledge of God overflows into the mainstream of society.

ious forms" (1 Peter 4:10). It is the Christian's obligation to use his or her gifts wisely according to the purposes given.

Experience-oriented learning activities provide one of the means by which these spiritual abilities may be used. They provide the external structure within which spiritual gifts may function effectively and efficiently. Within this framework, each person contributes his or her own special ability in order to help achieve God's purposes in the world, to help the group accomplish its goal, and to achieve a measure of personal fulfillment by making a meaningful contribution.

A fourth reason for having service projects, or—as we are now calling them, experience-oriented learning activities—is that they meet the needs of youth. Perhaps this goes without saying, yet it is important to underline the fact that experience-oriented learning is built squarely on the developmental needs, concerns, and interests of youth. It is their learning experience. It is not part of a curriculum written by the youth editor and staff of some publishing house, then approved by various boards, committees, and local church leaders. It is the youth's curriculum. It is their project. (Youth workers are player-coaches, participant-guides.)

In these experience-oriented learning situations the youth and youth workers ". . . have something at stake . . . which cannot be carried through without reflection and use of judgment to select material of observation and recollection. . . ."[2] What one already knows about God, Christianity, himself or herself, and oth-

ers becomes the foundation for interaction with the new data of the learning situation. Upon this base, youth build an understanding of God in the present. The great doctrines of God's person, his providential care, his love and mercy, his omnipotence, omnipresence, and omniscience take on vital meaning in and through youth's involvement with God in the experience-oriented learning situation. The faith that is worth dying for suddenly becomes meaningful enough to live for in the present. The youth know God because they have experienced him. They have "tasted and seen that God is good" for them now; their Christian faith is relevant and practical. No amount of preaching or sterile classroom teaching can be substituted for one's experience. As the needs of youth are met, they learn about themselves, others, and God.

A fifth rationale for service projects is that youth mature in Christ immeasurably through experience-oriented learning situations. Christian growth in these situations has a spiraling effect. Youth are confronted with a need for a greater personal knowledge of God and his activity. They seek him, therefore, in a concrete revelation of himself through their experience-oriented learning situation. They experience this and, as a result, change inwardly. This change opens them to further acknowledged needs for more of God's self-revelation, and they begin the process all over again. They never exhaust God's self-revelation, nor do they exhaust their own need of him in their growing experience. The lesson never ends. What they learn at one time becomes the stepping stone to additional experience-oriented learning situations. These situations become the impetus for further spiritual growth.

Finally, experience-oriented learning situations reproduce part of the experiences of the first-century New Testament church in this century. These learning situations produce a unity among the participants that is unachievable outside such a group. The group becomes the "fellowship of believers" as its members work, experience, and learn together. The group members share themselves with each other and, in doing so, grow to accept each other. They begin to reveal increasingly more of themselves to the others in the group. In prayer participation they learn to "carry each other's burdens, and in this way . . . fulfill the law of Christ" (Gal. 6:2). They minister to each other as well as to other people. This ministry results in a deeper spiritual growth; the group members are therefore increasingly able to aid both others within the group and people outside the group. The group then becomes a microcosm of part of the function of the whole church of Christ. It meets for fellowship, that is, sharing and mutual encouragement, work instruction, and worship. As the youth learn, they return to the world outside the church and become the light, salt, and leaven of the Gospel. Their personal knowledge of God overflows into the mainstream of society.

BENEFITS OF EXPERIENCE-ORIENTED LEARNING ACTIVITIES

The preceding section has shown several values of experience-oriented learning activities: (1) youth learn properly and effectively; (2) youth fulfill their God-given obligation to serve; (3) youth's needs are met; (4) youth mature in Christ; and (5) the activities produce a fellowship patterned on the New Testament church. There are also additional benefits from this type of learning that accrue to the church,

to the group which receives the ministry of the youth, and to the youth themselves.

The local church and the church universal benefit from experience-oriented learning in several ways. It is the youth from the local church who mature in Christ. They in turn will affect their peers, their families, and others within the local organization. They bring the spiritual dynamic of a growing faith into the atmosphere of the church. Through them many in the church are caused to reevaluate their own Christian lives. They become a living example and ideal to the entire body of believers (1 Tim. 4:12). From them comes the pulse of the church's life.

Youth bring benefits to both the local church and the universal church by developing and using their leadership potentials and spiritual abilities. Both the local and the worldwide church will reap these benefits for years to come as the youth increase in Christian maturity.

The young people also benefit by having their eyes opened to the possibilities and values of service to others through missions and other Christian or secular organizations. To most youth, church-related vocations are not a serious option. Yet their involvement in just that type of service enables them to see firsthand the rewards of organized service as a vocation. The result is that these vocations become live and exciting options.

Perhaps the most tangibly benefited group is the one which receives the ministry of the youth. Hospitals can see the new curtains made, donated, and hung by the youth. Patients and shut-ins can appreciate personally a friendly visit from concerned youth. A youth experience-oriented learning activity bestowed the following benefits upon a local church that received ministry:

> Let me itemize some of the responses that have come to light since you left. Before you had time to get out of the county, [he] . . . came looking for me to tell me that he was

turning his life over to the Lord. . . . It was simply you being there [holding church services] and demonstrating what the Lord means to you that got through to him.[3]

Sunday morning found the . . . congregations amazingly full of teenagers. . . . With a great deal of excitement and enthusiasm they decided that they wanted to meet each Sunday, not just to play (as had been the case in the past) but to "learn about God." What is happening in the lives of these kids is absolutely incredible.[4]

Not all benefits are so dramatic. Nevertheless, if youth have an adequate orientation to the learning situation and have already sufficiently learned from it, God will bless their ministry. (There is a basic assumption associated with the last statement. That is, the youth are truly involved in the learning activity, are prepared to minister, and are truly directed and empowered by the Holy Spirit.)

The greatest value and benefit of experience-oriented learning activities are for the participants. They learn to trust God for all things and, in particular, to trust him for strength in their weaknesses. They gain amazing insights into themselves and their interpersonal relationships. They find that God directs them through the day's activities, even in those things that are usually viewed as routine or trivial. They learn that God is the great King who in his power is triumphant.

Some of the value and benefits to participants are found in the following journal selections from several senior-high youth who participated in an experience-oriented learning activity:

What can I possibly say to express the feelings I had tonight as for four hours the group talked about themselves, others, and God. As I sat there my thoughts were . . . centered mainly on you. How I have cheated you, Lord. . . . Tonight I feel close to no one—not even You, and what a horrible feeling that is. I know I have let you down again and in your great love, in order to find you again, you are taking away the nearness

of those I love so I'll find you. A "service project" is nothing to play with, in fact, any commitment to you has got to be dead serious. Serving you is not for [me] fun, etc.—it is hard and needs a total self-sacrifice to you. . . . It's just that you've taught me this past week how little I really do depend on you.

―――

[This] . . . was a service project, but it was much more. It was God; it was loving; it was giving; it was experiencing; it was expressing; and it was finding. We found ourselves in Kentucky, too, as we found *Him*. . . . We found ourselves in those people's love and where there is love there is God, so we found God, too. We found ourselves in giving and sharing with them our King. We found ourselves in true values—without material crutches, without social crutches of home, friends or school, but only to rely on Him. The human heart can only be opened from the inside. Now that we've found ourselves and know our inside, we can open up our hearts to God's use and for other. . . . This experience was real—it was LIFE.

―――

Tonight after the meeting we really had a cool prayer and sharing meeting. It's really neat when you can look back and see the little and big things God has done. I really hope that this is just the beginning and that God will build us up. . . . In a way I felt jealous at first and disappointed that I didn't win anyone to Christ. But I know God was there tonight guiding everything that went on. I'm just happy now for those who have been helped. I have faith that God is going to keep working now. . . . I feel tonight like we've just begun but I know that it's not really us who's done any of this and that God is going to stay down here and carry on the work.

―――

I think this has been the happiest day of my life. . . . Up to this point I was kind of disappointed that I hadn't been able to talk to anyone. Well, as it turned out I was able (through God's help) to bring this girl to Christ. You wouldn't know the feeling that went through me to know that I had brought my first person to Christ.

More than I could ever express in words is what this trip meant to me. How can one measure treasured experiences of seeing God truly work in my life as He has—and through my life as I've always longed. I have learned better now to forget about me and reach out to someone else. And it's so exciting to see others respond.

—

Complete dependence in God is *the* one and only answer. I had a lousy time [at] the pot luck supper, because I was trying to rely on MYSELF AND IT WAS DISCOURAGING. . . . Tomorrow will be chock full of things! Help us God—we know you can, and you'll have to, cause we're bushed and wiped out. Thanks.

—

I got so sick of hearing other Christians telling me about the way God could work but then never saw it myself. It seems [now during this project] that everything we are asking from God, he is giving to us.

—

It's going to be hard now to get back . . . at school and to keep on because I won't be learning lessons about God half as quickly as in this one week probably. Also, something else occurred to me. This week I was expecting God to work in other people and in my life. Usually I don't expect Him to work like this. If I would just believe that he will I'm sure He is able to and will. This will make life so much more exciting!

These experience-oriented learning situations produced immeasurable benefits for all concerned. The value of this type of learning cannot be duplicated by any other means, nor can it be destroyed. It has been corroborated by both intellectual reflection and by the emotion of the direct experience. The youth involved know what they experienced; they cannot be easily shaken. As a result they have grown more mature in Jesus Christ. They have learned to show love and concern for each other under the trying circumstances of fear, excitement, fatigue, pressure, and illness. They have also seen their own God-given talents

blessed by him and, like the fish and loaves in Jesus' disciples' hands, multiplied over and over for God's own glory.

POSSIBLE NEGATIVE EFFECTS OF SERVICE PROJECTS

In fairness, it must be stated that there might be some negative effects from experience-oriented learning projects. The first one has already been alluded to elsewhere; that is, projects which are merely tacked on to existing youth programs might easily lead to a great disenchantment with traditional youth programing. This in turn could conceivably cause a desire for radical change within the program, a change to conform to the experienced learning concept. If the adult leadership of the church resists this change and modernization, the resultant friction and frustration might cause a serious issue within the church.

A second possible negative result is that some of the participants may reject God. They ". . . have once been enlightened, . . . [and] have tasted the goodness of the word of God and the powers of the coming age, . . . [and] they fall away . . ." (Heb. 6:4–5, 6a). Some, having seen God work and having experienced him in their lives, do not want him. It is too demanding. They deliberately reject him with full knowledge of his power and love. When a person chooses this path, there is nothing the leaders can do but pray for and seek to talk with him or her. The fact that it was done with due regard to the experiences of God and with full knowledge of the possible consequences makes the ultimate end doubly frightful.

Third, it is possible that some of the group will develop an attitude of super-spirituality. They may feel they are spiritually elite—above the rest of the youth or even the church. (The unfortunate aspect of this attitude is that their perception is too often on target.) Their spiritual pride is the stumbling stone that will eventually bring these youth back to their senses, but the damage to the ministry at their own church and among their peers will have already been done. They must be constantly reminded that God does not use his people for their own glorification and praise but for his own. God has said, "I will not give my glory to another . . ." (Isa. 42:8).

Fourth, there is a definite danger that the testimonies of the youth will result in misunderstanding and even censoriousness on the part of both their peers and the adults of the church. This might be caused by a lack of humility on the part of the young people and a negative reaction to that pride by those outside the group. But it might also be caused by the work of the Holy Spirit bringing conviction and rebuke to those not involved. Those who see the youth's sincerity and closeness to Christ might turn in defensiveness against them.

Lastly, there is the danger of the youth not having really learned the way to daily spiritual development through the experience-oriented learning activity. This becomes evident after the activity has ended. Instead of relating the project to one's total life, the youth may still treat it as an incident isolated from the everyday world. The result is the age-old problem of professing one thing while practicing another entirely different thing.

These negatives notwithstanding, the projects do produce great changes of character. They are much more valuable than any other teaching-learning activity. The negative aspects simply point out areas of deeper concern in youth work.

PRINCIPLES AND METHODOLOGIES OF EXPERIENCE-ORIENTED LEARNING PROJECTS

It is now time to turn from the theory to the actual implementation of experience-oriented learning in the church's youth program.

> *The value of experience-oriented learning cannot be duplicated by any other means, nor can it be destroyed.*

Operation

Experience-oriented projects are directly related to experience-oriented learning situations. It may be that the projects develop first, that is, that the idea to do something comes before any data are gathered. Or, some direct needs, concerns, or interests of the youth may suggest a worthwhile project. In either case these needs, concerns, and interests are primary. In the former case, an interest in some sort of work—summer missions, or spring vacation in-service project—stimulates the youth to learn. In the latter case, their expanding intellectual capacities cause them to want to experience knowledge directly.

For both cases the same basic steps are followed:

1. The *concerns, interest,* and *felt needs* of the youth are *determined* by the youth and by the adult youth workers through means of discussion and close personal contact. The adults should have a good idea of the unexpressed (but nevertheless real) needs of youth through their involvement with them in other contacts inside and outside the local church situation. Because of these contacts, a project may be related to the needs and interests of youth without the young people having to articulate them immediately.

2. As a group, the youth and the youth worker decide how best to structure the situation to provide maximum learning and involvement for all. They also decide on mea-

surable personal and group outcomes. That is, they set up definitely worded standards by which they will be able to measure success in reaching their intended outcomes. Each outcome will have some corresponding means of measuring the degree of its achievement. An example of such a goal would be, "to effectively teach Vacation Bible School to a certain group of children." The standard of performance would state that "this goal will have been achieved if the parents of eighty-five percent of those who attend all week mention the effect of the Vacation Bible School on their children's lives."

3. Together, youth and youth workers seek out relevant data in the Scriptures, in sociological studies of the area and the people, in methods and media of effective communication, and in other areas of knowledge necessary to successful goal achievement. They meet regularly to share the information they have discovered and to get to know each other in closer fellowship and love.

4. The group undertakes activities which are necessary for achievement of the anticipated outcomes and for producing within their lives a learning experience commensurate with their felt and real needs, their interests and concerns. This activity is not considered to be the "practical" phase of the learning process. It is rather the test of the cognitive data in the real world situation outside the classroom. In this experience the youth perceive the truth or falsity of their theory and gain additional knowledge which could not be found apart from testing and personal experience.

5. At the end of the activity or project the group evaluates its results. Group members ask such questions as: What was accomplished? What concrete results does the group have to show for its labor? Were the intended outcomes achieved? (This is measured by the standard of performance the group had established earlier.) If the outcomes and standards were not met, why not? Were the outcomes and standards realistic and attainable? Are changes necessary in either or both the outcomes and the standard? Should the group try again if it did not meet its outcomes, or should it turn its attention elsewhere?

Organization

Some group within the structure of the church must sponsor any service activity. Usually the project is directly related to the teaching-learning environment of the organized youth ministry of the local church. It would therefore be under the supervision and sponsorship of the head youth worker. Often the nature of the project is one of outreach as well as one of strict learning, in which case it would be related to some other committee(s) and/or board(s) of the church. In this latter case the group project should receive the approval of those various committees and boards before the participants begin to get seriously involved. If the project is of any serious magnitude the entire church should be directly involved in prayer support. The pastor(s) will also want to know in detail the nature and scope of the activity.

Before approval is sought, the group should have as much information about the project as possible. The pastor(s), committees, and boards cannot make an intelligent response until they know such facts as: the type of project; the work and service involved; the reasons for choosing this particular project; the location, transportation involved, and provision for transportation; the names of participating youth and adults; total costs, and the cost to participants and to the church; necessary leadership development and person(s) responsible for development.

Because finances are often involved, an inter-agency or joint committee may be necessary as the sponsoring group. This committee may consist of the youth worker, representatives from the missions committee, youth sponsors, several youth group members, and a pastor.

Youth Participants

Experience-oriented learning projects are not mere adjuncts to the church's youth program. Because of this, all of the youth of a local church should be included in the projects, if at all possible. If the projects cannot be added on to the youth program, neither can they form an adjunct to learning. They are the critical phase of the total learning activity. Therefore, it is not wise to select only a certain few participants from the whole youth group. Instead, all the youth should be part of the projects in order to more fully complete their learning experience. There should be as many groups as necessary to accommodate all the youth, and they should be small enough in number/group to make the experiences worthwhile and outcomes achievable. The groups would normally be coeducational.

Every person involved in a project, either youth or adult, has the potential for great spiritual growth. Even the most spiritually immature may take great steps in their overall spiritual development. A strong Christian life should not necessarily be a prerequisite to involvement, unless the nature of the project calls for highly spiritual participants. What is important is a desire to be involved and to learn. If God is God, he will teach the spiritually weak as well as the spiritually strong. If the project is properly handled, the individual's needs as well as the group's needs will be met. Thus both strong and weak, mature and immature, and spiritual and carnal Christian youth will grow according to their needs, capacities, involvement, and willingness to grow. The Holy Spirit does his work in the lives of all Christians, not just the most spiritual ones. The twelve disciples were not chosen because of their deep spirituality!

No special personality trait is a prerequisite to involvement; the youth are involved simply because they are part of the local church. This is an integral aspect of the teaching process of the church. That a person has or does not have a pleasing personality makes no difference to his or her involvement, for the personalities of all concerned will be somewhat changed through the group process. The one that is most irritating will eventually be told so by the group. It may take time, but the group will make the necessary suggestions for needed correctives. Both the overly meek and the one who irritates others will change through the project.

It is not unusual for some youth with great talent to go undiscovered in the church's youth program because they are more reserved than those extroverted persons who constantly take the noticeable lead. When the more reticent individuals are given opportunity to contribute to a project, they do so admirably. Individuals of dubious leadership qualities or with questionable personalities will also improve, first, as the group accepts them; second, as the group seeks to understand them as people; third, as the group seeks, through a loving and warm group environment, to help them understand themselves; fourth, as the group makes suggestions for positive changes in their personalities; and fifth, as the individuals respond to change with openness, love, and willingness, and actually initiate changes suggested by the group and by their own self-perceptions.

It is not necessary that a participant already be a Christian—one who has received Jesus Christ into his or her life as Savior-Lord. Here again the nature of the learning situation is not to have the answers prior to the learning. The non-Christians will soon find out through their own intelligence, the group's contribution, and the ministry and work of the Holy Spirit that they lack a most vital ingredient to spiritual learning: Jesus Christ.

The group of youth involved in the experience-oriented learning process must be limited to a workable number. This number is relative to the age of the participants, the capabilities and experiences of the adults involved, and the

> *Experience-oriented learning projects are not mere adjuncts to the church's youth program. They are the critical phase of the total learning activity.*

type and duration of the project envisaged. Usually, it would be easier to work with a larger number of twelfth graders than ninth graders because of the higher maturity level of the older group; less supervision and direct adult leadership is necessary with twelfth graders. The older group would also presumably have had more experiences on which to build, and in having developed their capabilities, they would need less practice to do something well.

The youth workers' previous experiences in an experience-oriented learning situation, and their innate and acquired abilities in group work are also factors involved in selecting the number of participants. Those youth workers who have had some amount of good experience with this type of learning group would usually be able to handle a larger, more diverse group than would adults with little or no experience in this sort of leadership capacity.

The type of project will also bear on the number of people involved. If the group will be conducting rural Vacation Bible School, sufficient participants will be needed to properly staff the school. This number could be anywhere from two or three youth to eight or even twenty, depending on the size of the project and on the number of schools being run simultaneously. The number of participants in a work project—building a house, for example—needs to be adequate to complete the construction in the given amount of time. A principle to keep in mind is that the number should be small enough to allow for maximum group participation and contribution from everyone and large enough to accomplish the intended outcomes within the time constraints.

Something to avoid, if possible, is the conflict that arises over intra-group dating. While this is a possibility within any coed group, it should be discouraged. The reason for this is that the individuals who date are concerned with making an impression on each other; they tend to think more in terms of their own peculiar problems and interests than those of the whole group. The resultant friction between the couple and the remainder of the group leads in turn to a polarization between those two individuals and the rest of the group. The entire group process stops while the emotional energies are focused on the couple and their behavior.

Another reason for discouraging intra-group dating is that couples tend to focus their energies toward non-group-oriented activities and goals. They want to be by themselves rather than share in the lives of the entire group. Fellowship and love become centered around their own "in" secrets and thoughts. The result is again fragmentation and polarization within the group. Not all couples would behave like this, of course, but those who do not are the exception rather than the rule.

When there is a dating couple within the group, the individuals concerned can be made to see their responsibility as a couple to maintain an open, sharing relationship with the entire group while still maintaining their own special relationship. The adult couple working with the youth can help teach this through their own actions. Adults can show that although they are husband and wife they do not have to be constantly together. They separate to sleep with the separate sexes, and they willingly give up part of their private lives to be with the rest of the group. With this loving example before them, the teenage couple should be able to overcome some of the difficulties mentioned.

Sometimes there is a case of siblings being in the same group. While the emotional attachment of a dating couple is not the problem here, it is still better to have siblings separated. In some instances, perhaps in many, siblings get along together wonderfully; in such cases, there is no reason to separate them. The adult workers and the youth themselves will have to make the final decision in this matter.

Adult Participants

The most crucial aspect of experience-oriented learning is the selection and development of adult leaders. They hold the key to success or failure of the learning process for the youth. Upon their shoulders falls the responsibility of helping students learn for themselves. The choice of adults to work with the senior high youth is the key to success in experience-oriented learning. (See chapter 3.)

Additional Program Components

Part III centers on the application of the basic philosophy of incarnational, agapic, and developmental youth ministry to additional program components. Chapter 8 examines the crucial need and requirements for leadership development and thus rounds out the emphasis on leadership introduced in part I.

Chapter 9 seeks to apply the developmental aspects of part I to administration and organization. It shows that good administration is developmental in concept and promotes the growth and encouragement of both the adults and the youth involved in the youth ministry.

Chapter 10 shows how camps and retreats form a vital element in an effective youth ministry model. Although the chapter deals mainly with camps, the planning of retreats is similar and the principles apply to both kinds of programs.

Chapter 11 lays out the basic principles of evaluation. It presupposes that all who help to design, develop, and administer a youth ministry are concerned to evaluate their work and to understand how to improve the ministry.

CHAPTER

8

Leadership Development

The first place to turn in discussing a philosophy of leadership is the Bible. Among the most pertinent biblical selections are Matthew 23:1–12; Acts 6:1–7; 1 Timothy 3:1–13; Numbers 11:10–17, 24–25; Romans 12:3–8; Luke 22:24–30 (cf. Matt. 20:20–28; Mark 10:35–45). From these readings, one can glean important information concerning God's idea of leadership: God helps identify leaders. Work is to be shared, not simply doled out from the top to the bottom. Leaders are to be filled with the Holy Spirit. Leaders are servant ministers. All of us are gifted to be servants and to become leaders in our own right. But all of us are also meant to be followers. Leadership is not necessarily a life calling (see the book of Amos). And, finally, leadership is a role to be filled, not a position or a station to be maintained.

TYPES OF LEADERSHIP

"There are almost as many different definitions of leadership as there are persons who have attempted to define the concept,"[1] says the renowned leadership thinker Bernard M. Bass. For the purposes of this book, however, we will limit our discussion to six classifications of leadership.

Management Leadership

In many ways the expression "management leadership" is an oxymoron. One either manages or leads; to do both at the same time is difficult at best and, for most people, almost impossible. Management traditionally has four functions—planning, organizing, leading, and controlling—none of which is truly leadership.

- *Planning* determines present and future needs, establishes objectives, assigns priorities to program elements, and determines procedures and processes by which work is to be done and the people are to be supervised.
- *Organizing* determines the structure of an organization, delegates work to others, and establishes and maintains relations between parts.
- *Leading* functions in making decisions for others, motivating others to follow and do the work of the organization, controls communication between individuals and between groups, selects people to become involved with the manager, and trains people.
- *Controlling* establishes performance standards, measures performance, evaluates the measurements taken, and provides feedback on performances.

Management is not leadership. Managers control people and things for predetermined goals and within limited resources of time, personnel, and raw materials. Through behavior modification, managers use rewards and punishment to achieve their goals. Managers look out for the bottom line because that is how they are judged. Managers are not leaders! The church is full of managers. But where are the leaders?

Youth workers who are managers may have a well-organized and planned program. They would tend to have every one assigned to specific tasks. They would be able to achieve many fine accomplishments in programing, assigning people to jobs, and generally controlling the progress of the youth ministry. But they would lack one major ability, that is, they would not be able to focus on leadership development. They would seek to train both

> *Management traditionally has four functions— planning, organizing, leading, and controlling —none of which is truly leadership. Management is not leadership.*

youth and adult leaders to do certain bottom-line tasks that the youth worker manager would then orchestrate into a whole. The idea of facilitating growth and development of both the youth and adult leaders would not fit into the manager's mind. They are more concerned with developing a well-operated youth program that shows their superior management-organizational skills. They are not concerned with the growth of those in the program except as that growth might happen as a result of the well-managed, efficiently organized program.

Laissez-faire leadership

"Laissez-faire leadership" is also an oxymoron. This type of approach to leading is characterized by a "laid back" approach. Little or no direction is given; no vision is developed and shared; no resources are amassed; not much of anything else is done by this type of person. He or she just lets others go about their task unfettered by any sort of intrusion from the leader and with little help from that leader. Too many pastors and officially elected church leaders function in this manner, to the detriment of providing direction and help to the local church or denomination.

A youth ministry characterized by laissez-faire leadership is almost the total opposite of the management leadership approach. If things are accomplished in the laissez-faire approach, it is because someone else got things organized, not because the youth worker was involved in initiating the planning, organizing, execution, and evaluation. Usually, this type of "leadership" is characterized by helter-skelter confusion. Plans may or may not be made. Leadership development occurs only if someone else takes the initiative. Planning, organization, leadership development, gift identification, and development are not carried out.

Pyramid Leadership

The pyramid approach to leadership is found in the military and other more authoritarian types of organizations. It functions in a "from-the-top-down" flow of authority, with those at the bottom following orders from those higher up. The lower a person is located in the hierarchy, the less opportunity there is for input and the less likely one will be involved in decisionmaking. Decisions are made at or near the top and are expected to be followed. There is a chain of command and everyone has his or her place and job in that chain. Everyone reports to someone else. This type of leadership plays an important role in certain social situations, namely, in the military. But there is serious doubt that under normal circumstances this form of leadership should be exercised in the church.

A youth ministry that has this leadership

mentality is operated like a military school rather than a place of learning to willingly follow Christ. The youth pastor usually considers himself or herself as the "general" who makes the decisions, which are to be implemented by the youth and the adult workers. This mentality has as its theme: "Yours is not to ask the reason why. Yours is just to do or die." Obviously, an agapic, incarnational, and developmental perspective of leadership is foreign. Youth and adult workers are seen as people to carry out the program ideas of the head youth worker. Information flows from this head worker or youth pastor to those below him or her. Concern for the "troops" and the "sergeants" is only in terms of whether or not they can carry out the mission of the "general." Concern is not for the development of the youth nor for the adults involved, unless it is to teach skills needed to carry out the "general's" orders.

Autocratic Leadership

Autocratic leadership is a dictatorship in which the king, queen, dictator, pastor, chairperson of an official board, or—mostly likely—the youth pastor decrees and commands absolute obedience. No one has the authority, power, or responsibility to question the decrees and commands and no one has the authority to do anything other than what has been decreed and commanded. Power resides in basically one person who is situated on top; all others are below him or her. This is absolute power focused in one person. This form of leadership is antithetical to all of biblical revelation. Even God does not command us to a relationship with him; he invites us.

The dictator approach to youth ministry is a lonely task. All authority and therefore all decision making resides in one person. He or she makes the decisions, issues the commands, and expects them to be carried out. Disobedience or lackadaisical follow-through

Developmental leadership is not concerned with power, authority, management, motivating, inducing, or reinforcing of behaviors. It is concerned with effectiveness, with doing the right thing and doing "right!"

on the parts of the underlings usually brings strong reprimand, if not firing.

Democratic Leadership

The democratic type of leadership functions in an ongoing debate over values, goals, priorities, and policies. Leaders seek to influence the debate, but after the debate is over, people vote and the majority wins. Leaders then take up the majority cause and make it happen. If, as is currently happening in many parts of the world, there is a slim majority, then democracy becomes difficult to operate. Since a democratic leader never knows when the majority will change its mind and will vote against a leader, democratic leaders stay tuned to the majority and likewise to the minority just in case the minority turns into a majority. This type of leadership is often found in churches, but it lacks biblical foundation and is ultimately disruptive or leads to paralysis by committee and consensus.

A youth ministry that follows democratic lines seeks to make everyone feel that he or she is important and should make their ideas known in the common debates about values, goals, priorities, and policies. Realistically, most democratic leaders are not as democratic as they might like to think they are. In reality, most democratic leaders are a combination of managers, autocratic military, or autocratic dictators. People may be asked to vote, but only after the leader has manipulated, massaged, molded, and controlled the information and experiences of those who will vote. In a

way, this type of leader is just as manipulative as any of the above except the laissez-faire leader type. The concern by democratic leaders is still to get the tasks done efficiently. Focus is on the program, with people as the means to achieving the program. People are secondary to achieving the outcomes.

Developmental Leadership

Developmental leadership is not concerned with power, authority, management, motivating, inducing, or reinforcing of behaviors. It is not just concerned with getting a job done efficiently. It *is* concerned with effectiveness, with doing the right thing and doing it "right!" It is characterized by being servants, ministering to people's needs, accepting and sharing with each other, and growing into a community of interdependent colaborers. This form of leader-teacher behaviors is the primary biblical model of Jesus and the apostles. It fits into the picture of the church as the community of believers who belong to each other and who minister to each other in order to build each other up in the faith (Rom. 12:4–8; Eph. 4:11–16).

Developmental leadership does not ask what style a leader should have. Instead, it asks the following questions to determine what leadership style to use in a given setting:

- Who comprises the group that I will lead?
- What is the group's particular vision?
- What are the specific circumstances of the group?

- What organization or institution is involved in the whole process of achieving the vision?
- What are the constituencies involved, besides the leader and the particular group?
- What are the gifts and talents already in the group?
- What are the developmental needs of the group and the individuals in the group?
- How can I as the "leader" be servant to these people and help meet their needs?

Notice that in the developmental leadership approach, the person is primary. Programs, though important, are seen as means to the outcomes of helping people learn, grow, and develop into Christlikeness.

Not all leadership styles are appropriate at any given time. Most, if not all, leadership styles may be appropriate at one time or another in a particular situation.

Ultimately, a developmental leadership perspective seeks to help those involved to learn, grow, and mature—to develop in the exercise of their God-given gifts and accomplish their God-inspired vision and God-revealed tasks. Developmental leadership does not seek to coerce or induce people to change their minds. Rather, the purpose of developmental leadership is to seek to help people get on with their own development as persons and to be effective in their calling to minister to the world.

Developmental leaders are characterized by the following:

1. They focus on people, seeking to help them go from what they are to what they are called by God to be.

2. They do not focus primarily on organizational thinking and tasks, nor are they concerned with the maintenance of an organization or the organization's rules.

3. They are "boat rockers" and iconoclasts who challenge the status quo and traditions, seeking for new and better ways to go about the ministry.

4. They are driven by a desire for people to become more than what they are now, for them to develop a vision of what God is calling people and organizations to be. They are compelled by a vision of helping people in an organization to become transformed, to keep on being transformed, and, in turn, to continually transform their group, organization, and society.

5. They are nurturers who facilitate others in becoming holistically more developed as God intended them to be, who facilitate others to identify, develop, and enhance their spiritual gifts, and who help in the deployment of people exercising their spiritual gifts for the ministry of Christ in the church and in the world.

6. They are driven by a vision that is shaped both by those in leadership and by those who are led. It is a mutually owned vision because it has been developed in community, not in isolation by those "in power."

7. They are keepers of the vision, charged with communicating that vision constantly to those within the organization, regardless of the organization's size and complexity.

8. They build trust in the community's vision, in the people themselves, in the ability to achieve the vision, and in the leaders.

9. They enable, empower, facilitate, and teach others so that all in the organization can achieve the vision, attain the outcomes desired, and accomplish the tasks determined through each of the operations of their spiritual gifts.[2]

Therefore, developmental leadership is a *process,* not a mechanical skill; it is an *art,* not just a technical, learned ability. Leadership is a *personal function,* not a power position. Leadership is the fulfillment of the kingdom of God, doing the will of the Father, and teaching the values of the kingdom (Matt. 5–7). It is a *relationship,* not a rank. Leadership is *empowering people* not a focus on one's own power. Leadership is *equipping and freeing people,* not controlling them. Leadership is *service and ministry*, not prominence, stature, or status. Leadership is *humility*, not ostentation and arrogance.

Leadership relates developmentally to people within an organization who are characterized by the following qualities: (1) They share a common vision, often helped to be identified and articulated by a leader. (2) They mold and shape the vision together. (3) They agree together upon desired outcomes for the vision. (4) They work together with agreed-upon tasks that draw them closer in shared vision and values because all have agreed to the outcomes and tasks.

Leadership helps others to (1) identify their spiritual gifts, (2) enhance those spiritual gifts, (3) deploy those spiritual gifts, (4) use their spiritual gifts, (5) evaluate the operation of their gifts, and (6) continually enhance their spiritual gifts. Leadership is not just getting a task done. Leadership is guiding people, not just manipulating them to obtain quantifiable, "bottom-line" goals.

The goal of developmental leadership is that all who "lead and follow" will be servants together. This means submitting to one another while being conscious of the various temporary and/or permanent roles assigned to each according to the Holy Spirit. Developmental leaders, or servants, must work together by supporting, building, and growing together into the ". . . whole measure of the fullness of Christ" (Eph. 4:13).

REQUIREMENTS OF LEADERSHIP

Analysis

Leadership calls for two types of analysis. The first is an analysis of *what* the leader is trying to do. The leader is either selfishly motivated to get himself or herself out front, or motivated to serve others and Christ. Before fulfilling this analysis, however, the leader needs to consider the task: What actually needs to be done? The practical step of listing subtasks will enable the leader to move on to the greater task of leadership. To do this, leaders also must make the second analysis of *whom* they will be attempting to lead.

In this second type of analysis, motivation is a key question. (Remember that motivation is not manipulation.) What is the source of the followers' desire to do the task? Is the motivation internal or external or imposed (manipulation)? Effective motivation stems from the other's sense of needs, drives, urges, and past experiences.

Motivation

Four major inner dynamics of motivation must be recognized:

1. *Self-aggrandizement*—behavior oriented around maximizing one's own pleasure.
2. *Other directedness*—behavior oriented around doing what significant others consider to be good or right.
3. *Principle*—behavior oriented around a basic commitment to a level of principled justice.
4. *Agape*—love for others, regardless of their condition, that produces agapic servant leaders.

It is the leader's task to help people become motivated. This can be done in several ways. One is to *share* one's self with others, using empathy for those persons' situations. Set an example of sharing for the others involved. Another way is to *encourage* others by selectively praising worthy deeds or attitudes. Or, try *stimulating* or gently "prodding." This type of psychological motivation must be done carefully, however. The prerequisites for its use are that the others respect and accept the leader, and accept the leader's prodding. It is too easy to slip into manipulation and a behavioristic molding of people's responses to conform to the leaders' demands.

Two more ways to motivate others psychologically are, by using associations and by facilitation. In the former, leaders help others see similarities between the present motivation state and a new experience to which the present motivation can be transferred. In the latter, leaders help others to accomplish something that will make them feel successful. This is a fine way to motivate others to want to perform successfully again.

Motivation of Team Members

On the pragmatic side of motivation, it must be recognized that most tasks in a youth group are accomplished by committees or teams of youths working together. Motivating people to work on a team is another element of leadership. How are people motivated toward this end? For one thing, team or committee responsibility is a spiritual effort. It is done for Christ (Col. 3:23–24). Therefore our work should be the best we can do with God's help and be part of our "reasonable worship" (Rom. 12:1). Challenge team members with the task before them. Ask, *Why is the job important? What difficulties will there be to overcome? What rewards do you foresee?*

In motivating a group, a leader should share both the *responsibility*—the doing of the task—and the *authority*—the making of decisions. Help the youth to think of the job as "ours," not "mine" or "yours." Be sure to give all the details of the job. Let the team know exactly what has to be done. And let them set their own goals for what they want to accomplish. Do ask them, however, how they will know when they have achieved their goal.

Express confidence in the team and the individuals' abilities to get the job done well (assuming you can do this honestly). A leader's enthusiasm about a task will rub off onto a group. Enthusiasm is not enough, though; a leader must be prepared. He or she

> *Leadership is* equipping and freeing people, *not controlling them. Leadership is* service and ministry, *not prominence, stature, or status. Leadership is* humility, *not ostentation and arrogance.*

should come to a team meeting with a few ideas to begin discussion, providing the members with paper and pencils to let them doodle or write ideas down. Especially important is knowing and using proper group techniques in leading discussion. Finally, evaluation of the previous work of the team or committee should take place. Ask them how they think the job went. Give praise when a job is well done. And give constructive suggestions when there is need for improvement. Help them come to a sober evaluation of their work, encouraging them to suggest both positive and negative observations for changes.

Creativity

Leadership must be creative. In a Christian leader, creativity begins with a commitment to Christ, in the full sense of the word commitment. He or she must be open to the direction of the Holy Spirit, ready to follow through any and all channels.

Christian creativity presupposes that any approach not forbidden in Scripture is open to Christians for their use and God's glory. With this presupposition in mind, a leader has an innovative mind-set that asks: What is the

> *Leaders must "forget" to criticize the past, thinking positively about how to affect* now *and* tomorrow.

spirit of the times? What are the needs of people involved? What are the outcomes desired? What resources of people and things and raw materials do we have at our disposal? How can we best coordinate and assemble resources of people, things, and raw materials together to achieve our intended outcomes?

A creative leader ferrets out *all* significant factors, exploring the greatest depths of the matter in order to become oriented to it. This kind of leadership demands a large amount of time and energy—10 percent inspiration and 90 percent perspiration. But it is worth the effort to become courageous and try something different. Those who are willing to take risks do so because God is leading them.

Positive, Fresh, and Contemporaneous

Leaders must "forget" to criticize the past, thinking positively about how to affect *now* and *tomorrow*. The past is prologue to today. On the other hand, the past is one way of learning how to do better. By looking at what has been done before, a leader can evaluate how to improve. Using a "can do" attitude, leaders should look at problems, ideas, suggestions, and tasks as challenges for the use of creative, positive thinking. Brainstorming for any ideas is a good way to prime the pump to get new, fresh, and creative input. The tendency is to try to determine as each idea is suggested whether it will work or not. But before any ideas are discarded, first consider serious-

ly how they could happen, not why they would not work. When modified, many "unworkable" ideas work extremely well. Try using new forms, approaches, or methods that are contemporary.

ROLES OF LEADERS (OR, SERVANT LEADERS)

Essentially, the role of a servant leader is to help people work together successfully for a common task. Effective servant leaders among youth do the following things:

1. They enter prayerfully into their role, preparing ahead of time by thinking through problems, issues, and potential solutions.

2. They depend on the Holy Spirit to use their own intelligence, gifts, and insights for preparation and the leadership role.

3. They act as a catalyst, facilitator, helper, and director, but not as a dictator. Leaders help the group process the issues and problems by coming with several options, none of which may be the best, but which serve to stimulate the group's processing.

4. They are knowledgeable of small group dynamics and processes.

5. They act as the servants of the group rather than as its masters.

6. They share leadership easily and willingly among group members, making use of the initiative and experiences of each person.

7. They know the tasks and goals that the group has determined.

8. They aid the group to own those goals, and to determine the tasks associated with those goals.

9. Effective group leaders are sensitive to the group and to each individual within it, recognizing that each group member comes with his or her own special needs that the group will have to meet in order for the group process to occur satisfactorily.

10. Group leaders reaffirm each member, helping them to perceive themselves as valu-

able and as having worthwhile roles to play in the group.

11. They look for compensating factors in each group member, seeing value in each person.

12. They work for feelings of equality among members.

13. They ask for input from each member to accomplish the group's tasks.

14. They listen sensitively and carefully to each group member and are able to restate the ideas of others concisely and accurately.

15. Effective group leaders moderate all sides of an issue, helping the group to integrate all ideas for the common goal.

16. They seek a consensus rather than a vote.

17. They facilitate closure to the tasks and goals by helping to determine who will do what, by when, and with what degree of success.

18. They are not afraid to ask the group to stop discussions and pray for guidance.

Finally, one of the most important roles of the group leader is that of facilitator in problem solving. This is done in a number of ways. Leaders ask provocative questions. They provide or suggest resources to the group. They encourage all to speak, and redirect questions to the group as a whole. Leaders are responsible to alleviate blocks and/or tensions within the group. They help to sift through varying viewpoints, yet avoid dominating the discussion—and avoid letting anyone else dominate. Group leaders must maintain a permissive atmosphere for interaction, one in which all ideas are welcomed. They keep discussion moving and to the point at hand, controlling irrelevant questions and comments by focusing on the goal. They also clarify the various options before the group, facilitating a listing of solutions to the tasks, as well as the means to achieve the group's goal. Finally, leaders aid the members of the group in accepting their own responsibilities of leadership.

ROLES OF GROUP MEMBERS

It is the task of a group leader to help group members function well. Thus, the leader is an enabler of development for the members of the group. And, in order for the leader to succeed at this task, it is important that he or she has a clear grasp of what roles the group members need to play. The major role of a group member is to function smoothly with other members of group on their mutual tasks. Each will contribute to the clarification of the goals of the group. They will also help enumerate the tasks required to achieve their goals.

Group members should help the leader facilitate problem solving by both their thinking and speaking. Hopefully, they will ask forwarding questions, and offer suggestions and ideas. They should help clarify discussion, encouraging and accepting each member. And, they must willingly accept responsibilities either as a volunteer or by appointment, fulfilling those responsibilities conscientiously.

EMOTIONAL CLIMATE OF THE GROUP

Each group member comes with his or her own affective needs and issues. A small group, whether it be a Bible study or a work group, reflects to a large degree the emotionality of those in it. Thus, each group leader should be aware of the emotional climate that is being created within the dynamic of group interaction.

The group needs to help meet the emotional needs of the individuals in that group. Failure to do so will cause either minor or major dysfunction of the group processes and will hinder achievement of the group's tasks.

The group needs to function in an atmosphere of agape, freedom, openness, and acceptance in order to do its tasks and reach its goals. Being a part of the group should be stimulating for each member in order for each one to make a significant contribution. Group members need to feel like they are all equal regardless of status or position in the youth group and/or church, and regardless of age or sex. A spirit of challenge, excitement, and adventure should permeate the group, and members should feel that it is fun and worth-while to give of themselves to meet together.

Group members should demonstrate empathetic acceptance of others and an ongoing desire to understand each other. Such acceptance and knowledge are based on fellowship of group members with each other. This fellowship allows all to begin to get to know each other and to know what each is like. And needs of group members can become apparent in such fellowship and can be met through the group process. Such fellowship reduces any threat to any one member as positive, interpersonal relationships develop. Such a group should be relatively small, normally less than thirteen. Groups larger than this become less manageable and tend to be more impersonal. Some people can hide in a group of more than twelve and consequently their contribution is limited or omitted.

Members should feel that they are in the group for a purpose, normally to resolve an issue or problem or to design and develop a plan of action. Group members need to understand the reason for their being called together. They need to be helped to formulate outcomes or goals and then work on plans to achieve these.

Small groups, even those whose primary task is to do a job, will often produce conflict. Any change is almost bound to cause some sort of disagreement. That every group is composed of less than perfect people also suggests that conflicts will arise. Group members should be helped to realize that conflict, and sometimes even real hostility, are normal occurrences in any healthy group process. The issue is how to deal with these. Positive growth should be the result of such conflict because it is dealt with rather than swept aside

by a majority vote. The group should therefore strive to make a decision by consensus, not majority opinion. Group members should seek for the unity of the body of Christ by seeking the mind of Christ in each matter. The Holy Spirit does not stutter or send out conflicting guidance to a group. If the group does not know which decision to make, then it should stop discussing and spend time praying to the ultimate head of both the youth group and the church, asking for his divine guidance.

Keeping the atmosphere relaxed and informal helps youth feel more comfortable. Sitting around a table may cause adult youth workers to feel more like they are in a business meeting at work, but the youth group is not a secular business situation. The goal is to produce an atmosphere in which youth feel comfortable and in which they can all participate as equal members in the group process.

PROFESSIONAL YOUTH LEADERS' RELATIONSHIPS WITH VOLUNTEERS

Professional youth workers, that is, those employed by the church, have a special relationship to the nonpaid adult youth workers. The professional serves as a model of the servant leader who is concerned for the development of not just the youth but also of the adult youth worker. Professional youth workers are not authoritarian bosses nor laissez-faire bureaucrats. Nor are they idols or "models" to be copied or duplicated by youth or adults. The professionals are coaches of coaches, teachers of teachers, enablers of enablers, helpers of helpers, and models who are demonstrations or examples of a Christian leader.

Professional youth workers should work on the same basic philosophy with their adult co-workers as they want those co-workers to use with the youth. That is, the professional seeks to develop adult leadership just as both the professional and adult co-workers seek to develop young people into leaders. Thus professional youth workers should not do anything that adults could be helped to learn to do themselves just as the adults in turn help the youth learn to function as leaders. Adult coworkers and youth leaders need help to grow, experience, and develop into leaders.

Professional youth workers need to spend time with their adult co-workers, getting to know them and helping them become the leaders that God has gifted them to be. Professionals have the responsibility to help their adult co-workers identify their gifts, develop those gifts, find places to use those gifts, and to continually sharpen them.

LEADERSHIP DEVELOPMENT PLAN FOR YOUTH AND ADULT YOUTH WORKERS

Leadership begins with childhood, continuing throughout the local church's youth ministry and into the adult ministries. The leadership development program depends upon the age and developmental maturity of the youth involved. Early adolescents have different responsibilities; less expectations will be placed on them than on older adolescents. Leadership development and the deployment of youth and adult youth workers must be sensitive to the developmental needs and capabilities of those involved.

Two venues exist for the leadership development of both youth and adult youth workers. These two venues need to be kept in balance: one is a "one shot" leadership retreat, and the other, on-the-job development.

Leadership retreats are a time to focus on

- Developing both spiritually and in personal relationships with other leaders,
- The meaning of being a servant leader,
- A biblical concept of ministry,
- One's own church's youth ministry,
- General leadership roles,

- Definite roles of youth leaders described in detail,
- An outline of general plans for the next six to twelve months.

Participants should include all the youth who are in any form of leadership, all the professional youth workers, all the adult co-workers, and, at least for a few hours, the senior pastor. These should meet for a day and a half at some location away from both church property and people's homes. An office meeting room, though rather formal, is often available on Friday night and all day Saturday. Other locations could be a motel/hotel conference room, a conference center, or a camp.

The duration of a leadership retreat is crucial. Having the retreat over one night enables people to get to know each other informally and in a less hectic atmosphere. By laying out major issues on Friday night, one allows the informal discussions that go on late into the evening and around breakfast the next morning to be dealt with in an unpressured and creative atmosphere.

On-going, on-the-job leadership development is the responsibility of all the leaders. Professional youth workers are responsible to see that their co-workers are developing in leadership. And these same professionals are ultimately responsible to assure that the adult co-workers are encouraging youth to develop into leaders.

On-the-job leadership development means that the broad outlines of program and leadership developed at the leadership retreat are being implemented in the youth ministry's program. People are encouraged in the tasks and responsibilities that they are given. They are held accountable for their commitments and are helped to continually evaluate both their own actions and the outcomes of their leadership.

Perhaps no other form of leadership development is as effective as the on-the-job method. One does not learn to be a leader by just attending a retreat on leadership. One learns to be a leader by taking up the activities of a leader. Leadership is an action, not a set of data stored in one's mind. To be sure, cognitive data about leadership, including philosophy and principles, are crucial for leadership development. However, one is a leader as one does the work of leadership.

Thus, on-the-job leadership is where the principles of leadership taught at a retreat are experienced. Those who have responsibilities for leadership development should be sensitive to the numerous opportunities to help others exercise their leadership. A leader will, for example, ask a less-experienced leader how he or she thought something could be improved. This same leader can offer advice or make suggestions based on observing a less-experienced leader in action. The issue is not a formalized program of leadership development. Rather, it is taking advantage of the many opportunities to give input into the lives of developing leaders as these less experienced youth exercise leadership.

9

Principles of Administration and Organization

M any horror stories surround the organization and administration of youth ministry in the local church, from absolute fiascoes of disorganized youth pastors to iron-fisted, no-nonsense youth committees dictating every organizational detail. Anecdotal evidence suggests that if there is one serious flaw in many church staff youth workers and youth pastors, it is that they have little sense of administration and organization. Yet there are enough current problems in church youth ministries to make good administration and organization not only important, but imperative. Several of these key problems are as follows.

First, there are *overlapping functions of agencies and programs* in a local church. Churches probably have youth Bible studies, Sunday school, camps and retreats, and more—all of which purport to teach the Bible and help youth study the Bible on their own. Just who is responsible to teach the Bible systematically and for application in life is never defined. Each agency follows its own curriculum materials with little communication between adult leaders and little or no joint planning. One church found that its younger youth were involved in memorizing about a dozen Scripture verses per week if they were active participants in all four of the church's programs. No one had ever stopped to ask what each of the agencies that were working with the youth were doing.

Too often a unified program—a comprehensive, all-inclusive plan—is lacking in church youth ministries. The program is neither well thought out nor planned. It lacks unified purpose, vision, and general outcomes held in common with the local church, and it suffers from a lack of separate outcomes that are germane only to the youth ministry itself. Often, this is the case because the church does not have a unified plan either. There is also a lack of connection and correlation of programs, both within the youth ministry and within the entire church. Each particular agency within each of the church's various ministries does what it wants with little more than budgetary accountability. Finally, often none of the agencies within the church, and in particular within a youth ministry, work together in common action toward some common outcomes, driven by common vision and purpose.

Second, *agency-itis has set in;* there is a multiplication of agencies in a local church. The result is that a multitude of church organizations exist, all calling for loyalty from the youth and from adult youth workers. Youth are urged to join all the youth activities in their church. If they do not, they are considered less spiritual or more carnal Christians. Adults are pressed into serving in several capacities in the youth ministry, teaching Bible here, leadership development there, attending a social, helping to direct a youth team. These calls for loyalties are confusing and obfuscate the real heart of ministry, namely, the people whom the youth ministry is attempting to serve.

Third, *programs grow in a haphazard manner.* Someone gets the idea that another program is needed in the youth ministry, and it is organized. Once something is begun, it never dies or gets killed off. It just seems to continue in perpetuity, even if it no longer meets a known need and even when neither youth nor adult workers see any need for it. The theme seems to be, "what is shall be, forever."

Fourth, *administrative and organizational responsibilities are unclear.* No one knows who is in charge, who helps whom, or who does what and when. This causes lack of accountability. Evaluation of the programs and the ministry in general can never occur. Each leader and each agency does what is right in its own eyes with no one to help them determine what works, what requires modification, and what should be dropped. Any form of systematic evaluation is unheard of.

An objective person looks at many youth ministry organizations and administrative structures and recognizes a classic mess. It is little comfort to know that many businesses operate in this same manner. Books and articles proliferate that are aimed at helping businesses become better organized, more effectively administered, and sensibly managed. But local churches have a spiritual responsibility to do the Lord's work "decently and in order" (1 Cor. 14:40 KJV).

PRINCIPLES OF ADMINISTRATION

What Is Administration and Organization?

Administration and *organization* are the means by which a group of people, bound together by some common purpose(s)/mission, structure and arrange themselves in order to accomplish their purpose(s) or mission. Administration is the human endeavor to govern those plans within the given parameters of an organization's purpose(s) or mission. It exists to help organize the group into an effective pattern of relationships (leaders, workers, etc.) to serve and minister to the target audience(s) of that group, and thus accom-

> *If there is one serious flaw in many church staff youth workers and youth pastors, it is that they have little sense of administration and organization.*

plish the purpose and achieve the goals of the organization.

Organization is the effective, efficient arrangement of personnel, materials, facilities, and finances in order to accomplish the purpose(s) or mission of the group. This is governed by developmental leadership that enables a ministry to become effective in achieving its purposes and outcomes with as much efficiency as possible. It avoids doing the wrong thing well. Rather, it facilitates doing the right things correctly.

An effective administrator, usually a paid youth worker (youth director, youth pastor, or assistant or associate pastor), is the one who helps an organization function developmentally through *enablement.* Administrators provide the impetus and stimulus for an organization to apply developmental leadership to the organization, in order for that organization to function developmentally.

Effective administrators function as follows in working with all members of the church/organization:

1. They help provide clearly defined purpose(s) or a mission statement. But administrators are not responsible to define these; they must enable the youth ministry participants to produce these.

2. They help identify the target population's needs that are to be met.

3. They help establish definite goals or outcomes.

4. They help develop a clear plan of action. Note that effective administrators do not develop the plan, but rather help develop it.

5. They help organize youth, adults, and equipment into a viable program to achieve goals in line with its purpose or mission for the accomplishment of its plan.

6. They help assemble resources needed in a coherent, interrelated and interdependent, organized manner. This is basically a curriculum for program and people. Resources include

- Personnel who have job descriptions, regardless of how minor their tasks are
- Recruitment and enlistment of personnel
- Both initial and continuous leadership development
- Deployment of personnel
- Continued enhancement of people's gifts, talents, and areas of expertise
- Gathering of materials to support the program
- Engagement of appropriate facilities for the program
- Development of finances to support the program
- Evaluation

7. They oversee the implementation of the plan through the program. The major task of administrators, once the program plan has been devised, is to ensure that the plan is carried out with accuracy and dispatch. Administrators usually do not have the authority to make major changes in the plan; they do have authority to make adaptations caused by unforeseen circumstances. Both freewheeling and straight-jacketed administration should be avoided. The object is to implement the program plan in an effective and efficient manner, not to give license or cause undue constraints on the implementation of the program.

8. They continually evaluate the process

and the outcomes, recycling information and data of evaluation as appropriate. The leader in continuous evaluation should be the administrator. He or she should want to know before anyone else whether or not the program will accomplish its intended outcomes as it is being planned and implemented. Administrators should use that evaluative data to help effect appropriate changes based on evaluation.

9. They continue and maintain the organization's operations as long as its purpose(s) and mission are valid and viable. Administrators need to be sensitive to both the mission and outcomes of the youth ministry, as well as to the actual program as it is being implemented. In one sense, administrators use both intuitive and objective evaluation to maintain the youth ministry's operations. If one senses that something is awry, he or she should begin to make changes and/or alert others involved in the planning of the ministry program concerning any problem.

10. They maintain communication between all parts of an organization. Improper or ineffective communication is probably a major cause of all sorts of controversy, dissensions, frictions, struggles, and clashes that lead to open conflicts between staff members and others involved in youth ministry. Wise administrators avert this conflict between those involved in the program planning and execution by keeping everyone current on its implementation and the outcomes.

11. They help people function smoothly and well by resolving conflict, not continuing conflict. Conflicts of various magnitudes *will* occur. But the wise administrator will not allow them to continue. Instead, he or she will bring the parties involved into conflict resolution so that the work of the Lord will go forward effectively and in peace. If the administrator is the one in conflict with others, then he or she must get involved as a participant in conflict resolution. This sets the pattern for others to follow and for others to anticipate when they get into a conflict situation.

12. They encourage people to continue to develop, while providing the means for this to happen. One of the key ingredients in a developmental leadership approach is that all leaders need to be encouraged in their continued development as people and as leaders. One

> *An effective administrator is the one who helps an organization function developmentally through enablement.*

does not achieve a leadership role and then stop learning about leadership. Effective administrators budget finances for leadership development events and publications. Continued leadership seminars are held for youth workers. It is vital that such leadership development is holistic, dealing not just with the tasks and behavior of youth ministry, but also with the whole person of the leaders involved. This means that the spiritual, psychological, social, cognitive, moral, and even physical development of the adult youth worker need to be in the purview of the administrators.

13. They focus people's attention on vision, purpose, mission, intended outcomes, and agreed-upon tasks. There is a relative single-mindedness about administrators; they seek to help people get the job done. Thus they are keepers of the vision, mission, purpose, outcomes, and tasks. It is their job to help achieve what has been decided by the greater group. And the more developmentally the administrators function, the more likely they are to enable people to use their gifts in accomplishing the plan.

14. They provide experiences that will enable leaders to be successful. One of the eas-

iest ways to discourage workers is to give them responsibilities they cannot carry out and at which they will surely fail. The opposite is also true. The way to encourage paid and unpaid youth workers is to ensure that they will be successful.

Success is never guaranteed unless the responsibilities are very simple. More complex responsibilities call for a greater risk both for the administrator and for the youth workers. The success can be relatively ensured if the youth workers have been given help to know *what* to do, *how* to do it, and *how to involve others* in the doing. Administrators are responsible to produce and empower new, effective, developmental leadership. Such leadership development is the major way to ensure success.

15. They celebrate with their church's paid and nonpaid staff. Special thank yous are appropriate several times a year, especially for the nonpaid workers. For example, hold special recognition dinners, a Christmas party, picnics, or outings for the nonpaid and paid youth staff, along with the adolescent leaders themselves. All of these help to say "thank you" to those who give unselfishly to minister with youth. It is also important to recognize the youth worker staff in church services, prayer meetings, prayer request lists to the congregation, and in front of the youth themselves.

A church should be constantly telling its staff how much they are appreciated. This is not some manipulative device to get more work out of people, although some may use it as such. Rather, it is a way of recognizing that the church notices the "good and faithful" work that these people are doing. Nonpaid staff, because they are serving without monetary compensation, especially need to be encouraged by public and private ways of thanks. For example, notes of appreciation to adults who were counselors at a week of camp or for a winter weekend retreat are effective ways to thank them for their ministry. Too

many churches want God to give the thanks when the ministering staff meet him face-to-face. Surely God will do so at that time, but the church paid staff need to express their own appreciation as well as the Lord's to those who give of themselves without monetary reward to work with the church youth.

PRINCIPLES OF ORGANIZATION

There are several basic principles of organization that, if followed, should lead to the relatively effective planning and execution of a youth program. The first and most basic principle is the well-known acronym KISS—Keep It Simple Stupid. The less complex the organization, the more likely it is that a youth ministry will operate smoothly; the more complex, the more likely it is that crucial elements will malfunction at the least propitious times.

1. Simplicity requires well-defined program outcomes, clearly stated tasks, clear authority lines, and the involvement of as many as possible of those affected in the decision-making processes. The responsibility for organization and program plans should be clearly given to various adult youth workers and leaders from among the youth themselves. Officers and workers in the youth ministry should know their tasks, know when those tasks are to be completed, and seek to involve all youth in the ministry in the execution of the tasks.

2. Any organization should be based on the needs of the group, desired outcomes, and actual program plans. The organization, both of the whole youth ministry and of particular parts of that ministry, is secondary—is servant—to the program. When the organizational aspects take on a life of their own, the organization becomes a life of its own and no longer serves to make the program happen. All organizations, whether they be the whole church, a particular Sunday school class, or an entire denomination, are only means to an

end—an orderly means no doubt, but still simply a means to the desired outcomes.

3. Organization should be the product of group planning, involving all those affected by the program. These youth, leaders among the youth, and adult workers all have a major investment in the outcomes. Hence they should be involved in determining the best way to become and stay organized to achieve those desired outcomes.

4. Whatever form the organization of the youth ministry takes should be comprehensive, unified, correlated, coordinated, and well planned.

Comprehensive means that all the agencies involved with youth in the local church should be included in the organizational planning processes. *Unified* means that there are agreed-upon mission, vision, and purposes for all agencies involved. The youth ministry must also fit into the unified vision, mission, and purpose of the church as a whole. Within the youth ministry itself, individual agencies should have clear reasons for existing, clear outcomes, and should avoid overlapping outcomes.

Correlated means there is a systematic connection between agencies and all the parts of the youth program. Agencies within the youth ministry should build on each other, showing mutual concern that the youth come under consistent, relevant, correct and effective teaching and experiences.

Coordinated means that all aspects of the youth program take part in harmonious, common action, working toward common outcomes based on common values and commitments to the mission, vision, and purpose of both the local church and the youth ministry. *Well planned* means that what is to be executed has been well thought out, the details have been worked through, and the personnel and material needed can be assembled.

5. The organization should reflect the youth involved, their natural groups and interests, and the geographic dispersal of the youth in the civic areas from which they are drawn. For example, it would be foolish to seek to organize a chess club if none of the youth are interested in playing chess! Nor would it make sense to have a highly centralized organization if the youth are many miles from each other—such as is true in large city churches and mega-churches.

6. Whatever organization structures that are developed, whether they be long- or short-term, should be flexible. Rigidity and traditionalism should be avoided. The way a particular program or the entire youth program is organized one year does not necessarily suggest the way it should be the next year, or in five years. Organization serves the program and changes as the youth and program change.

7. Whatever organizational structures are determined, they should provide for maximum participation on the parts of all those involved in the youth ministry. Participation of youth, leaders among the youth, and adult youth workers is crucial. One should also not omit parents of the youth nor the official boards of the church and the pastoral staff. How much the parents, boards, and pastoral staff should be involved depends on the local situation. Whatever the involvement, it should be at a level which ensures that none of these groups is surprised by any new aspects of the youth ministry program.

Providing for maximum participation of the youth makes them feel that they are an important and integral part of the youth ministry and the church. They will have positive encounters with adult leaders not only from within the youth ministry but also from the rest of the official leadership of the church. Likewise, positive encounters with adults who are parents of youth within the group will enhance their attempts at positive communications with their own parents.

8. All responsibility for program planning must have a commensurate amount of authority. If youth are given the responsibility to plan

> *Nothing can frustrate leaders more than to be given much responsibility and have little or no authority to fulfill that responsiblity.*

something, they must be given the authority—within legitimate limits of the law and the church's own operational procedures—to make decisions and carry them out. The same holds true for adult workers. Nothing can frustrate leaders more than to be given much responsibility and have little or no authority to fulfill that responsibility.

The feeding of the five thousand is an interesting example of responsibility. Jesus told his disciples, "You give them something to eat," without at first giving them the authority to do so. It was not until after Jesus gave thanks and broke the bread and gave it to them that the disciples had the authority necessary to fulfill their responsibility (Matt. 14:16–19 and parallel passages).

9. Accountability to higher authorities must be built in. Youth who are given appropriate responsibility and authority should not be left to fend for themselves. Nor should any adult workers, paid or nonpaid, be left to execute plans without someone giving supervision to the administration of those plans. No one works in a vacuum, especially those in youth ministry. The overseers of the program and the youth ministry in general should clearly spell things out. The workers should know to whom they are responsible. And all within the youth ministry should know who has final authority over the youth program plans. Clear lines of authority and administration should be explained to youth, adult youth workers,

pastoral staff, official boards, and parents.

10. Whatever the organizational structure, regular evaluation should be included within the design. Ongoing evaluation that begins during the planning processes, continues throughout the implementation phase, and ends with the final aspect of the program is vital. (See chapter 11.)

11. The smallest organizational unit is usually the Sunday school class or small group Bible study. These smaller groups are places of intimacy, warmth, acceptance, and close, person-to-person contact. They provide contact with caring people who can come to know the youth and whom the youth can come to know. Regardless of the organizational plan determined, one of these two smaller groupings should be the building blocks on which the rest of the organization is constructed.

VARIOUS PLANS OF ORGANIZATIONS

There are as many youth ministry organizational charts or plans as there are churches. We explain three generic plans, outlining the basic principles that underlie each, along with their advantages and disadvantages. One needs to identify the organizational pattern that best fits the local situation; enables the youth ministry to fulfill its mission, purpose, and desired outcomes; and is workable, given the people, resources, and economies involved.

Integration Plan

(See figure 1.)

The organizational pattern of the integration plan is based on several principles:

1. The Sunday school is the primary agency for the whole program. Sunday school classes are the units through which all ministry is done and all programs are carried out. This enables the youth ministry program to touch each individual in a personal way through the

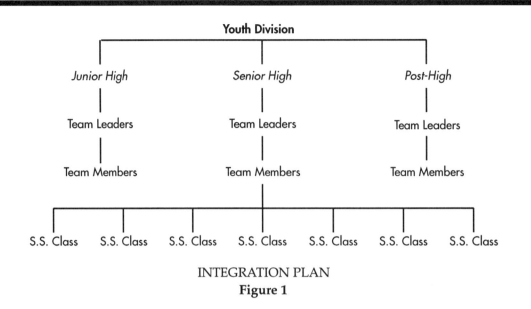

INTEGRATION PLAN
Figure 1

adult teacher and through any of the youth who are leaders within the class.

2. It provides three departments for youth, thereby covering the usual entire youth age span.

3. All the teachers are involved in other aspects of the youth ministry program; teachers work in Sunday school and in other agencies of program.

The advantages of the integration organizational plan are, first, that it is graded by age groups that usually hold certain characteristics in common. Developmental age groups are not mixed, thereby providing programs that are developmentally appropriate. Second, it is centralized, affording staff people ease in communication and detailed planning. Third, there is an economy of leadership in which each knows his or her roles. Teachers and other youth workers can function within their roles in order to produce the outcomes planned. Fourth, it is unified and coordinated, yet flexible. Further, the integration plan keeps the youth from having multiple appeals for their allegiance and

time/energy commitments. Still further, it is a good plan for leadership development. Leaders' roles and responsibilities can be clearly described and communicated and leaders can be equipped to do definite tasks.

The disadvantages of the integration plan are several. It makes authority and responsibility for the administration and policy rest on "professionals," or at least on those not intricately connected with youth and the program. It also places too much responsibility on the individual teacher: Does he or she have that much time, talent, and leadership to offer a balanced program? It fails to recognize the contributions that other local church youth agencies can and have made. It is not wise to totally omit these other agencies since they have definitive roles to fulfill. Further, the plan is difficult to implement in a small church. And still further, if a church continues a closely graded organization it can tend to be too segregated, isolating even those within the various age groups from others within the same department.

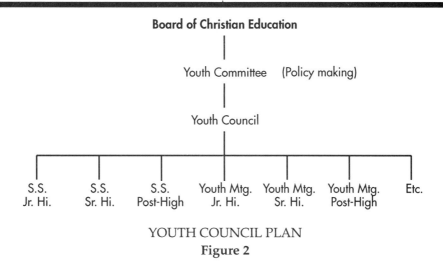

Board of Christian Education

Youth Committee   (Policy making)

Youth Council

| S.S. | S.S. | S.S. | Youth Mtg. | Youth Mtg. | Youth Mtg. | Etc. |
| Jr. Hi. | Sr. Hi. | Post-High | Jr. Hi. | Sr. Hi. | Post-High | |

YOUTH COUNCIL PLAN
Figure 2

Youth Council Plan

(See figure 2.)

The principles on which the youth council plan is built are twofold. First, it recognizes existing units and assigns program elements and executions to the various agencies within the youth ministry. Second, policy is made on the Youth Committee level, which is close to those with leadership authority in the church as a whole. This plan provides for coordination and integration on the Youth Council level. Thus, there is an allocation of responsibilities with no single group being charged with too much responsibility or too many tasks.

The youth council plan creates greater interest among youth because they are on the Youth Council making plans and administering their own program. And it avoids duplication. It provides for an integrated, coordinated, correlated, and unified program, supporting a central clearing house function for planning. The youth council plan is a means of expediting details of a balanced program; it relates each agency to the others, yet retains the identity of each agency involved because each agency is represented. Finally, it helps adults know the youth involved because they are working directly with them in planning.

The disadvantages of this plan are many. It does not relate to the whole church; rather, it splits youth into agencies. It might work in a small church where few would be on the Youth Council. But in a large church, it would soon become unwieldy. It requires youth to become involved in many different agencies in order to achieve balanced spiritual formation, nurture, and discipleship experiences. It allows "agency-itis" to creep in, that is, the proliferation of multiple agencies to meet the ever-increasing needs of youth. As more agencies are organized, the older agencies usually are not replaced. Instead, the new are added to the old ones. Representatives tend to be parochial, looking out for their own agencies' interests, thereby politicizing the organizational plan and sometimes thwarting progress, to the detriment of youth.

The youth council plan asks too much of each member on the council; not all would be interested in the whole youth ministry if they represented just one aspect. Communication between agencies, which is supposedly enhanced by this plan, would probably actually break down because of communication gaps between agencies. There would be just

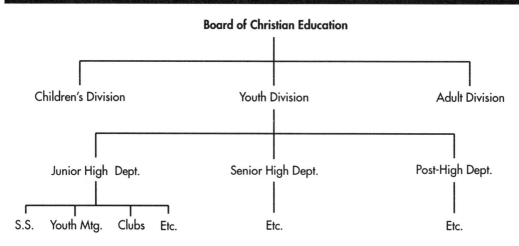

MODIFIDED INTEGRATION OR DEPARTMENTAL PLAN
Figure 3

too many plans for all on the Council and Committee to deal with. There is undoubted overlap between the Youth Committee, the Youth Council, and the agencies involved in each age division. This plan requires an enormous number of workers and continued problems of ongoing leadership development. Church staff workers would have an enormous amount of administrative work to do in order to keep all the agencies in balance. And they would be always fighting the parochial interests of each youth agency involved. There is no true unified vision, mission, purpose, and outcome in such an organizational plan.

Modified Integration or Departmental Plan

(See figure 3.)

The modified integration, or departmental, plan is built on the principle that the separate organizations necessary to deal with the needs and interests of the age groups involved are provided for. It recognizes that various agencies make a contribution to the youth ministry program, and it provides for keeping each

agency if it fits with the youth ministry. This plan provides for integration on the departmental age level, not on the agency level.

The advantages of the modified plan are as follows: First, it provides for integration, coordination, correlation, and unification, which are possible on each level and throughout the program. Second, planning takes place on several levels and therefore responsibility is spread. Third, it provides for flexibility regardless of church size; it can work in small or large churches. This plan can be made as complex or simple as needs dictate. Fourth, those most interested in organization are responsible for its smooth functioning. And finally, it is simple, based on needs, yet visionary.

There are disadvantages of the modified plan. First, this plan will often require reorganization of programs. It is not the way that churches usually operate. Second, it is possibly not too democratic. The individual who leads either the Age Department or the entire Youth Division could become a dictator if too much authority is given to him or her. Third, this plan might not work well for a small church with only a few youth. Fourth, it must be decided from which direction responsibilities and authority will come—from the top down or from the bottom up. And last, it almost demands that professionals be at the head of each division.

In conclusion, the organizational format chosen is dependent on the types of adults and youth involved, the conditions of the church sponsoring the youth ministry, and, in many cases, the denomination involved. Some denominations declare how a local church is to be organized, right down to its youth ministries. In such cases, one can only hope that those running the denomination—usually far removed from the local active youth ministry—have insights that are relevant to all the youth ministry organizational plans for all the denomination's churches.

10

Camp and Retreats

Christian camping can be a unique and irreplaceable experience. It can be one of the most effective ways to effect evangelization and Christian growth, surpassing the effects of Sunday school. Consequently, camping has the potential to be one of the most powerful means available to the church of Christ. What the program of a camp is, what its facilities provide, and what its staff can give in their leadership will determine whether or not a particular camp can achieve its potential effects. A number of people have observed that two weeks of Christian camping are much more valuable than a year of Sunday school. More than one person has also noted that Jesus took his disciples on an extended, three-year camping trip to teach them about himself. Moses also led Israel on a forty-year, nonresidential, tent-camping experience!

Christian camping and retreats need to be integral and planned experiences in a local church's youth ministry. Camping and retreats in various forms provide long-term exposure for evangelism and Christian living. They provide for teaching, worship, fellowship, service, and leadership development, all within the span of a few days to a week or more. This concentrated time apart from the ordinary regimens of life provides for in-depth experiences and life-changing events.

Consider that all the basic elements of an effective youth ministry plus leadership development can be experienced through camping and to a lesser degree in weekend retreats. It would take many weeks or possibly years to accomplish in a church's regular youth program what can be accomplished in a week or two of camping. Given a choice between Sunday school or two weeks of camping, I would choose camping. Concentrated time, real-life situations, opportunities for worship, fellowship, and service, and direct application of Bible teaching to life at camp are far superior to a weekly dose of a few Bible verses in a Sunday school class or even in a Bible study.

Camping should not be viewed as just another option for youth ministry. It can be one of the most fruitful means for helping to make life-long changes in young people. Camping and retreats, like all other aspects of ministry, must be well planned, executed effectively, and evaluated for continual improvement. This chapter proposes a basic philosophy of Christian camping and retreats.

TYPES OF CAMPING

Camping may be divided into two major categories. The first is *residential,* in which most or all of the program and activities are centered at the camp facilities and on camp property. The second category is *nonresidential,* meaning that most of the program and activities are centered away from the actual camp property. In the latter, the camp serves as the home base for various trips, programs, and activities.

Most nonresidential camps are counselor-centered with the program focused on small groups of campers with their counselors and assistant counselors. Counselors are the leaders of the program and of all activities, including spiritual ones.

Residential camping can be subdivided into conference-centered and counselor-camper-centered camping. Conference-centered camping is oriented around the entire group of campers going through the program. The whole group is together for most of the time. Speakers, chapel services, and large group studies and activities are the program.

Organized Christian camping incorporates into its program a balance among physical, cognitive, social, affective, moral, and spiritual aspects of life.

While some residential camps are counselor-centered, most are camp-centered with specialized staff operating various activities on the camp property. Counselors often double as program specialists, though this is not recommended procedure. Counselors' main roles are to control campers at night, get them up for breakfast, and generally "baby-sit" when campers are not occupied in activities. The spiritual task of counselors may be limited to leading bed-time devotions and prayer, leaving the main spiritual input and program activities to specialists.

Counselor-camper-centered camping is oriented almost totally around the counselor-camper relationship. Very little large group programing is used—usually campers all eat together and may have a worship service together. Almost all the activities are in small groups, counselor- and/or camper-led.

Retreats are minicamps, two to four days in duration. They can be held at almost any location that has the facilities needed to service the group: recreation, lodging, food, meeting space. Obviously, when looking for a retreat location a youth worker seeks more than just the barest minimum in facilities. Yet, the bare minimum may be all that some can find and/or afford. The issue is not the luxury of the retreat site but whether the use of the particular site facilitates the achieving of desirable outcomes. Camping outside in the rain is usually not first choice for most youth workers or youth, yet such an experience can make a huge difference in the lives of the youth if they can be helped to use their creative resources to make "sunshine" out of the rain.

What is said below about Christian camping is valid for retreats as well. The principles of Christian camping and retreats are the same even though their length of time is different. The remainder of this chapter focuses on Christian camping from the perspective of a church actually owning and operating its own camp. While this may not be in the purview of many churches, the concepts associated with operating a camp are the same whether a church owns or rents a camp.

When a youth ministry rents a camp, it should be aware of the issues that go into choosing an excellent camp site and developing an effective, safe program. Thus, even though a church may not actually own a camp, they will be the users of a camp facility and they should know what makes a location excellent for Christian camping. A church youth ministry should also know how to determine the most effective programming for its youth. Some churches merely send their youth to a camp that is operated by full-time summer camp staff. This is one way to avoid much responsibility for the camping program, but it does not excuse youth workers from becoming knowledgeable about the program at that camp.

As you read the following, keep in mind that these principles apply in one way or another to camps and retreats in general, regardless of whether or not a youth ministry owns or rents a camp, or sends its youth to one operated by others. What the program of a camp is, what its facilities provide, and what its personnel can give in their leadership will determine whether a particular camp can achieve its potential of being a very effective means for spiritual formation, nurture, and discipleship of youth.

ASSUMPTIONS

The first assumption we will make is that the target groups for Christian camping are children, youth, adults, and families. Thus, planning, buildings, properties, and program should all reflect these target groups. However, the priority listing is youth, children, adults, and lastly, families. Second, year-round use of the facilities is a goal for two reasons: It provides for more efficient use of the investment, and it provides for increased opportunities to affect people's lives.

A third assumption is philosophy must dictate program and program must dictate site planning and building. Fourth, the first steps in developing or renewing a camp program are to determine a basic camp philosophy and general program. From these two preliminary and vital steps, subsequent physical plans should be developed. To do the steps in any other order is to impose restrictions upon the camp's program before it is even developed.

Our fifth assumption is that both long- and short-range goals must be developed, along with a timetable for completion, definite assignments of the goals to responsible leaders, and periodic reporting and evaluation on progress to the goals. A sixth assumption is that a quality program and facilities are desired. These are not to be luxurious, but neither are they to be so minimal as to detract from the cause of Christ or the effectiveness of the program. The site, facilities, equipment, buildings, and program should reflect a high standard of excellence. And, finally, the day of the inadequately supplied camp with very limited facilities, program, and personnel is over.

PHILOSOPHY OF CAMPING

A philosophy of camping gives the general purpose, definition, and intended outcomes of camping. It delineates in general terms what camp is all about, and provides the conceptual foundation on which all future plans for programs and facilities are based. Without a philosophy, all the whims of individuals and leaders are brought to bear on the camp. The philosophy is therefore a planning compass or rational blueprint to guide the board of directors and all the leadership of the camp.

Definition

Organized Christian camping is an experience in group living in a natural setting. It incorporates into its program a balance among physical, cognitive, social, affective, moral, and spiritual aspects of life. This is done through a proper relationship between campers and the total camp environment, and the personal relationship of campers to each other, to counselors, and to other leaders.

Developmental Purposes

Spiritually, the purpose of organized camping is, first, to introduce Jesus Christ as Savior and Lord to those who do not know him. Second, it is to continue to nurture those who do know him as Savior and Lord toward continued growth in Christ and increased service to Christ as he leads through the Holy Spirit, as well as to provide increased knowledge and application of the Bible to life. These are the priority ultimate goals.

Physically, the purpose is to provide activities, resources, and facilities to help campers (children, youth, and adults) to develop their physical bodies to greater usefulness and to develop and improve coordination and skills in various leisure and recreational activities. *Cognitively,* organized camping provides stimulus to develop greater understanding of the issues, problems, and answers facing today's campers in various aspects of their lives. It introduces campers to new concepts and viewpoints consonant with biblical doctrines which are a normal part of Christian camping. *Socially,* the purpose of organized camping is to help foster better interpersonal relationships in a camper's life. This is done first by helping the camper to a better understanding and acceptance of himself or herself as created in God's image, loved by him, and of the utmost value to him. Second, it is realized through understanding and accepting others in the camp program.

Affectively, camping's purpose is to help campers learn to understand who they are, their own emotions, their responses to others, and to control their own emotions in various situations. *Morally,* campers are encouraged to integrate higher stages of moral judgments into their behaviors, moving from egocentric moral perspectives to concerns for others' input, to a godly view of justice, to making moral decisions and taking moral actions based on the agape love of God.

In summary, Christian camping is a total life experience that takes place twenty-four hours a day in the lives of campers. The sixfold purposes are not easily relegated to limited, individual program areas. The whole of the camp experience should be geared to meeting these basic purposes, which should be integrated into the entire program. Thus, for example, physical skill development and activity can also be seen in the light of cognitive, social, affective, moral, and spiritual developments.

Educational Approach

In setting forth a structure for effective learning, remember that individual growth in all of the areas above occurs best in a blend of individual, small group, and larger group experiences. A counselor-centered approach is the best for children and youth. This means that Bible study and discussion occur under the direction of counselor leaders rather than just from a monologue by a "preacher" or speaker. Likewise, various skills and activities should be taught and practiced in small groups. Opportunity and guidance need to be given in the use of unstructured time for personal growth in all of the sixfold developmental areas above. And larger group meetings are the best place to provide general information, inspiration, and corporate worship.

The rest of this chapter is written with a counselor-camper approach.

Living Together

Campers and a counselor living together twenty-four hours a day provide the "stuff" of real life situations for camp. An organized camping program can take advantage of this unique learning situation by molding this interaction to foster growth in the six developmental purpose areas. This is done best in homogeneous, small group, counselor-led accommodations and learning units. Homogeneous means units of campers of the same sex and approximately the same age, with small groups consisting of no more than eleven campers per counselor. The counselor is the key person to help campers to develop and grow successfully. As such, he or she should be the main leader of the group, and must lead in Bible study and in one or more of the camp program activity and skill areas. Often an assistant counselor (sometimes called a "junior counselor" or "counselor in training") assists the senior counselor.

Outcomes

Intended outcomes or goals are somewhat more specific statements derived from the purpose statement. They provide more defined limits to the development of program and site usage. These are some proper outcomes:

1. Introducing Jesus Christ as Savior and Lord to those who do not know him. Christ should be presented in a nonthreatening atmosphere through the informal personal witness of counselors and Christian campers, and through more formal program elements.

2. Providing for spiritual growth in Christ toward the ultimate goal of being mature in him. Christian campers should be discipled to bring their lives under Christ's control more and more.

3. Increasing knowledge of the Bible. Spiritual growth occurs as the Holy Spirit takes the Scriptures and applies them to lives of campers.

4. Providing worship experiences. The natural setting of camp should be used to inspire awe and worship of God. Both structured and unstructured experiences can provide for individual, small group, and large group worship of God.

5. Taking advantage of the natural setting of the camp property. The natural terrain, setting, and environment must not be disturbed unless absolutely necessary, and even then as little as possible. The program, buildings, and site usage should conform to the natural surrounding and terrain. And campers should be helped to appreciate the beauty and magnificence of God's creation. Stress ecological features, as well as our response of "how great Thou art!" to God in worship.

6. Providing challenging fun and adventure. Campers need to enjoy themselves. At the same time, they all must be challenged to grow spiritually, physically, intellectually, socially, and psychologically. The program should be challenging—providing for growth experiences—and adventuresome—providing

excitement and stimulation—within a reasonable and safe framework.

7. Providing learning, inspirational, and worship experiences in both small groups and larger groups. Bible studies should emphasize both Bible content and practical application to daily Christian living, starting at camp and extending to home. This is most effectively done in small groups. Other instructional and practice periods in various camp skills and activities should also be in small groups. Inspirational and worship experiences can be achieved through both small and large group activities. A "preacher" or speaker could be used in this area, though such is not necessary.

8. Providing an unobtrusive framework around which a camper could build or improve his or her own philosophy or approach to life. The camp experience should give help and guidance in value and attitude development, and in actual, proper Christian behavior for the camper toward himself or herself, God, humanity, and the physical world. A camper should be a "better person" and a "better Christian" as a result of his or her experiences in camp.

9. Providing for increased social adjustment and democratic living. The camp experience should help campers in their relationships with each other as they live together twenty-four hours a day. They will improve their relationships with both their peers and their leaders.

10. Teaching campers new skills and a degree of proficiency in their use. Camping should focus upon skills not normally experienced in the camper's own home environment. These skills should be taught safely and well by qualified leaders. And campers must be given opportunities to practice their newly acquired skills under the guidance of these leaders, in order to develop full utilization and proficiency.

11. Providing a safe, healthful, and physically nourishing environment. The safety and

health of campers must be guarded continually: food, activities, and facilities should contribute to the safety, health, and physical nourishment of campers. Ill campers are unhappy campers. Unpalatable food and/or poor facilities make for unhappy campers, too. Unhappy campers miss the spiritual benefits of camp. Appropriate medically trained person(s) must be on staff or nearby for routine and immediate emergency aid. The highest sanitary and safety standards should be set up and jealously maintained. And all of the health and safety laws of the state and county should be followed closely.

> *The counselor is the most influential person in relation to campers. On his or her shoulders rests much of the effectiveness of the entire camp experience.*

12. Providing freedom of choice within a flexible, structured experience in order to foster mature, responsible decisions by campers. Camping should not be a completely planned program with little or no freedom of choice. Within the larger structure of the program, campers should be allowed to make their own choices, both as individuals and as homogeneous units. The program must be flexible enough to accommodate changes without disruption or the need for immediate readjustment of the physical facilities. Campers as individuals and as small groups should be helped to make reasonable decisions based upon their own spiritual, physi-

cal, intellectual, social, and psychological development and to live with the consequences of those decisions.

Counselors and Program Staff

The counselor is the most influential person in relation to campers. On his or her shoulders rests much of the effectiveness of the entire camp experience: safety, enjoyment, challenge, fun, growth, and the holistic development of campers. Much of the maturation of campers will occur mainly under the counselor's direction or influence. Counselors should be of the highest quality spiritually; they should be dedicated, competent, and maturing Christians with a good grasp of the Bible. They should also be intellectually maturing, well-adjusted, and stable socially and psychologically. And they will need abilities to lead Bible studies and at least one camp program skill (water sports, archery, handicraft, horsemanship, etc.).

Organization

The board of directors or the official board of a local church is responsible for approval of the camp philosophy, general programing, hiring and releasing the director, approval of the staff, financial acquisition, and the real property. The director is responsible for implementing the entire philosophy and program of the board. He or she develops program details with the approval of the board and appoints program and counselor staff as well as other staff as needed, with the board's approval.

The assistant and/or associate director assists the director as determined by the board of directors and the director. The program staff are program specialists who help develop, oversee, and operate the program and assist in the leadership development of counselors and campers. Counselors work directly with

campers. The ratio of counselor to campers should be a maximum of one counselor to eleven campers; a more effective ratio is one to eight. Nonprogram staff are the resident caretakers, maintenance personnel, kitchen and dining hall staff, and others as needed. All of these should demonstrate Christian living and relationships, too.

PROGRAM

The program of Christian camping consists of every hour of each day the camper is at camp. The program, therefore, should be planned, graded, and supervised with the campers and their needs in mind. The age, sex, and developmental needs of campers should be ascertained as much as possible, and accordingly, suitable activities should be developed. Ideally, camp program activities should be those not normally experienced "back home." Many campers go to camp in order to learn new things and have new experiences. Keeping this in mind, "These principles should govern the choice of program content in camp:

1. Activities should be *indigenous* to the natural setting. . . .
2. The program should be *simple* so that the important values can be emphasized.
3. It should be *flexible*, to allow for individual differences.
4. There should be provision for *creativity* so that the campers may discover and use their God-given abilities.
5. The program should be *geared to meeting the needs* of individuals and therefore provide much opportunity for personal and small-group contact.
6. It should allow for *participation* by every camper.
7. The program should be *graded* according to the ability and interest of the varying ages of campers."[1]

Following is a suggested program for youth:

7:30 a.m.	—	rise
8:00 a.m.	—	breakfast
8:30 a.m.	—	quiet time, devotions
9:00 a.m.	—	clean-up
9:30 – 10:30 a.m.	—	Bible study in small groups
10:30 a.m.– 12:15 p.m.	—	camp skill instruction in small groups
12:30 p.m.	—	lunch
1:30 p.m.	—	camp skill practice or small-group activities
3:00 – 5:30 p.m.	—	free time
6:00 p.m.	—	supper
7:00 p.m.	—	evening special program and activity in large or small group
9:00 p.m.	—	evening worship and inspirational devotiona program, large group
10:30 p.m.	—	cabin devotions, small group sharing, and prayer
11:00 p.m.	—	lights out

In conjunction with the above program, out-of-camp trips (backpacking, canoeing, horseback riding, etc.) of one to four days could be undertaken by small groups led by counselors, but planned jointly by counselors and campers. Tripping, with only relatively minor adjustments, can be used for all campers from fourth grade through post-high age.

These components make up the program:

Bible study and instruction. This should be accomplished in small groups, with the counselor leading the Bible study. Bible study should be definitely geared to the ages and developmental needs of the campers. And it could be held either in living units or in smaller parts of other buildings. On nice days, it could be held outdoors, away from noise and other groups.

Worship and inspirational experiences. The world of nature is inspiring in and of itself. Both outdoor area(s) and sheltered area(s) for worship of God should be provided. Daily worship should be planned, with both campers and counselors sharing in the leadership. Also, a speaker or "preacher" who can relate to the campers could be part of this activity, although a good counseling and program staff would do as well, if not better.

Handcrafts. These include various leather, paper, and other kinds of craft activities, depending on the depth of craft programming and the interests of the youth.

Water skills and activities. These include swimming and life-saving instruction and practice in the camp pool or nearby lake, river, or ocean; free swimming as recreation; canoeing or kayaking instruction and recreation in a nearby river or lake; boating, windsailing, and sailing in a nearby lake, river, or ocean; fishing in a nearby lake, river, and ocean, and; water-skiing in a nearby lake or river.

Land skills and activities. These include, but are not limited to, such things as archery, riflery, basketball, softball, tennis, volleyball, gymnastics, wrestling, and trampoline. Added to these would be horseback riding and care of horses and tack (also burros); camping skills such as fire building, tent pitching, outdoor cooking, and backpacking; and other land games and sports as personnel, facilities, and equipment permit. The emphasis should be on land activities that are not usually available at home. So such sports as basketball and softball, for example, would not be emphasized, whereas archery and riflery would tend to be more highlighted if these are not readily available at home.

Nature study and lore. Local flora and fauna should be studied, and local and regional ecology and geology should be explored. Astronomy can be studied with both the naked eye and with a small telescope and map of the stars. Weather, weather forecasting, and record keeping could be studied, as could orienteering with a compass.

Tripping (one to four days). The essentials of trip planning and safety should be covered. Trips themselves might include canoe trips down regional rivers (within a maximum two-three hour drive from camp), backpack and biking trips, day hikes, horseback and burro trips, and sailing on a large body of water.

Lore of the local area. This would include the study of and experiences with the various and interesting lore of the area, experiences with select peoples of the area, and the study of the history, geography, and movement of the local people.

IMPLICATIONS OF THE PHILOSOPHY OF CAMPING

If one were to apply the above philosophy of camping immediately to a specific camp, the following dozen steps would be necessary. Foremost, a philosophy of Christian camping should be adopted, including a commitment to a *counselor-centered* program over against a *speaker-oriented* program.

1. Short- and long-range goals need to be decided, and a definite timetable should be established for fulfillment of the goals. Leadership must be assigned for each goal, periodic reporting to the governing board must be called for, and periodic evaluations by the board must be made regarding achievement.

2. A basic program should be outlined.

3. Adequate land should be purchased or rented. It would be wise to find land on a large lake, a river, or on an ocean in order to provide for swimming, boating, waterskiing, and canoeing.

4. A definite *site study* should be made to determine drainage, flooding risk, and the flood plain. Other factors will also be considered: frost and snow effects; sun directions;

major rain, hail, and windstorm directions; subsoil conditions; forest and vegetation conditions; and other such matters. The natural setting in and near the site should be studied to determine what is already available for programing. Often camps adjacent to state or federal parks are wise choices, since they can usually be used for camp activities.

5. A basic site usage should be developed, based on the first four steps. This should include buildings for sleeping, dining, and recreation. It should also include road access, water supply, sewage disposal, garbage disposal, placement of a swimming pool (if needed), and availability and access to other properties needed for program activities such as hiking, horseback riding, canoeing, waterskiing, or sailing.

6. A camp director should be appointed to implement the decisions of the board, to develop program specifics, and to publicize the camp. This person could serve on a part-time basis for several years. He or she should, however, be experienced and knowledgeable on current camp skills and philosophy, and be committed to Christ-centered camping for the "whole" person.

7. Publicity should be begun to churches and other Christian groups nearby stating the availability of the camp for rental for fall, winter, and spring retreats and camping. Various retreats could also be planned by the camp for junior high, senior high, post-high, and adult groups on appropriate weekends in the fall, winter, and spring.

8. A large publicity and public relations campaign should be begun to acquaint interested and potentially interested people in the camp, to enlist their prayer support, and acquire financial backing.

9. A resident caretaker should be acquired. He or she would be expected to live on the property and help maintain it year-round.

10. Sleeping accommodations, multipurpose buildings, and outdoor facilities need to

be built to fit into the overall philosophy and program as outlined above.

Sleeping accommodations should house a maximum of twelve persons per room with sufficient space—walking and clothing storage—for residents to stay for at least two weeks. (This could accommodate a "cabin group" and counselor for a children's or youth camp, or could be used for family camping.) The accommodations need to be winterized, with toilet, shower, and wash facilities contiguous.

The multi-purpose buildings need to be large enough to accommodate all campers and counselors at one time for recreational activities and meetings. These must also be winterized, with toilets and wash facilities under the same roof, and have large, open spaces for large muscle activities.

Kitchen and dining hall, with toilets and wash facilities under the same roof are needed.

Finally, outdoor recreation facilities to shelter outdoor activities and provide suitable areas for particular activities—archery and riflery range, basketball courts—should be erected.

11. Profiles of potential campers should be delineated. These involve describing their age, sex, socioeconomic status, and spiritual knowledge. The profiles include also determining what cities and states they will be coming from, and how they can be contacted. Ask, would transportation have to be furnished from various geographic points?

12. A decision must be made on the length of the camping season—how long camp will be open for each age group for summer camping and for retreat and school-year camping. Effective summer camping usually requires a minimum of six days in camp. Most effective camper-centered camps do not plan for less than two weeks, while some camps run three- to eight-week sessions.

Camps and retreats require much planning and hard work to be effective, but the results will prove to be worth the effort. Young people will meet Christ in new ways or, in some cases, for the first time. They will see Christ in the creation, in Scripture, in fellowship with each other, and in their personal reflection and introspection. They will benefit from spiritual formation, nurture, and discipleship. They will experience leadership firsthand as they help to plan and execute the camp/retreat event. Young people can be significantly changed because of Christian camps and retreats.

CHAPTER 11

Evaluation

There is no shortage of ideas and models for youth ministry, and no shortage of willingness to try new solutions for old problems. Local and national conferences on youth ministry specialize in youth program ideas. Books, journals, newsletters, and curricular resources purport to give program ideas that are almost guaranteed to work. New products seemingly come out on the market monthly, promising the best in youth materials for youth groups. These tout the use of current media, such as videos, movie analyses, small group Bible studies, support groups, and discussion groups, to name just a few. Herein lies a matter of great concern: through what processes will all these program ideas be identified as promising and worthy of emulation, adoption, adaptation, or just plain copying?*

Youth workers are particularly prone to copy others' ideas, partly because of their own relative freedom from traditions and because of their pragmatic concern for getting a job done. It is not

---

*Some of the concepts in this chapter have been contributed by Ted W. Ward of Trinity Evangelical Divinity School.

at all uncommon for youth workers to attend a youth conference and then return to their churches and begin implementing new ideas presented at that conference. These youth workers often have their antennae finely tuned to the latest idea that some more creative youth worker has developed. Wholesale adoption is more the norm than the exception.

Almost in contrast, many youth workers have been known to repeat the same basic program ideas and skits and activities year after year. They can sometimes get away with this lack of creativity because they seem to stay no more than a few years in any one particular church ministry. If they change churches every three to four years, they only need that many years of program ideas to be recycled. Seldom is the question of effectiveness asked of these programs and their activities.

Evaluation often has a bad name. It is usually equated with what happened to us throughout our formal schooling: examinations, papers, and standardized tests all measured us and told us how much we did not know in order to grade us. Few teachers took the time to help us learn from those evaluations of our learning. And fewer teachers viewed student tests as an evaluation of their own—the teachers'—teaching effectiveness. In most formal schooling, grades are viewed as an evaluation of learning by the students, not as an evaluation of how effectively the teacher taught.

EVALUATION AND LEARNING EFFECTIVENESS

Youth ministry is a highly volatile activity. Youth whose needs are not met will stop attending. Or if they do attend because of parental or peer pressure they demonstrate through their actions that they are bored and their needs are not being met. Evaluation needs to be interlocked with learning effectiveness. Although an established form of min-

> *Youth ministries are not apt to survive unless they can demonstrate that they are performing intended functions and meeting the needs of intended audiences.*

istry—especially the formal worship service—may survive for many years on its own momentum, youth ministries are not apt to survive unless they can demonstrate that they are performing intended functions and meeting the needs of intended audiences. The realization of the intended outcomes and the effectiveness of the youth ministry program cannot be taken for granted. Evaluation is indispensable because it helps identify what is effective, where ineffectiveness lies, and what to change to make the youth ministry more effective.

Christians have a built-in reticence when it comes to evaluation. Not only are we fearful of the "grade" we might get, but we also have a fear that we might intrude into God's realm. (Of course, we have no problems doing so in medicine, science, and many other areas of life.) Somehow one gets the feeling that evaluation of youth ministry should be left for the Final Judgment.

There is a solid basis for evaluation in Scripture. The two Greek words that are translated "testing" suggest the idea of testing for reliability and genuineness. The concepts come from the testing of metal in order to determine its purity and genuineness. We are told that God tests believers (see James 1:12; 1 Thess. 2:4; Jer. 11:20; Mal. 3:1–4). But in addition, believers are to test themselves (see Rom. 1:1–2; 1 Cor. 9:27; 11:28; 2 Cor. 13:5; Gal. 6:4).

Testing or examination is a part of every believer's experiences and character development (see Rom. 5:3–4; 1 Peter 1:6–7). It is not unspiritual to evaluate oneself or what one is doing. Nor is it unspiritual to do the same for our youth programs. Testings or evaluations help us identify the "dross" in order to become more effective in ministry.

In scientific terms, evaluation is an important process that should be associated with every youth ministry and its program. The basic outcomes of evaluation are

- To describe what has been accomplished,
- To determine which intended outcomes have been achieved,
- To identify what weaknesses or failures have occurred, and
- To decide what importance should be ascribed to each of these.

One needs to know if a particular program, an entire year of youth ministry, and several years of youth ministry have been effective. But this alone is not sufficient. One also needs to know what produced the desired outcomes. Was it some particular aspect that needs to be repeated? Or was it cumulative—many meetings and discussions and one-on-one times with adult leaders? Or was it something unplanned that happened serendipitously?

Research of any sort is generally limited by the questions it is able to ask with precision. For example, the findings of an evaluation can be no more precise than the questions posed. Three problems enter at this point: cost, time, and specificity.

Sometimes too many questions are asked. When youth workers begin to design evaluative instruments for the church's youth ministry, they tend to assume that as long as an evaluation is underway, they might as well find out ten kinds of information rather than just five. But evaluators know that answering questions is costly. The more questions there are, the higher the cost and the more complex the evaluative design must be.

Another problem arises when important questions require long periods of time to obtain reliable and valid responses. For example, longitudinal studies lasting months or years are necessary to evaluate certain long-term impacts of ongoing youth ministry. Even more difficult than the problem of time and cost is the lack of clearly specified outcomes for specific programs, or for an entire year of youth ministry. When only generalized statements of outcomes and platitudinously spiritualized goal statements are available, few questions can be asked in a precise manner. Thus, the first task for the design of an evaluation is to identify worthy questions which could be answered specifically within the time and cost constraints of the requested study. Following are four types of evaluation that are germane to youth ministry.

CONTEXT EVALUATION

Context evaluation focuses on the adequacy of describing both the sponsoring agency or agencies and the intended target groups of the ministry. First, by describing the sponsoring agency or agencies youth workers will know who is sponsoring the youth ministry, what the values of the organization are, and which part of the organization (for example, the Sunday school) is responsible for particular aspects of the Bible teaching and fellowship ministry elements. The evaluative question here is, "Have the sponsoring organization and agencies been adequately described? Do we have a good idea of who we are and what our organization's basic operational values are?"

Second, by describing the target groups—the youth themselves—one is able to answer the basic question, "Do we know whom we are trying to reach? Do we have a detailed description of the youth involved? Do we know their needs, concerns, interests, values, culture?"

Information determined in these first evaluative actions provides the base for the whole planning process that follows. This information becomes the ground for determining program outcomes. Without knowing who the organization is, what agency is responsible to act and who the youth are, program planning for ministry is a shot in the dark.

PROGRAM PLANNING EVALUATION

The main question of program planning evaluation is, "Will we hit our target?" This is a future-tense action, examining the plans as they are being made. It asks, "Can this program, as it is being designed, adequately meet the needs and outcomes determined? Is it a realistic program, given the context?" Feedback in program planning evaluation is vital in order to make changes in the ongoing planning process.

FORMATIVE EVALUATION

The time frame of formative evaluation is that of the present program. It asks, "Are we hitting our intended outcomes?" Formative evaluation seeks to determine the degree to which the intended outcomes are currently being achieved, continuously measuring intended outcomes with observed outcomes. Formative evaluation does not determine the value of a program, because the program is still ongoing. Rather, it assumes that any program operated by humans will have imperfections and will need mid-course corrections.

Formative evaluation provides feedback that will continually shape and reshape the youth ministry and its particular programs so that each will more likely achieve its intended outcomes. It avoids the major weakness of the fourth form of evaluation—summative—by not waiting until the end of a program or time frame of ministry to determine whether it has been effective. It provides for input that will help summative evaluation show whether what was being evaluated has indeed achieved its intended outcomes.

Virtually any information that sheds light on ways to improve an ongoing youth ministry experience can qualify as formative evaluation. The issue for designers of this evaluation is to assure responsible validity and reliability of such information. What is valued as the learning outcomes must be synonymous with the nature of the youth ministry experiences. Assessments upon which evaluations will be based will have to compare the actual learning experiences with the specifications of experiences that theoretically contribute to the intended outcomes. Thus the key question for a formative evaluation of an instructional material or procedure is, "To what extent are the observed experiences that result from the program, instructional material, or procedure consistent with the intended outcomes for the experience?"

From this question two others are derived, and thus are established two pursuant lines of inquiry: (1) What are the greatest deficiencies of the youth program, instructional material, or procedures in comparison with the appropriate learning experiences for the intended learning outcomes? (2) What suggestions about improvement of the instructional material or procedure can be deduced from descriptions of their uses?

The second of these questions is the crux of formative evaluation. It leads to the gathering of descriptive data about the usefulness of the learning which occurred, the level of motivation involved, and the learning gains at several points in the series of instructional experiences. The particular data collected and the resultant findings are used in the creative process of improvement of the materials and procedures. Thus, formative evaluation is a major means of improving learning effectiveness.

The probability of any given brief teaching experience or a one- or two-hour program leading directly to life-changing consequences is remote.

Formative evaluation is ordinarily associated with the pilot study of effectiveness of a new instructional material or with the early assessment of a new program. As such, formative evaluation is expected to lead to changes. After a youth program has gotten up and running, continuing to carry on formative evaluation makes sense only if change and improvement is possible. If, however, the only decision the program will face is whether or not to continue, formative evaluation is less important than summative evaluation.

SUMMATIVE EVALUATION

As its name implies, summative evaluation occurs at the end of a program. It is the final form of evaluation, asking, "Did we accomplish our intended outcomes?"

When summative evaluation occurs, there is no longer any time to make adjustments in the program; the program is completed. Summative evaluation does provide, however, the basis for making changes in the program the next time it is operated. Summative evaluation gives a basis for judgment of the worth of the effects of a youth ministry program, material, or experience. It is generally based upon measurements of the learning that are applied in real situations. Such measurements are assessed against either pretest data, taken before the program experience, or against the specifications of intended outcomes, or both. Summative evaluation, at its best, is a judgment of the ultimate value or worth of a series of youth programs, certain materials, a series of experiences, several months or even a year's worth of youth min-

istry, or even several years of youth ministry. These agreed-upon value positions determine the degree of achievement acceptable for the desired outcomes.

When issues regarding value positions are left unresolved, summative evaluation is often diverted to focus on other, less worthy questions than the worth of the learning gained. For example, it is common to find summative evaluations concentrating on the leaders' and/or parents' opinions or estimates of the worth of the experience, the students' liking or disliking of experiences and materials as reported by opinion surveys, and the use of highly subjective and nonrepresentative anecdotes as a basis for passing judgments. This sort of evaluation is potentially misleading unless kept in its place within a more comprehensive evaluative framework.

Measurement problems also thwart well-intentioned summative evaluation. Verbal responses in the affective and existential domains often bear little resemblance to the actual behaviors. ("What you *are* speaks so loudly I cannot hear what you say.") Verbal data on written tests or interviews rarely can be taken at face value. It is too easy to misrepresent oneself, enhancing one's ego or suppressing guilt and fears; and even when people want to be "open" and honest they may not be sure enough of their own feelings to be able to speak or write with confidence. Since unobtrusive observation of the behaviors that reflect true emotion are awkward and usually costly, verbal self-report is usually utilized to get quantifiable data. The validity of such data is always open to challenge. It is better to use less expensive means to obtain limited unobtrusive measurements that are reliable than to obtain much more data of unknown and unknowable reliability. Unreliable data are dangerous.

Currently, the accepted way to begin the design of an instructional system or component is to carefully specify intended behavioral outcomes or objectives. This causes another problem of evaluation: an overly ambitious assumption tends to accompany the emphasis on behavioral objectives—if a learning objective is well-defined it is likely to be achieved. The tragedy of this assumption is that one tends to overanticipate results from a given learning experience. Behavioral objectives have a characteristic tone of finality. For example, when confronted by the question, "How do you know God exists?" a young person might respond, "I know because the Bible tells me so." This has the ring of "always and forever." But experienced educators are familiar with the tentative nature of new learning and the distinct possibility that a learner will know something today, and yet tomorrow will know it in a different way with a different meaning. The probability of any given brief teaching experience or a one- or two-hour program leading directly to life-changing consequences is remote. Thus it seems unfair—if not irresponsible—to take a list of ambitious intentions for a particular program or a given teaching material or experience and evaluate them exclusively on the basis of pretest and posttest of these traits or behaviors in the youth.

Instead, responsible evaluation looks at the larger scope of a series of learning experiences. Rather than picking out the minor contributions of some small portion of the series, such as the learning gain in a particular lesson, the particulars are better examined as they relate to some larger whole. Obsession with objectives at the expense of concern for the larger picture or outcomes can result in a fragmented and faulty evaluation.

The sources of worthy questions for summative evaluation will certainly include whatever general statements may already exist, yet inference and extrapolation will be needed in order to convert generalizations into appropriately specific questions. Useful questions that can lead to summative evaluation of youth ministry experiences usually can be inferred from the values implicit in the program's stated purposes and general intended outcomes.

For example, if a value is held that a learning experience should be meaningful, then it is possible to evaluate by comparing the intended messages with the messages received. Youth can be asked directly what they thought was meaningful. Their replies would then be compared to what the designers of the learning experience thought would be meaningful. Or, if the capability of a learning experience to hold the interest of the learner is valued, an evaluation can be based on an assessment comparing immediate and long-term recall, or comparing the intended and actual responsiveness of a learner or group of learners. Evaluations may also be based on investigation of the target audience through an intermediary person or group, for example, asking teachers or parents if they thought the experiences were meaningful or of interest to the youth.

Sample questions of the sort that a summative evaluation might attempt to answer through descriptive research are the following:

1. Did the learning experience or program carry a message that is meaningful to the intended youth?
2. Was the learning experience or program recognizable in relation to needs the youth see as significant?
3. Did the learning experience or program tend to cause the youth to apply themselves to higher levels of spiritual commitment than those they currently hold?
4. Did the learning experience or program affect behavior and being, and, if so, in

desirable directions? To what degree are they changed?

The heart of assessment in the typical summative evaluation is this:

5. Did the particular program or ministry accomplish what was intended or needed? A secondary but also important question asks whether or not it was the actual program itself or some other event that led to the actual outcomes.

The basis for assessment in summative evaluation is usually the intended outcomes. What actually results from an educational program is compared with what was intended, and is judged to have reached or not reached satisfactory levels of outcome. These five questions are *summative* in nature. Their answers, in the affirmative, would seem to be basic to any claims for the satisfactory performance of any nonformal education program.

FOUR STEPS FOR MAKING SUMMATIVE AND FORMATIVE EVALUATIONS

Since the distinction between formative and summative is concerned with the *purpose* of evaluation, these terms do not necessarily indicate separate kinds of data gathering or different kinds of concerns about reliability and validity. Formative evaluation is intended to provide information on which judgments can be made about the effectiveness and worth of the educational experience and the materials and procedures that produced it while the experience is occurring. Summative evaluation's purpose is limited to the value of repeating the experience, modifying it, or dropping it completely.

Most competent evaluations are based on a series of four steps or stages. The first stage is *description;* on this is built *measurement;* on measurements are built *assessments;* and then, by bringing values to bear on the assessments, one can make *evaluations.*

The *description* of observed effects is a necessary first step. What has happened as a result of the program being evaluated? Usually these descriptions are verbal, though graphic and pictorial descriptions are often more meaningful. The *measurement* step is necessary if clear-cut assessment is to follow. That differences may exist can sometimes be determined "by inspection," but without measurements (expressions of the descriptions in quantitative terms) the significance of the contrasts can be stated only subjectively.

Comparisons of two or more measurements constitutes *assessment.* Two scores representing two youth can be used to assess that one has achieved more than the other. Two measurements taken on the same learner at different times can be used to assess that a learning gain has taken place. But to say that the gain is important, that the learner has achieved well, or that the competency is adequate requires a step beyond assessment; such judgments are *evaluations.* Evaluation is the process of putting a value judgment on the conclusions of an assessment. Or, putting it another way, evaluation is judgment of the worth or importance of assessments.

That "goodness" or value is very much a relative matter in evaluation is illustrated by the contrast between conclusions one draws from two different value positions: assuming that youth workers are concerned about both *growth* and *competency,* each can be taken as a value position. Assume that the scores in figure 1 are for a set of five learners. (The students are named Angela, Bob, Carlo, Dominique, and Eric.)

Which learner did *better?* Who is the *best* or who is *better* cannot be answered until we take a value position. For example, if one assumes that competency is the value ("competency is more important than growth") and thus the highest score is better, then clearly Angela is more competent in this behavior or knowledge—before and after the learning experi-

PreTest Scores	PostTest Scores	Assessment (Discrepancy)	% Change
A 14	A 18	A +4	A +26%
B 12	B 14	B +2	B +17%
C 10	C 14	C +4	C +40%
D 7	D 14	D +7	D +50%
E 4	E 9	E +5	E +125%

Figure 1

ence. Eric remains the least competent. Bob, Carlo, and Dominique seem now to be equally competent. This evaluation is based on an assessment of the differences of the various posttest scores in light of the competency value position. Thus, when we note that Angela "did better," we are evaluating on the basis of competency.

If we accept another value position, that growth is more important than competency, then Eric "did better." In terms of growth, Eric's 125 percent gain is the largest, and for this value position the largeness of gain is the basis of judgment or evaluation. Note that this evaluation uses assessment data from the pretests and posttests expressed as amount of percentage differences between the two.

In evaluating an instructional material or procedure, we are sometimes concerned more about growth than competency. This is especially true when no common agreement exists about what constitutes competency in a given area. In youth ministry, however, the skills and concepts being taught are commonly "practical," with fairly easily observed applications and consequences. Thus it is especially important for youth ministry to accept responsibility for providing effective learning experiences, to state the levels of both growth and competency intended, and to evaluate accordingly.

The quest for learning effectiveness is a continuous process. Providing experiences that will lead to spiritual changes and transformations in a learner's life is a most demanding

task. It is not enough that a certain experience would "reasonably" or "logically" lead to transformation of life; the real issue is whether the experience does, in fact, lead to effective learning that is transformational. Effective, transformative learning requires a process of continual development, not merely a good delivery system or a charismatic, fun-loving youth pastor.

The process through which learning effectiveness can be assured is a series of four steps. The first and fourth steps are both concerned with design and planning, thus three different types of activities can best be seen as a recurring cycle (see fig. 2).

The *design* step consists of three functions: First, *specify intended outcomes*, being as specific as one can, given the nature of spiritual formation, nurture, and discipleship. Second, *describe* in as much detail possible the youth group population. Third, *plan* the program or teaching-learning experience.

The *operate* step consists of four functions. The first step is to *develop* the program and/or instructional materials. Second, *teach* those who will operate and use it. Third, *develop* logistic and administrative support systems. The final step is to *operate* the program.

The *evaluate* step is made up of six functions. First, *establish* criteria and state value positions. Second, *collect* pretest data on the target population, whenever possible using quantifiable data. Third, *observe and describe* the program or experiences. This can be both

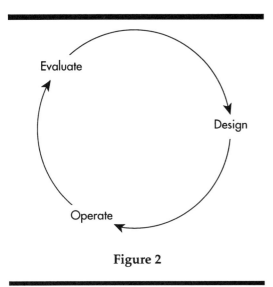

Figure 2

qualitative as well as quantitative data. The fourth step is to *collect* quantitative posttest data. Fifth, *assess* (compare) data; this also should be quantitative. Lastly, *evaluate* against criteria and values.

Some common mistakes occur in the process of building an evaluation component for any program; these can be avoided. Primary mistakes arise when rival hypotheses—that is, some other reasonable ways—are equally valid to explain the outcomes observed. It is important to be able to rule out these rival ways of explaining the observations, thus making evaluation honest. Several actions help rule out basic rival hypotheses.

The first rival hypothesis is that the youth already had acquired the learning that was said to have resulted from the program or instruction. The way to rule out this explanation is to collect pretest and posttest data, observing the youth before and after the program or instruction. One could give a quiz or an adult could spend a week or more selectively observing the youth before and then again after the program. These would determine that indeed the young people did not possess the qualities being taught before the teaching-learning experience, but that they did subsequent to it.

A second rival hypothesis is that those who participated in the program are somehow different from others who did not. In fact, this is true because some did attend and the others did not participate, for whatever reasons. The only way to avoid this problem is to do a random sample to observe both those who attended and those who did not. Or, on the other hand, one could observe everyone in the group, both participants and nonparticipants of the experience being evaluated.

A third rival hypothesis is that the evaluators see what they want to see. The best way to avoid this is not to rely on personal judgments and others' opinions. Rather, seek to quantify as much as possible all the observations. This may be more difficult to do in some youth ministry settings, but it should be attempted as much as possible. Relying on personal judgments and others' opinions may lead to subjectivism rather than objective observations.

Lastly, a rival hypothesis may be that youth will tell the evaluators what they think the evaluators want to hear. The way to avoid this is not to use direct opinion questions. Instead, use nonobtrusive observations, such as asking someone to observe youth for a week in a certain environment and to note their behavior on a checklist. The checklist becomes a quantified measurement device that will help fulfill the evaluation.

EVALUATION MODELS

The simplest model for evaluating youth ministry programs and experiences is to measure intended outcomes compared to the actual outcomes. The simplicity of this model is that it requires that the program state from the very beginning what it will strive to accomplish in the lives of the youth involved. Measurements taken look for these intentions to be actualized in the lives of the learners. Assessment discrepancies between the intended outcomes and the actual outcomes are the raw data to which one applies the criteria for the success or failure of the experience being evaluated. Judging the value of that discrepancy is the crucial evaluative action.

A more complex evaluation is of even greater benefit, however. Such an evaluation takes time and energy, but for what it requires in work, it more than returns in thoroughness. If youth workers are interested in determining the effectiveness and value of their ministry, then what follows will give adequate support for understanding the process of evaluation. Figure 3 provides a more detailed approach to evaluation.

EVALUATION MODEL
Rationale

Adequacy of philosophy, theology, and purpose of organization.
Relevance and significance of rationale for today's situation.

1. Intentions	2. Observations	3. Discrepancies	4. Criteria	5. Judgments and Feedback
A. Intended antecedents	A. Actually observed	Column 1 – Column 2 = Column 3	Criteria to be used to determine acceptable levels of discrepancies.	Ascribe worth to findings of discrepancies between intentions and observations.
1. in youth	1. in youth	Differences between what was intended and what actually was observed. Note: one should not assume that observations are 100% accurate and represent what actually occurred. There is always the chance that one's observations were inaccurate and that actual effects were not adequately measured.	Two questions: 1. What are criteria for A, B, C? 2. Have they been achieved? Example of criteria or standard: "85% of learners will . . ." implies effectiveness of progress being evaluated.	Based on criteria. Judgment = good, bad, medium. Feedback = where does improvement need to be made?
2. in youth worker	2. in youth worker			
3. in environment	3. in environment			
B. Intended Transactions and Interactions	B. Actual Transactions and Interactions			
1. Youth behavior	1. Youth			
2. Youth worker behavior	2. Youth worker			
3. Total experience	3. Total experience			
C. Intended Outcomes	C. Actual Effects found in youth:			
1. Know	1. Knowledge			
2. Feel	2. Feeling			
3. Do	3. Behavioral change			
4. Be	4. Core of being changed			

Figure 3

Rationale Questions

The rationale questions in figure 3 focus on the philosophical issues. They ask whether there is sufficient reasoning behind program design and development. Many people ignore this step, but if they do so they have no definitive rationale for either the program or subsequent evaluation. These are basic rationale questions:

1. Are purposes defined relevant to contemporary needs and conditions?

2. Has the present statement of purpose been reviewed within a reasonable period of time? Does it clearly delineate the roles of youth ministry in the church? Does it specify the long-term outcomes and constituencies clearly? Does it express a philosophy and theology of ministry and teaching-learning that is congruent with modern knowledge about youth as learners? Are the purposes significant and relevant in the light of contemporary conditions?

The previous comments regarding the first part of context and program evaluation (pp. 155–156) are germane here.

Intended Antecedents

Intended antecedents (fig. 3, col. 1A) are those requirements needed as foundational input to do effective program design and development. The previous comments on the second part of context evaluation (pp. 155–56) apply here. The issues associated with intended antecedents are as follows:

1. Have surveys of these needs and interests of individuals, organizations, and communities been made within a reasonable period? Is some individual or group taking responsibility for sensing the changing needs and interests from contacts with community leaders, the mass media, and professional literature? Are the techniques we are using for the collection and analysis of data about needs and interests in step with advancing survey technology? Do

the assessed needs include predicted future needs as well as identified present needs?

2. Have the outcomes been reviewed within a reasonable period of time? Are they clearly related to assessed needs?

3. Is the desired youth target group clearly defined? Is the promotion campaign adequately planned and efficiently carried out? Do promotion materials accurately reflect the quality and spirit of the program? Are the various media being used appropriately and effectively? Are the results of the various elements of promotion evaluated adequately? Is the program being adequately interpreted to the church at large and to the community?

4. Are the youth workers and supporting staff adequate in number to the needs of the program? Does the staff perform in accordance with stated expectations? Is there adequate differentiation and yet flexibility in role definitions? Is there a spirit of teamwork? Do staff members involve participants and committee members in sharing responsibilities and rewards imaginatively? Are there good working conditions, adequate salaries (where appropriate), and sound personnel policies and practices for paid and unpaid ("volunteer") staff? Are staff members paying adequate attention to their own continuing self-development? Are they good role models for youth and new staff?

5. Are the criteria of selection of staff clear, adequate, and in keeping with principles of developmental learning? Are they applied? Is compensation on a professional basis? Is it competitive with other churches? Are new youth workers given adequate orientation and individual coaching? Is adequate in-service leadership development and supervision given to all the youth workers? Do they perceive it as a program of continuing self-directed self-development? Are the performances of youth workers periodically assessed?

6. Are the meeting rooms adequate in number, size, flexibility, comfort, and attractive-

ness? Do leaders and instructors arrange rooms for maximum informality and interaction? Are the lighting, ventilation, and storage facilities adequate? Are the physical facilities maintained in good condition? Is there adequate program equipment? Are facilities and equipment properly safeguarded and maintained in good condition? Are the youth workers given sufficient help in using the physical facilities well? Is provision made for the replacement or renewal of equipment and facilities before they deteriorate? Are the space and equipment used as close to capacity as is practicable? Are the facilities adequate, attractive, and efficient?

Intended Transactions

Intended transactions (fig. 3, col. 1B) focus upon the interpersonal relationships that are part of the design, development, and execution of a youth program. The issues for intended transactions are as follow:

1. Are all participants (youth and youth workers) treated with warmth, dignity, and respect at all points of contact? Are the rich experiences of participants being used to the fullest extent in policy making, planning, management, learning, and evaluation? Do we know in what way the participants feel they are being treated as more or less human and appropriately for their ages and stages in their experience with us?

2. Is a sense of continuity provided by a dynamic theme, activity sequences, and time schedule? Does an interesting space pattern emerge from the rhythm of activities, varying depth of activities, and control of size of activities? Is the tone of the program one of warmth, varying emphases, and personalization? Is the color of the program bright and warm, as conveyed by publicity materials, the arrangement and decoration of physical facilities, and the youth workers themselves? Is the texture of the program interesting, rich, and functional?

Does the design make use of a variety of formats for learning appropriately? Does the program design demonstrate unity, balance, and integrity with other programs in the church?

3. Are transactions clearly related to assessed needs? Are they developmentally based, that is, on the developmental stages/levels of the youth and for their development?

Intended Outcomes

Intended outcomes (fig. 3, col. 1C) focus on anticipated, desired, and planned-for results of the execution of the program. The basic questions here are as follow:

1. What will the learners be expected to *know* when they finish? (Cognitive outcomes)
2. What will the learners be expected to *feel* when they finish? (Affective outcomes)
3. What will the learners be expected to *do* when they finish? (Behavioral outcomes)
4. What will the learners be expected to *be* when they finish? (Existential outcomes)

Observations

Observations (fig. 3, col. 2A, B, C) are made in each of the areas already stated under Intentions (col. 1). The goal of this part of evaluation is to determine what actually happened during the teaching-learning process. At this point, no value is placed on outcomes observed; that comes later (col. 5).

Youth workers who seek to evaluate a part or all of their program need to be sensitive in making ongoing observations about the youth ministry. Data can be collected through written instruments such as surveys or even "tests" that seek to determine how much of what was taught has actually been learned.

Observations can also be made less obtrusively by watching youth in action or soliciting comments from other people who are with the youth through the week. For example, parents, peers, or school teachers can be asked what differences they have observed in youth behavior.

Evaluation instruments need not be major written documents or complicated endeavors. The simpler the instrument, the less likely that errors will be made. Youth workers are not concerned with scientific studies such as might appear in a psychology journal; they merely need to know what happened as a result of the intended actions planned for youth. Observation will provide adequate answers.

Discrepancies

Discrepancies (fig. 3, col. 3) are determinated according to a simple formula: Column 1 minus column 2 equals column 3. This formula discloses the difference between what was intended and what was achieved. In the real world we seldom achieve all that we hope for; many things can go wrong—and *do* go wrong—and do not work out as we planned. Programs do not run with 100 percent efficiency. There will almost always be some discrepancies between planned outcomes or intentions and what we observe.

So far, however, we still have not reached the point of making an actual evaluation. We are still on the way, and there are two more steps to fulfill.

Criteria

Criteria (fig. 3, col. 4) that will be used to make judgments of value—the actual evaluation—need to be stated before we make observations. Youth workers should state what level of accomplishment they will accept as valuable. That is, they should be willing to commit to a definite statement that they will accept a certain level or degree of achievement. This might be expressed as a percentage of intended outcomes achieved or as certain repeated behaviors or as a certain level of responses to survey questions.

The critical issue is that before the evaluators begin to observe, they determine the criteria for acceptable levels of accomplishment. For example, a unit of personal Bible study might have been taught with these intended outcomes:

- Learners will be able to list and describe the major elements in three means of Bible study. (Cognitive outcome)
- Learners will choose one of the three means of personal Bible study for their own use. (Affective outcome)
- Learners will use their chosen means four out of seven days per week, for a minimum of fifteen minutes per day, for the next twelve weeks. (Behavioral outcome)
- Learners will continue to do personal Bible study for the next forty weeks after the twelve-week minimum is completed. (Existential outcome)

With these outcomes in mind, we can state criteria looking for 95 percent accomplishment of outcome one (cognitive), 85 percent of outcome two (affective), and 65 percent of outcome three (behavioral). The percentages would be determined beforehand by the evaluators.

The critical question is what criteria to use in determining the acceptable degree of discrepancy between intentions and observations. Realistic expectation is an important consideration. We humans strive for perfection, knowing that we will not measure up completely; therefore, the standards must be realistic. Evaluation should not be a means to depress us or make us feel like failures. Rather, evaluation should help us to know where we need to continue to work and make improvements.

Judgment and Feedback

Judgement and feedback (fig. 3, col. 5) complete the evaluation process. These require the evaluators to determine the work or value of the ministry—that is, to make an evaluation or judgment of the worth of the findings. Intentions were stated at the development of the program, and criteria established at the beginning of the evaluation process. Observations were made during the program (formative evaluation) or at the end of the program (summative evaluation), and discrepancies were noted. Criteria were used to determine the degree to which intentions were actually achieved. Now the values inherent in the criteria are used to express a final judgment: *good, bad, medium,* or some other evaluative word.

Judgment, however, is still not the final step. The last step is to determine what should be done next with the program: Should it be continued as it is, or discontinued or modified? The judgment must therefore include not only the worth of the program, but also what feedback should be given regarding the program (or unit of study or planned experience of the youth ministry).

Only when feedback has been expressed is the evaluation process completed. The process calls for responses to what has been determined. Evaluation is never sufficient if it only judges something *good, bad,* or *average.* Rather, evaluation always ends in feedback for improvement.

BASIC PRINCIPLES OF EVALUATION

Principle One. When less-than-effective spiritual learning has occurred, it is more likely a flaw in the program, instructional process, and/or the plan than an inadequacy or failure of the learners. Lack of effective learning is a sign that the program must be evaluated from start to finish, beginning with context evaluation, program planning evaluation, formative, and summative evaluation.

Principle Two. Evaluation is part of the planning process. In that process it appears toward the end of a flow chart. But in reality, it begins at the beginning and continues throughout the whole planning process. Context and program planning evaluations should flow throughout the whole process of planning. Formative evaluations are operative from the beginning of the execution of the program.

Principle Three. Evaluation is not grading. It is feedback for improvement, growth, and development. Youth workers should be helped to feel positive about evaluation rather than threatened by it.

Principle Four. The process of evaluation places a value on certain outcomes and their relative success or failure, on the accomplishment or nonaccomplishment of outcomes, on the achievement of predetermined competencies, and on observed strengths and weaknesses. These value perspectives need to be agreed upon *before* formative and summative evaluations begin.

Principle Five. The evaluation process answers certain basic questions before the process begins. (1) Why evaluate? (2) Who requests the evaluation? (3) What use is planned for the evaluation and by whom? (4) Who will pay for the evaluation costs and how much resources can be given to it? (5) Who will oversee and direct the evaluation? (6) Who needs to be involved? (7) Is there anyone with a hidden agenda who wants to make the evaluation say something? (8) What are the value positions to be used to determine if something is successful?

Principle Six. Ownership of the planning and execution of the evaluation process needs to be shared. Ownership extends to the evaluators, the evaluatees, the users of the program, and the decision makers in the youth ministry and the church.

Principle Seven. Many things and people could be evaluated, such as the following:

- Cost-effectiveness of the program
- Teachers' or leaders' behaviors

- Behaviors of the youth
- The learning environment (such as facilities and equipment)
- Curricular materials
- The degree to which leaders fulfill their roles
- Effectiveness of planning
- Leaders' or teachers' characteristics
- Preparation for leading
- Handling a group of youth
- Facilitation of learning by the youth
- Development of close relationships with youth
- Actual change in knowledge, feelings, behaviors, and being on the part of the youth involved

There are more items that could be evaluated than time and money allow. Evaluators need to determine ahead of time what is most important to know, and to major on those, leaving minor issues alone.

Principle Eight. The plan for evaluation must start at the beginning of a youth program plan. After-thought evaluation is better than none, but it is less effective when it is tagged on at the end of the plan. When evaluation is planned for from the very beginning, it can then be viewed as a means for feedback to improve the program all along the planning and execution processes. Leaders are less likely to fear something that they help to develop and operate.

Principle Nine. Evaluation needs leadership. A leader must grasp the importance of evaluation and operate it as if the program's and ministry's lives depended on that evaluation. In a way, they do!

Appendices

A ppendix A is a handbook for youth workers developed and used in one church. We include it here to illustrate one relatively successful attempt to help adult and youth leaders know what their roles were, what the youth ministry entailed, and why. The handbook is founded on the basic philosophy of youth ministry explained in this textbook, but it also reflects the particular emphases of that church and should not necessarily be imitated in every part. Therefore it is not the final word, but it demonstrates one way to design and develop an effective youth ministry that is incarnational, agapic, and developmental.

Appendix B is an annotated bibliography of books that focus on adolescents and youth ministry. Even though the bibliography contains a large number of entries, it should not be regarded as complete, because many pertinent books, video and audio tapes, and other resource materials are not included.

Appendix A

A SAMPLE YOUTH WORKERS' HANDBOOK

The following document is a handbook written for a local church's youth ministry. It is included here as a sample. Each church should prepare its own handbook for youth ministry. The particular contents will vary from church to church and from year to year even though the philosophy on which they are based does not change.

Youth Workers' Handbook

YOUTH DIVISION

Contents

1. INTRODUCTION

2. OVERALL OBJECTIVES AND PHILOSOPHY

3. ORGANIZATION OF THE YOUTH DIVISION

4. PERSONNEL

5. THE PROGRAM OF THE JUNIOR HIGH DEPARTMENT

6. THE PROGRAM OF THE HIGH SCHOOL DEPARTMENT

7. THE PROGRAM OF THE POST-HIGH DEPARTMENT

8. FINANCES

9. USE OF CHURCH PROPERTY

10. TRIPS AND INSURANCE

11. HOURS

---

1. INTRODUCTION

This handbook has been developed at the urging of various youth workers who over the years have expressed a desire to have a written body of information at their fingertips regarding the Youth Program in the church.

It is hoped that this handbook will be a useful tool for leadership development in the Youth Division and also be a primary source for information and reference for the youth workers. It is not exhaustive by any means nor does it purport to be so. It is a handbook and should be used therefore in conjunction with leadership seminars and informal leadership discussion.

2. THE OVERALL OBJECTIVES AND PHILOSOPHY

The Youth Program of the church exists to provide for Christian fellowship, instruction, worship, and service on the age levels of our various youth groups. It is an integral and necessary aspect of our total church program of spiritual formation, nurture, and discipleship. Its primary function is hardly one of baby-sitting teenagers. Nor does it exist to provide "Christian" entertainment or a substitute for public school events. The church is not equipped for either entertainment or competition with the public school program.

The church desires that the Youth Ministry provide an atmosphere in which young people will come to know the Lord Jesus Christ as Savior and Lord, will submit to the authority of the Scriptures in their lives, and will become Christian leaders in both the secular and religious communities.

It is for the achievement of these goals that we have a Youth Division, adult and adolescent leaders, and a professional staff to help administer the program.

3. ORGANIZATION OF THE YOUTH DIVISION

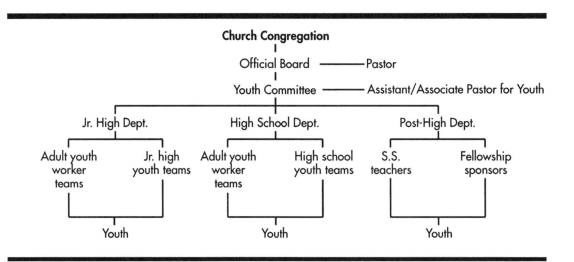

4. PERSONNEL

I. The role of the Youth Pastor in relation to the various agencies and personnel of the Youth Division. The Youth Pastor:

A. Functions as executive secretary of the Youth Committee to carry out the directives of that Committee.

B. Provides leadership for the philosophy, direction, goals, and forward movement of the youth program of the church.

C. Is the chief administrator of the total Youth Program.

D. Is directly responsible to the Pastor for supervision.

E. Wworks with the Chair of the Youth Committee, the General Sunday School Superintendent, the Assistant General Sunday School Superintendent, departmental superintendents, and all youth leaders as an advisor, helper, and leadership development facilitator.

F. Provides for an effective program of coordinated and meaningful spiritual formation, nurture, and discipleship of, for, by, and with youth. (Youth pastor and all paid and unpaid youth ministry workers work together.)

G. Meets monthly with youth workers and youth team leaders and quarterly with Sunday School leadership to discuss plans, program, activities, and problems, and for prayer.

H. Is always available for questions; any problems should be brought to him or her.

I. Provides effective resources and sources of program ideas and materials.

J. Is responsible for the Youth Program materials and equipment.

K. Makes informal contacts with youth by visiting their "turf"—schools, games, plays, sports activities, etc.

L. Is pastor to all adult and adolescent workers and to all the youth in general. He or she is *the* guarantor of the church's youth.

II. The Youth Committee shall be appointed/elected and shall serve its terms and provide for the execution of its role as provided in our Church Constitution and By-Laws and denominational book of order. The Youth Committee:

A. Is responsible for over-all policies and direction of the various parts of the Youth Program.

B. Is responsible for the recruitment, selection, enlistment, leadership development, appointment, reappointment yearly, and supervision of all youth leader-sponsors, including Sunday school teachers and Sunday school departmental superintendents.

C. Functions as a sounding board and advisory board for the Youth Program.

D. Works with the General Sunday School Superintendent and other Sunday school officers and departmental leaders in correlating and planning the total program for our youth. This is done by a quarterly planning session involving all the youth leaders of all agencies. They will meet according to age departments to accomplish the above. The Youth Committee shall sponsor these each quarter.

E. Is responsible to supervise and encourage the various youth leaders in all agencies of the Youth Division. These youth leaders should attend Youth Committee meetings when they are invited to do so or when they have a personal desire to conduct business with the committee. Written reports should be submitted semiannually in writing to the Youth Committee from each age department in the Youth Division. The superintendent of each Sunday school department shall be responsible to provide this semiannual report.

III. Adult Youth Workers

A. General Qualifications. They shall:
1. Be called by God to the work.
2. Be spiritually minded:
    a. A Christian
    b. Giving evidence of the "fruit of the Spirit" in personal life
    c. "In the world, yet not of it," and
    d. A person of the Word and prayer
3. Understand or seeking to understand the age group with which working.
4. Love youth and want to work with them.
5. Be emotionally stable.
6. Be able to inspire and lead.
7. Be consistent in temperament and dealings.
8. Be intelligent, self-confident, desirous of success.
9. Be able to share leadership with others.
10. Be willing to work into and within the program of the church under the various appointed and elected leaders, including the youth themselves as leaders.

11. Be willing to participate in the leadership education provided by the church through its own facilities and the facilities of outside organizations: monthly Sunday school leaders classes, leadership seminars, conventions, workshops.

12. Be allowed to lead though they are not members of this church. However, in place of membership they will be interviewed by the Youth Committee; their acceptance will be based on the results of said interview.

13. Generally be responsible to provide leadership and enabling of youth to grow and develop in all areas of their lives.

B. Youth Workers—Sunday School Teachers (See also III.A)

1. Selection—by the Youth Committee
2. Responsibilities—teachers shall:

   a. Know youth: general characteristics of age group and personal characteristics of each youth.

   b. Prepare Sunday school lessons conscientiously with the learners and their needs in mind; remember the responsibility that God places on leaders of young people.

   c. Present the lesson in a way that will help transform the lives of the learners.

   d. Provide informal get-togethers for the class to enable the teachers to know and understand their learners and to help the class to be a fellowshipping small group. These activities should be coordinated with the Youth Calendar to avoid conflicts.

   e. Set an example as a mature believer in church attendance, devotional life, and daily Christian conduct.

   f. Work with the other agencies of the Youth Division by being willing to help when called upon, attend occasional meetings and socials, ball games, school activities, etc.

   g. Work under the direct supervision of the Departmental Superintendent and the Youth Pastor.

   h. Seek to meet the personal needs of the learners regarding the Christian walk.

   i. Visit each learner at least once each year in

his/her home or take each one out on a special occasion, for example, birthday or spiritual birthday.

    j. Contact absent youth.

    k. Work with the Sunday school Departmental Superintendent.

C. Youth Workers—Sponsors (See also III.4)

  1. Selection—by the Youth Committee

  2. Responsibilities—sponsors shall:

    a. Know youth: general characteristics of the age group and personal characteristics of each young person.

    b. Act as coach, not chief or chairperson.

    c. Work especially with the youth officers and youth in leadership to accomplish the anticipated outcomes of the program.

    d. Attend activities on a rotation basis with the other sponsors.

    e. Encourage the youth by setting an example in church attendance, personal Christian life, and daily devotions.

    f. Be responsible to the Youth Committee in particular for the general direction of the program; meet with the Committee when requested or when sponsors ask to meet with the Youth Committee.

    g. Work directly with the Youth Pastor to plan and execute the entire program.

D. Youth Leaders—Sunday School Department Superintendents

  1. Work closely with the Youth Pastor and the General Sunday School Superintendent for the general planning for the department.

  2. Help to develop, along with the Sunday school general staff and Youth Pastor, the appropriate curriculum for the department.

  3. Order the correct kind and amount of curriculum materials through the appointed channels for each session.

  4. Encourage the youth workers—teachers, sponsors, department leadership, Youth Committee.

  5. Lead the quarterly departmental meetings, in conjunction with the Youth Pastor of all workers in the department from all agencies of the departments. This meeting is to coordinate and plan for

the forthcoming quarter and evaluate the quarter just being completed.
6. See that each class in the department is properly organized, staffed, and taught.

E. Baby-sitting for Youth Workers' children. Baby-sitting service will be provided for or underwritten by the Youth Committee.

5. THE PROGRAM OF THE JUNIOR HIGH DEPARTMENT

I. Sunday School
A. Meaningful worship consisting of:
1. Music—this is the time to introduce both new and old hymns and contemporary songs of the church in an understanding and meaningful setting. Just singing to sing is an unworthy motive for worship singing.
2. Prayer—make this personal and real for all involved. Perfunctory prayer without relevance, or a vain repetition of last Sunday's prayer, has no place in worship.
3. Scripture reading—meaningful and relevant and understandable passages should be chosen. Use a modern translation (make copies for all to have the same version for the reading). Vary it with choral readings and responsive readings. Help youth to know the setting and general gist of the passage before they begin so they can understand what is being said. Reading Scripture in a void or just to read is unworthy of Scripture.
4. Offering—have a definite use for the offering and tell the young people how it is going to be used. Report back to them periodically what their monies are doing and how much they have given. Just taking an offering because it has always been done is an unworthy motive.
B. Announcements—make them short and to the point, but creative and interesting. Be brief!
C. Class period—every effort should be exerted to give as much time to the teacher as possible for his or her lesson. This should be done consistently each week so teachers can count on a weekly, specific minimum time of 45 minutes.
D. As much as possible, work with the various teenage leaders so that they can have as much actual leadership experience as possible in the Sunday school worship.

E. It is not necessary to have a worship time each Sunday as part of the Sunday school program.

II. Evening Program (Sunday night and/or week nights)

A. Singing—a singing group is a happy group. This is the place to teach new songs and to use the lighter gospel songs. Through the song leading program of the Youth Division, help the teenagers to lead singing, that is, encourage them to take the song leading course offered and then encourage them to actually lead in the meetings. Give them opportunities to do so. The same goes for accompanists.

B. Prayer—this is an opportunity for the junior highers to express themselves to God in front of a group.

C. Offering (if there is one)—it is the responsibility of the adult youth workers to help the young people decide where the offering should be used. Suggestions: support an orphan, buy books for church library or equipment for the Sunday school or Youth Division, or help a missionary child of the same age. Be sure to report back to the young people the amount collected, disbursed, and how it was used. Obtain thank you notes for the young people from persons helped by the youth.

D. Program—this is a presentation usually by the youth themselves of some relevant concern of the Christian life. The sponsors should work with a small group in preparation for this presentation. The sponsor is responsible to close the meeting with some pertinent, brief remark or summary. Occasionally a junior higher could do this. The program can also include adult workers or other adults or a media presentation.

E. Begin at the appointed time and end when the program is finished. There is no need to "fill up" the remaining minutes of the hour. Be finished by the designated time.

F. Suggestions for working with Jr. Highers

1. Help them to think and plan programs and socials—make it theirs.

2. Keep ideas within reason. Junior highers still do not have a tenacious spirit.

3. Remind them during the week of their forthcoming responsibilities. They forget too quickly and are not yet dependable.

4. "Love them and feed them."

G. Organization
   1. Diagram:

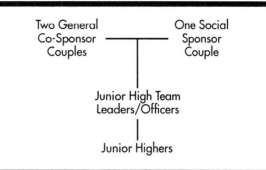

Two General Co-Sponsor Couples ——— One Social Sponsor Couple

Junior High Team Leaders/Officers

Junior Highers

2. Social Sponsor Couple works with the other sponsors and the social team in planning and executing the socials. There should be at least one social every four weeks and some more often than that at the discretion of the social committee. In planning and executing socials seek to get as many junior highers involved as possible.
   3. From year to year the actual offices of the group change so they have not been included here. The Sponsors and the Youth Pastor, with the approval of the Youth Committee, work out the offices.
   4. Nominations are by the Adult Workers/Sponsors through any of several methods.
   5. Officers should be elected for either a half-year or a full year. The young people should decide this for themselves *before* the election takes place.
H. Characteristics of a good Junior High Program:
   1. Variety—in people, activity, and materials
   2. Social activities
   3. Activity, liveliness
   4. Enthusiastic
   5. Accomplishes something worthwhile
   6. Spiritual
   7. Meets needs of youth attending
   8. Develops whole youth
   9. Leadership development

6. THE PROGRAM OF THE HIGH SCHOOL DEPARTMENT

(What follows is the handbook for one church's high school ministry, only slightly modified to serve as an example for other churches. It is included to demonstrate how one church sought to think through a ministry to, for, with, and by high schoolers. It illustrates the whole planning process for a high school ministry of spiritual formation, nurture, and discipline that is incarnational, agapic, and developmental. It should not be imitated in every part, but is offered as a commendable example.)

Preface

It is hoped that the following information will be of help to those involved in the Spiritual Formation, Nurture, and Discipleship (SFND) of our Senior Highs. The material presented is intended to give to each youth leader a picture of the total process of SFND in our High School Department and thereby help that leader see where he or she fits in. This in turn should produce a more meaningful participation on the part of that teacher or sponsor.

Not all of the following material is relevant to all leaders in the department, yet each should find that all of this gives a total picture of what is going on in the Senior High Department.

The material is still "rough"; it needs improvement in many respects. But only as it is put to the test will it have the rough spots smoothed out. Your comments, criticisms, and ideas will be greatly appreciated. Please feel free to express yourself in either a group or in personal contact. Together we will be able to make this work and thereby increase our own ministry to, for, with, and by Youth. The material is structured around six topics:

I. **Needs** (a lack that must be met) of our young people. We minister to the whole individual not just to his/her spiritual self. Therefore we must take into consideration the total individual and all the areas of his/her needs.

II. **Anticipated Outcomes** (anticipated goals, objectives toward which we strive, our goal in working with the young people) derived from the **Needs**.

III. **Program** (how to meet the **Needs** and **Anticipated Outcomes,** the various parts or agencies that help meet our objectives and needs).

IV. **Methods and Materials** (how to accomplish the **Program,** the ways and means of the work).

V. **Organization and Administration** (the most efficient way to accomplish all the above items).

VI. **Evaluation**—this is not included on the following pages because **Evaluation** comes only by careful reading of this material, criticizing it, modifying it, putting it into practice, and investigating to determine the results. Then an **Evaluation** can be made and the whole process begun all over to keep the total program working and meaningful to both leaders and senior highs.

I. NEEDS
(A lack that must be met)

A. Personal commitment to Jesus Christ as Savior and Lord
- Not just a decision (Jesus Christ is not just an "insurance policy" from hell)
- Find that Christ is a *real* Person with whom we have fellowship
- Learn to communicate with Christ
- Learn that fellowship with Christ is not relegated to "devotions," but is integral to each part of one's daily routine

B. Know and practice personal Christian living
- Seek to demonstrate the fruits of the Spirit in daily conduct
- Show Christ in all activities
- Know and practice what it means that Christ is relevant to all parts of life—school, recreation, work, home, church, etc.
- Make Jesus Christ Lord
- No division between the Christian life and daily existence
- Learn that love is from God and for the world. God "so loves" is a Christian's motivating force
- Motivate individuals to live for Christ daily in all places
- Know by experience the work and power of the Holy Spirit in one's life
- Service to the church and the world that God is love.

C. Understand and practice the Spirit-led life
- Lead a life filled by Spirit and demonstrating the fruit of the Spirit
- Know what the dangers of worldliness are
- Know the biblical principles of separation
- Help in applying principles to specific situations of life
- Know that the separated life is not only negative ("from" something) but also positive ("to" God)
- Begin to recognize, develop, and use our spiritual gifts

D. Have the feeling of being wanted and accepted, fitting into the group, feeling secure, belonging (this would be especially true of the fringe young people who are not very active in the program presently)

E. Social integration in Christian fellowship
- Know and practice social graces
- Expect that young people practice social graces
- Learn how to act in a group
- Learn how to act in various environments, for example, home versus retreat
- Learn how to act with and toward the opposite sex
- Learn how to have fun in a group without being destructive or overly boisterous
- Learn and respect property rights of others
- Learn to accept visitors and make them feel welcomed in the group

F. Self-acceptance
- Recognize and accept self for what he/she is regardless of personal development levels and thus enjoy a certain amount of security and personal worth

G. Direction in formulating a consistent philosophy of life, that is, a world and life view that includes a value system based on the revealed will of God. Philosophy of life includes: epistemology, metaphysics, ethics, morality, values, theology, culture, society
- Integrating these segments of reality into a biblically consistent pattern
- Ability to live consistently within this framework

H. Help to discover the will of God for one's life
- How God directs a Christian in general and the individual in particular
- Motivate the individual to be submissive to God's leading

I. Help in selecting a college, trade school, or vocational goal, in light of honest knowledge and an evaluation of gifts, assets and liabilities, opportunities, and circumstances

J. Learn how to control oneself in the light of one's increasing drive for independence and temptations to rebel
- Learn that parents are not as bad as they really seem to be
- Learn to continue to honor one's parents
- Continue to loosen the emotional and dependent ties with home and parents
- Learn to make and abide by one's own decisions
- Be responsible for one's actions regardless of the course of events

K. Be given the needed tools with which to grapple with the intellectual problems being confronted in school and in one's own thinking

- Tools: a strong personal faith in God based on Scripture
- Direct and honest answers to questions
- Foundation in understanding the contents and purposes of Scripture
- Help in thinking through questions and problems in the light of Scripture and present-day knowledge

L. Know and practice a Christian attitude toward sex

- Sex and sexual differences are God-given and therefore good
- Recognize the role of the sexes in our present culture and examine these demands in the light of the Scripture
- Dating and how to have a successful date: what to do and not to do; petting, necking, intercourse; realistic view of dating
- Preparation for serious dating, marriage, and family; correct ideas about all of this
- Premarital sex and homosexuality in light of Scripture and within one's culture and youth subcultures

M. Proper use of time, talents, and abilities

- Challenge to use these for God's honor and glory

N. Direction in using present energy, talents, and emotions for the church and Christ

- Becoming involved in ministry to the church, community, and world

O. Become engaged in personal sharing of one's faith

- Recognize the need for sharing the Good News
- Learn how to do it
- Provide opportunities for doing so

P. Direction and help in controlling emotions in relationship to all areas: physical, cognitive, affective, social, moral, and spiritual

Q. General psychological needs of all ages for all people to one degree or another:

security	self-confidence	popularity
acceptance	self-expression	importance
recognition	interdependence	self-determination

183

status	approval	excitement
usefulness	belonging	self-identity
independence	achievement	

R. Being able to cope with the social pressures of the peer group in high school with regard to Christian distinctives

S. Loyalty to the local church and to its program
- Encouragement to support the program of the church and especially the youth group
- Encourage young people to invite and bring out their friends

T. Continued development of a coordinated body

II. ANTICIPATED OUTCOMES
(Goal toward which we move based on the needs)

A. So teach the Word of God that the following will be possible:
  1. Know the Trinity and understand it as:
     Father—the Revealer, Worthy of Worship, Seeker
     Son—Jesus Christ, Savior and Lord of life, Creator, Begotten of Father
     Holy Spirit—Leader, Guide, Convictor of sin, Regenerator, Empowerer of daily spiritual walk.
  2. Understand one's role on earth in relation to God's will for him or her, applying this to the concrete facts of one's existence in society and especially the local community, including all the spheres of contact made by the teenager.
  3. Continue to mature in Christ by the power of God through the work of the Holy Spirit to grow as children of God, well-rooted in the local church and active in its support and in the propagation of the Gospel.
  4. Recognize the Bible as the inspired Word of God which is the revelation of himself to us through which we may come to know him.
  5. Become adequately equipped to handle the biblical materials so that questions and personal problems will be answered through use of the Scriptures.
  6. Have a working and practical knowledge of the biblical material and data.
B. Help realize that life plans can best be discovered and a philosophy of life can best be developed through a continual commitment to Jesus Christ.

    C. Help each individual formulate a consistent philosophy of life that is grounded in the Word of God and that can stand in a secular society.

    D. Give guidance from both adult guarantors and Scripture in making the great decisions in life: commitment to Christ, vocation, schooling, marriage, and ministry.

    E. Present opportunities to practice social graces and proper relationships between the sexes; fulfill the need for group activities.

    F. Develop a program that utilizes all the young people in its various parts and functions; put all to work and recognize their individual contributions to their teams.

    G. Provide instruction in how to use the Bible, how to study it.

    H. Provide instruction in how to have devotions and why.

    I. Help individuals understand themselves, accept themselves, and relate themselves adequately to others.

    J. Provide opportunities to use exuberant physical, emotional, and spiritual energies in constructive ways through various means (sports, projects, community service, church work, missions).

    K. Show the importance of the separated life for the believer.

    L. Give instruction and encouragement for witnessing in present situations and circumstances.

    M. Present needs and challenges of full-time Christian service.

    N. Present an understandable and realistic Christian view of sex, dating, marriage, and the family.

    O. Provide for basic psychological needs through the adult youth workers, staff, and program.

III. PROGRAM

    A. Parts of the Program, Various Agencies
        1. Sunday School
        2. Sunday evening or weeknight meetings
        3. Weekday activities and sports
        4. Socials
        5. Service projects
        6. Camping
        7. Informal, unplanned counseling and fellowship opportunities
        8. Winter Retreat

    B. General Role of the Above Agencies of the Program
        1. Sunday School
           a. To teach the Bible

    b. To confront each learner with the need to accept Jesus Christ as Savior and Lord

    c. To stimulate growth in Christian life and attitudes

    d. To provide opportunities for leadership development and exercise

    e. To provide a basis from which to work and numerical support for the other agencies of the youth ministry

    f. To provide for a limited amount of fellowship

    g. To provide for a limited amount of worship

    h. To provide for outreach

2. Evening Youth Group (Sunday or Weeknights)

    a. Determine a creative name

    b. To provide direct avenues for leadership development and exercise of leadership

    c. To provide another type of forum for spiritual growth and discipleship. Usually this is issue-centered and not a direct Bible study (as is Sunday school)

    d. To provide opportunities for formal and informal worship experiences

    e. To provide opportunities for outreach and informal evangelism

3. Weekday Sports Activities

    a. To evangelize young people

    b. To vitalize individuals' relationships to the church

    c. To provide opportunity to expend physical and emotional energy and to help in the coordination of the growing body and the acquiring of skills

    d. To instill in the individual that every part of one's activities has spiritual significance and implications

    e. To challenge each individual to consistent, daily Christian conduct

    f. To provide a means for reducing barriers to true Christian fellowship

4. Socials

    a. To provide a means of outreach for unchurched, unsaved, and infrequent attenders

    b. To provide opportunities for self-expression, fellowship, learning, and the practice of Christian social graces within an appropriate Christian environment

    c. To provide opportunity for leadership education and development

    d. To provide opportunity for use of gifts, talents, and abilities

    e. To introduce new members and prospective members to the department

    f. To provide means for reducing barriers to true Christian fellowship

    g. To demonstrate that Christian youth do know how to relax, have fun, and enjoy life

5. Service Projects/Ministry

    a. To provide opportunities for the constructive expression of one's Christian faith in the community at large and in the church

    b. To develop leadership qualities, abilities, and personal skills

    c. To provide experience-oriented learning opportunities

6. Camping

    a. To provide leadership development in an informal, relaxed atmosphere

    b. To help individuals acquire special outdoor skills

    c. To provide for social and fellowship activities and relationships

    d. To provide opportunities to appreciate the outdoors, nature, God's creation, and thereby God himself

    e. To provide opportunities for further outreach to the unsaved and unchurched and for a numerical increase in the department by bringing in new members

    f. To influence each participant by close personal contact with a counselor, encouraging Christian commitment, and/or continual, practical, daily Christian living

7. Informal, Unplanned Counseling and Fellowship Opportunities

    a. To influence the individual through personal, intimate contact, fostering Christian commitment and daily Christian living

    b. To help the individual in problem areas

    c. To discover the effectiveness of the total spiritual formation, nurture, and discipleship program of the High School Department and of the church

8. Winter Retreat

    a. To bring new youth into the group in an informal, fun atmosphere

b. To win unsaved to Christ

c. To build up Christian young people in Christ

d. To provide an opportunity for uniting group into a unified body through fellowship and common spiritual experiences

e. To have good, clean fun

IV. METHODS AND MATERIALS

A. Sunday School

1. Methods:

a. Teacher-directed activities (primarily teacher-led; on many occasions, youth should take a major and active part in actual teaching)

b. Small groups

c. Bible study emphasizing life-related situations

d. Provides for instruction and some worship on occasion

e. Outcome: transformation through information

2. Materials: Materials that enable study of appropriate portions of Scripture that are related to the lives of the learners, that enable active learning by youth, and that provide for the outworking of cognitive data in learners' lives. These materials need to fit into an overall curriculum plan.

B. Evening (Sunday/Weeknight) Youth Meetings, Socials, Weekday Activities, Service Projects, Camping

1. Methods:

a. Youth-centered activities. Youth learn by doing, active participation, therefore, use young people in planning and execution of ideas

b. Adult leaders are coaches, not chiefs or chaperons

c. Sufficient number of youth team leaders to enable the program to run smoothly

d. Enroll all members of the department in active participation as either team leaders or team members (all have some leadership function)

f. Obtain support of parents so they will encourage their youth to actively participate in the program

g. All programs including Sunday school programs stress active participation

2. Materials: Adapt "canned" programs, develop own, use videos, tape recordings, films, outside speakers (adults from church and in the community).

C. Counseling

1. Methods: Done by individual sponsors, peers, and

Youth Pastor as they are contacted by youth, or as leaders see need for it

2. Materials: None. "Counselors" should be competent to provide nonprofessional, noncrisis and crisis help. The church will enable youth workers to achieve at least a modicum of competence in this area and knowledge of community resources and people for referral.

V. ORGANIZATION AND ADMINISTRATION

A. Sunday School. High School Department Superintendent, teachers (youth workers), and youth. All team leaders of the high school program—teachers, Sunday school superintendent staff, and Youth Pastor—comprise the Sunday school leadership. This group will meet at least quarterly or on call to provide for the effective use of the Sunday school team.

B. Sunday/Weeknight Meetings. To be organized along the following lines and to include opportunities for the Sunday morning youth workers (commonly called "S.S. Teachers") to become better acquainted with their learners:

1. Youth Team Leaders of High School Department and Duties: All are automatically part of the High School Sunday school leadership [The following is one way—not the only way—to organize the leadership teams.]

a. President
(1) Presides over business meetings, keeping them running smoothly
(2) Knows team members personally
(3) Plans with adult youth workers and Youth Pastor for work sessions and retreats for cabinet
(4) Inspires cabinet with enthusiasm, presents new ideas, proposes projects, and communicates with other groups to gain these new ideas
(5) Ex-officio member of each standing committee
(6) Remains responsible for all regular meetings yet endeavors to have other team leaders do their part
(7) Makes all feel "in" during socials and fellowship hours
(8) Have firmly in mind the purpose and function of the President as a Christian leader, as well as know the purpose and function of the group

189

b. Vice-President and Executive Program Chair
    (1) Presides in the absence of the President at team meetings
    (2) Exercises leadership within the group
    (3) Responsible along with a committee for one program per month
    (4) Be generally responsible for smooth operation of all programs each month through Associate Program Chairmen and Missions Chairman
c. Secretary-Treasurer
    (1) Handles all monies (offerings, socials, retreats)
    (2) Reports at all business meetings and cabinet meetings the financial standing of the group
    (3) Keeps business meeting minutes
    (4) Writes thank you notes to various hostesses and outside speakers
d. Two Associate Program Chairs
    (1) Work under the direction of the Executive Program Chair and adult youth workers
    (2) Each responsible with a team of his/her choice for one Sunday evening (or other weeknight) program per month
e. Social Co-Chairs
    (1) Plan and execute the socials
    (2) Plan a social calendar with adult youth workers, social team, and Youth Pastor
    (3) Choose a committee for each social to work out details
f. Publicity Chair
    (1) Works with other teams, committees, and Chairs to get out effective publicity
    (2) Have a team that is available to produce catchy publicity
g. Retreat Chair
    (1) Chooses a team with which to work out details of retreats with adult youth workers and Youth Pastor
    (2) Plans and executes the retreat
    (3) Works with Publicity Chair and Social Chair with details of the retreat
h. Visitor Chair
    (1) Works with team, President, and Vice-President in setting up and following through on new contacts, visitors, and delinquent members

        (2) Do this either by a phone call or a casual contact in school

   i. Missions Chair

        (1) Keeps missions before group: emphasize home and foreign missions

        (2) Responsible for planning and running one meeting per month on missions

        (3) Chooses missions team to help in work

        (4) Responsible for a missions display or poster each month

   j. Each team leader is to choose his/her team/committee members from the full enrollment of the High School Department and submit the names to the adult youth workers for a final check to avoid lopsided teams or overduplication. Each team leader is to hand in his/her list of suggested team members during the first week after the election. Each team leader is required to attend the Team Leaders' Retreat.

2. Qualifications of Team Leaders

   a. Must be a church member (President only)

   b. Must be a Christian and be living a consistent Christian life

   c. Must demonstrate leadership potential

   d. Must be willing to work—hard!

   e. Must be acceptable to the adult youth workers, Youth Pastor, and high school group at large

3. Nomination and Election of Officers

   a. Principle: Get *all* of the youth in the High School Department involved

   b. Application of Principle: Present the offices available and the responsibilities of each on a Sunday morning during Sunday school. Let those who want to run for an office nominate themselves by speaking to an adult worker. During the week, each nominee should meet with the Youth Pastor for an interview to discuss the office and qualifications for the particular office. The following Sunday evening hold the election. The weekend following the election have the Team Leaders' Retreat (Friday and Saturday).

4. Adult Youth Workers/Sponsors of the High School Department

   a. Three (3) adult couples to sponsor the group

   b. The Youth Pastor works with the Sponsors. There

will be a monthly planning and leadership development meeting of Sponsors (at least one from each couple) and the Youth Pastor.

  c. Qualifications of Adult Youth Workers/Sponsors

    (1) Spiritual: A Christian who knows why and how he/she believes; capable of leading others to Christ. Evidence the fruit of the Spirit in daily life. A person of the Word and prayer

    (2) Called of God to this position (vocation)

    (3) Understand Senior Highs, or try to understand them; acquiring an understanding through contact with them

    (4) Love for the youth; learning to love those who are hard to love

    (5) Emotionally stable

    (6) Able to inspire and lead

    (7) Consistent in approach

    (8) Intelligent

    (9) Self-confident

    (10) Desire to succeed

    (11) Able to share leadership with other adult youth workers, with Youth Pastor, and with youth

    (12) Must attend Leadership Retreat each year

  d. Delegated Responsibilities of Sponsors:

    (1) One Sponsor represents High School Department on Youth Committee

    (2) Sunday Programs

      (a) 1st and 3rd Sundays' programs (work with #1 Assoc. Program Chair and Missions Chair)

      (b) 2d Sunday's Program (work with Vice President and Exec. Program Chair)

      (c) 4th Sunday's Program (work with #2 Assoc. Program Chair)

      (d) 5th Sunday's Program (special speaker, outsider; all Sponsors arrange for this)

    (3) Weekday Activities

      (a) Sports and other activities for boys

      (b) Sports and other activities for girls

      (c) Coed recreation activities

      (d) Socials (rotate one sponsoring couple per month in charge of working with social cochairs and supported by other Sponsors, Sunday school teachers, and Youth Pastor). Include sports, games (football, basketball, baseball, swimming, field hockey, soccer, etc.); local college games; regular socials each month; "Fifth Quarter" after an occasional football and/or basketball game; service projects that combine work and play

    (e) Counseling (by adult youth workers, Sunday school teachers, and Youth Pastor as needed)

7. THE PROGRAM OF THE POST-HIGH DEPARTMENT

  I. Sunday School

    A. If the youth determine they need a worship time during the Sunday school hour, they themselves should plan it.

    B. Announcements and any other "opening activities" should be executed by the young people themselves.

    C. Bible teaching should occur with methods and materials appropriate to this age group and with their needs and concerns clearly in mind.

  II. Sunday Evening or Weeknight Program

    A. This program should be distinct from the High School and Junior High programs. It should provide for total involvement of the youth themselves in the design, development, and execution of the program. It should have a clearly stated reason for being. Otherwise, it should not be attempted.

    B. Generally, Post-High youth, especially college youth themselves, need opportunity for searching, analyzing, and synthesizing their faith in relation to their daily lives. Emphasis should be placed, therefore, not on "speakers" as much as on leaders facilitating discussion, study, reflection, and action.

  III. Social Activities

    A. These need to be planned by the youth themselves and should occur with a frequency that they set, probably once a month.

    B. Types and kinds of socials will depend on the particular youth involved in the group, the location of the church, and the resources within the church itself, within the immediate community, and within an area of reasonable driving distance.

  IV. Service Projects: This age group has plenty of energy to expend and needs profitable experiences in which to channel those energies for evangelization and the meeting of social needs.

V. Camps and Retreats: This age group has more discretionary time than senior or junior highers. Thus retreats and camps can and should play an integral and important part in the Post-High Department program. Weekend retreats, rather than many longer camping experiences, are more easily attended, are less disruptive, and can provide for enriching experiences of instruction, fellowship, and worship. In the end, retreats (along with camping) may well be the most productive activities for ongoing encouragement of spiritual formation, nurture, and discipleship.

8. FINANCES

I. Each social activity should be self-financing through assessments from the participating members. Youth leaders are not expected to pay for any social activities unless the group is engaged in a public activity, such as bowling or miniature golf.

II. There are exceptions to the above: The church through its youth budget assumes the cost of bus transportation for retreats and outings for all youth groups.

III. The youth budget provides for materials needed for the proper running of youth ministry. The Youth Office is well supplied with materials and equipment for any and all reasonable demands. Typewriter, computer and printer, and a copier machine are available for leaders' use.

IV. The church provides for baby-sitting for youth leaders on Sunday evening. Baby-sitting expenses incurred during the week will also be reimbursed if requested.

V. Offerings (Sunday school and any other)
   A. These should only be taken after the youth team leaders and adult workers have discussed their purpose.
   B. Be sure to have a definite place for offerings to be used. See "offerings" under the Department Program sections.
   C. The monies should be deposited with the General Church Treasurer each week. The Treasurers and Sponsors should keep accurate records of the deposits and debits.
   D. Disbursement of offerings will be made by way of a voucher, signed by the youth group's treasurer, a designated adult sponsor, and the Youth Pastor.

9. USE OF CHURCH PROPERTY

I. Access to Buildings

A. Arrangements should be made through the Church Secretary for use of the buildings. She will instruct the head Custodian of the youths' plans and he will be responsible for opening and closing the building. Only as a last resort should you call on the pastoral staff for help.

B. The church will be opened at the time requested. At least one youth worker is expected to be there *at that time.* An adult worker is also expected to remain with the young people until the last one has departed. If you leave the church building before the custodian returns to lock up, please leave the lights on. This discourages prowlers, we hope!

II. Phone: There is a church phone available for use in calling parents or for any emergency. Please encourage the young people to use it for those purposes only. Conversations should be brief so that others may use it also. The phone is not meant for general conversation.

III. Kitchen: The kitchen will be locked at all times. Permission for use of the kitchen and/or its utensils should be obtained ahead of time with the kitchen Hostess. She will arrange for you to have a key. Please return all utensils immediately, and clean.

IV. Furniture: If you desire to have a room arranged in a special way, please notify either the church office or the head Custodian in writing no less than 5 days in advance. The custodial staff will arrange the room according to plans. Otherwise they will merely clear the chairs from the main part of the room. The custodial staff is responsible for setting up the furniture after you leave, but please cooperate in leaving the floor clean and the room neat.

V. Sports Equipment: For use of the various sports equipment see the Custodian.

10. TRIPS, CARS, AND INSURANCE

I. Junior High Group

A. Trips are an expected and anticipated part of any youth program. It is natural that the parents of these age groups will be called upon from to time to provide transportation for the young people.

B. It is important that the various adult youth leaders do not feel obligated to serve as taxi service. Youth leaders should notify parents in advance of the time and the location at which their young people will be available to be picked up.

II. High School and Post-High Groups
   A. Most parents feel obligated and want to provide the use of their cars for their teenage drivers since their children have been riding with others previously. This is commendable and desirous. However, the youth leaders do have two responsibilities in this matter:
      1. As much as possible, to protect the family that owns the cars and would be liable for any damages
      2. To protect passengers and drivers from any foreseeable problems
   B. The above responsibilities are fulfilled by careful scrutiny of the number of passengers in a car. It should be no more than the car can safely hold. It is also important to casually inquire concerning—or to investigate—the stability of the youthful driver. An unsafe driver is a hindrance to the work of the church and a danger to life and limb.
   C. Again, the youth workers are not to provide taxi service. Arrange ahead service to pool rides.
III. Buses: It is advisable when a large group is going some distance to arrange for a bus. If you would like to have one, please contact the Youth Pastor with the details and he/she will arrange for the transportation.
IV. Insurance Coverage: The church maintains accident and liability coverage for all church-sponsored activities except interchurch competitive sports. If you have any questions about this or if something happens that might be covered by this policy, please contact the Youth Pastor.
V. Reimbursement for Car Expenses: Youth workers will be reimbursed for car expenses. Mileage and toll charges should be submitted to the Youth Pastor. Youth workers should be sure that they have adequate automobile and home liability coverage.
VI. Permission Slips: Be sure to have up-to-date, signed permission slips from parent(s) or legal guardian(s). Any trip or program whose risk is above the normal range should be so described clearly on the permission slip to be signed by parent/guardian (for example, backpacking trips).
VII. Medical Slips: Carry signed medical permission slips with you on all trips. These will be needed for medical treatments in case of sickness and/or injury. Special medicines required, and allergies, for example, should be stated by the parent/guardian on the slip.

HOURS

I. Principles
   A. Most parents do not appreciate their youth staying out very late. This is especially true on Saturday evenings.
   B. The state curfew law must be obeyed by all youth groups.

II. Suggested Hours—Home by:

   A. High School and Post-High:

Friday evening	12:00 midnight
Saturday evening	11:00 p.m.
weeknights	11:00 p.m. (no school next day)
weeknights	10:00 p.m. (school next day)

   B. Junior High:

Friday evening	11:00 p.m.
Saturday evening	10:00 p.m.
weeknights	10:00 p.m. (no school next day)
weeknights	9:00 p.m. (school next day)

It is further recommended that events be scheduled if possible for Friday evenings and not Saturday evenings. It is best not to hold special events in the church building on Saturday night.

Appendix B

YOUTH MINISTRY BIBLIOGRAPHY

[Developed by the Youth Ministry and Theological Schools Project funded by the Lilly Endowment to Union Theological Seminary in Virginia; Sara Little, Project Director. Used by permission. Additional entries by John M. Dettoni.]

Professors from twenty-two theological schools, meeting in two seminar groups from 1985–1992, in addition to other activities, have exchanged syllabi, including bibliographies. These are persons with interests in youth and youth ministry, most of them within the context of broader teaching responsibilities.

In deciding to combine bibliographies and create a general list available to interested peers, seminar members did not intend to make a definitive selection. For books earlier than 1975, selections are limited to those considered to be of particular significance. Especially with respect to the overabundance of program resources, illustrative materials only are included. Most audio and video materials fall into the program resource category and have therefore been omitted. What is offered, therefore, is primarily a compilation of publications used by a particular group of professors in their work relating to youth ministry, either in specific age-group courses or in basic ministry or general educational courses.

Special appreciation goes to Mary-Ruth Marshall, graduate assistant (doctoral student from the Presbyterian School of Christian Education), who did the major work of compiling, annotating, and categorizing. Assistance was also provided by Carol Fisher and Stephen Earl. Mickey Lumpkin, administrative assistant for the project, is the major contributor to the actual production of the bibliography in all its phases.

Additions have been made by John M. Dettoni. While this is an extensive annotated bibliography, no claim is made that it is an exhaustive bibliography on youth ministry.

CODING

Part I: Youth and Adolescence
 c *Context:* Historical, sociological (including family) background
 d *Development:* Surveys or investigations of some aspect of ado-

199

lescent development: cognitive, moral, faith, personality, physical, or psychological

r *Reports of research:* Various types of research on youth

t *Theories of adolescence:* Interpretation of the phenomenon called "adolescence"

Part II: Youth Ministry

a *Approaches to youth ministry:* Theories and models as related to various approaches

g *General:* Comprehensive overviews, often collections of essays

o *Organization and leadership manuals:* Aids to adult and/or youth leaders in organizing and offering leadership

p *Program planning:* Helps in planning for various aspects of youth activities

r *Program resources:* Materials to be used in program development, worship, outreach, recreation, or other

Part I: Youth and Adolescence

```
                      CODING

            c  Context
            d  Development
            r  Reports of research
            t  Theories of adolescence
```

d Adelson, Joseph, ed. *Handbook of Adolescent Psychology.* New York: John Wiley, 1980. 624 pp.

Ideas, perspectives, and findings from recent scientific research literature about adolescents. Includes essays and reports focused on themes significant for the future. Considers current thinking, central processes common to adolescence, and significant variations in physical, social, and intellectual development.

dt Adelson, Joseph. *Inventing Adolescence: Political Psychology of Everyday Schooling.* New Brunswick, N.J.: Transaction Books, 1985. 320 pp.

The invention of adolescence was the result of a search for a problem child that foreshadowed problematic adults. Teenagers today are well balanced, but their educational administrators, whose vested interests conflict with the requirements of learning, are caught up in ideological generalities and are ignoring empirical data. Focuses on the politics of the adolescent and the educational administrator.

ct "Adolescence," *Religious Education.* Vol. 81, no. 2 (Spring 1986): 162–294.

A collection of articles, some of which are based on research relating to the present approaches to Jewish, Catholic, and Protestant youth ministry.

dt Aleshire, Daniel O. *Understanding Today's Youth.* Nashville: Convention, 1982. 160 pp.

A general overview of adolescent development, contexts, history, faith formation, and morals from the perspectives and resources of Scripture, psychological and sociological literature, and the author's experience.

c Allen, Steve. *Beloved Son: A Story of the Jesus Cults.* Indianapolis: Bobbs-Merrill, 1982. 241 pp.

Personal report by actor/comedian Allen about the Jesus cults in general, and his son's involvement with a particular cult. Results of Allen's ten-year study of religious and quasireligious cults. Offers assessment and findings.

dt Ausubel, David P., Raymond Montemayor and Pergrouhi (Najarian) Svajian. *Theory and Problems of Adolescent Development.* 2d ed. New York: Green & Stratton, 1977. 572 pp.

Undergraduate and graduate text, presenting a unified theory of a universal transitional stage of personality development. Reviews professional literature from 1950. Describes adolescents in terms of actual behavior in the 1970s, focusing on the particular cultural variant (U.S.) of a pancultural stage. Details biological and cultural determinants of adolescence.

ct Babin, Pierre. *Crisis of Faith: The Religious Psychology of Adolescence.* Translated by Eva Fleischner, New York: Herder and Herder, 1963. 251 pp.

Sets the crisis of faith (the interior decision to keep the promises others have made for the individual at baptism) within the broader framework of adolescent crises and becoming. Delineates the components for an appropriate Christian education of youth: education for freedom, awareness, Christian meaning, communal life, love of Jesus, Christian disciplines.

dt _____. *Faith and the Adolescent.* Translated by David Gibson, New York: Herder and Herder, 1965. 128 pp.

Report of an investigation of the views of modern French teenagers on the meaning of God in their lives. The three categories of response (God of Creation, God of Man, God of Jesus Christ) are analyzed from the perspectives of psychology, sociology, and pedagogy.

c Bacon, Leonard W., and Charles A. Northrup. *Young People's Societies.* New York: Lentilhon, 1900.

Classic description of early denominational societies for young people.

r   Barna Research Group. *Today's Teens: A Generation in Transition.* Glendale, Calif.: The Barna Research Group, 1991. 57 pp.

This is a national survey of 13 to 18 year-olds from across the United States that focuses on core values, future expectations, and the relationship of spiritual beliefs and practices to their beings. That it focuses on being and not just doing is very commendable, making the conceptualization of the survey different from the usual counting of responses.

r   Benson, Peter L., Dorothy Williams, and Arthur Johnson. *The Quicksilver Years: The Hopes and Fears of Early Adolescence.* San Francisco: Harper & Row, 1987. 245 pp.

The official, comprehensive report of a major study of 8,000 young adolescents and their parents. Search Institute is the sponsor of the study in which 13 national youth-serving agencies of churches and community participated.

cdt   Bernard, Harold W. *Adolescent Development in American Culture.* Yonkers-on-Hudson, N.Y.: World Book, 1957.

Broadly based text, tracking the growth and development of adolescents through their twenties. The analytic approach is enriched with helpful graphs and statistics. Text covers psychology and multiple developmental parameters including both the hierarchical potentials as well as the task requirements of this period.

cd   Berzonsky, Michael D. *Adolescent Development: A Conceptual Approach.* New York: Macmillan, 1981. 615 pp.

Aimed at developing a conceptual approach for use in viewing and interpreting adolescent behavior. Uses developmental psychology to explain why adolescents act as they do, and rounds out the picture with consideration of social, cultural, and historical influence on adolescent behavior and belief.

r   Bibby, Reginald Wayne, and Donald C. Posterski. *The Emerging Generation: An Inside Look at Canada's Teenagers.* Toronto: Irwin Publishing, 1985. 220 pp.

A report of the major recent empirical study of 3,600 Canadian youth with respect to values, beliefs, outlook, and behavior.

d   Blos, Peter. *The Adolescent Passage: Developmental Issues.* New York: International Universities, 1979. 538 pp.

A compilation of essays from a Freudian perspective of various dimensions of adolescence.

dt   _____. *On Adolescence: A Psychoanalytic Interpretation.* New York: Free Press of Glencoe, 1966. 269 pp.

Freudian and psychoanalytic perspective in describing five chronological phases of adolescent development (latency, preadolescence, and early, middle, and late adolescence) which must be completed, but at varying and uneven rates not fixed to age reference.

c Brake, Mike. *The Sociology of Youth Culture and Youth Subcultures: Sex and Drugs and Rock 'N' Roll.* London: Routledge & Kegan Paul, 1980. 204 pp.

Suggests subcultures originate in communal attempts to resolve problems arising from defects and weaknesses in the social structure, and that the collective identity of the subculture makes possible individual identity beyond that of class, education, and occupation. Analyzes and categorizes postwar youth subcultures in the U.S. and Britain, with special attention to those arising from sexism or racism.

ct Clark, Ted. *The Oppression of Youth.* New York: Harper & Row, 1975. 178 pp.

Clark's basic argument is that many adolescent problems are the result of oppressive relationships within the family and the school contexts. The chapter on sexuality provides research data from interviews with young people; concluding chapters propose a psychosocial understanding of the issues.

ct Coleman, James S., et. al. *High School Achievement: Public, Catholic and Private Schools Compared.* New York: Basic Books, 1982. 289 pp.

This book provides information about the different modes of organization reflected in the public-private dichotomy, particularly the two principles of organization around residence (the principal mode in the public sector) and a religious identity (the principal mode in the private sector).

ct Coleman, James S., ed. *Youth: Transition to Adulthood.* Chicago: University of Chicago Press, 1977. 193 pp.

Report of a presidential panel, this document is still one of the most widely used historical and sociological resources for those planning youth ministry. See especially the section on objectives.

cr Coleman, James S., and Thomas Hoffer. *Public and Private High Schools: The Impact of Communities.* New York: Basic Books, 1987. 254 pp.

A major study, building on the "High School and Beyond" project, with implications for the future of youth education.

dt Coleman, John C. *The Nature of Adolescence.* New York: Methuen, 1980. 214 pp.

Outlines both psychoanalytic and sociological theories of adolescence and adolescent development but suggests they are inadequate in the light of current evidence. Reassesses common concepts such as identity crisis, generation gap, and turbulent stage.

c Coleman, John, and Gregory Baum, eds. *Youth Without a Future?* (Symposium) Edinburgh: T & T Clark, 1985. 118 pp.

Worldwide studies collected in 1985, the International Year of Youth, on the situation of youth.

t Conger, John J. *Adolescence: Generation Under Pressure.* San Francisco: Harper & Row, 1979. 128 pp.

Here adolescence is described as an exclusive international culture, the arbiters of fashion, the wealthy target—as a group—of everybody with something to sell, and divided as never before from the world of adults. The author shows their antics and the adult perception of their drug-dominated, pop-crazed promiscuity to be instead a dauntingly difficult reaching out for values and understanding. Growth, parents, sex, peers, drugs, moral growth, alienation, and the resulting psychological problems are explored.

cd Conger, John J., and Anne C. Peterson. *Adolescence and Youth: Psychological Development in a Changing World,* 3d ed. New York: Harper & Row, 1984. 732 pp.

Describes biological, psychological, cognitive, and social change in the years surrounding and including puberty, with particular attention in this edition to the past decades' extensive research in adolescent development. Highlights principles of development and the effects of change and challenge in the seventies and beyond.

r Csikszentmihalyi, Mihaly, and Reed Larson. *Being Adolescent: Conflict and Growth in the Teenage Years.* New York: Basic Books, 1984. 332 pp.

A study of 75 adolescents, given "beepers" by the researchers, to allow random check-ins. The questions covered moods, activities, a variety of thoughts and feelings.

c Damrell, Joseph. *Search for Identity: Youth, Religion and Culture.* Beverly Hills: Sage, 1978. 231 pp.

Firsthand sociological report of a "church," an improvisational youth group providing an alternative to "growing up" in the technological society and emphasizing the adolescent search for identity as a permanent way of life. The author sets this example into its historical and social context and describes other such groups characteristic of the prolongation of adolescence. The nature of religious experience is explored.

c Demos, John. *Past, Present, and Personal: The Family and the Life Course in American History.* New York: Oxford University Press, 1986. 215 pp.

Covers the history and contexts of the American family and its influence on the individual's life course. A chapter is devoted to adolescence, highlighting the implications of the author's research in the history of adolescence.

cr Dragastin, Sigmund E., and Glen H. Elder, Jr., eds. *Adolescence in the Life Cycle: Psychological Change and Social Context.* New York: John Wiley, 1975. 324 pp.

A collection of papers prepared for a research conference on the psychology and sociology of adolescence. In the epilogue,

Dragastin discusses the emergent research themes within the conference papers and proposes future issues.

c Eisenstadt, Samuel Noah. *From Generation to Generation: Age Groups and Social Structure.* Glencoe, Ill.: Free Press, 1971. 357 pp.

A comparison of societies, from primitive to modern, and the way in which they classify or organize age groups, including age as qualifier for social obligations.

ct Elkind, David. *All Grown Up and No Place to Go: Teenagers in Crisis.* Reading, Mass.: Addison-Wesley, 1984. 232 pp.

Case studies, research, and examples from the author's practice as a psychologist support the contention that contemporary teenagers are confronted with adult challenges and social pressures for which they are unprepared. Teenage responses to such stresses are detailed, and coping strategies are suggested.

d _____ . *A Sympathetic Understanding of the Child: Birth to Sixteen.* 2d ed. Boston: Allyn and Bacon, 1978. 211 pp.

A brief survey of development (emotional, intellectual, social) written in nontechnical language. This edition eliminates sexist language and sexual role stereotypes. Adolescence (ages 12 to 16) is discussed in chapters 9–11, and the development of religious concepts is considered in chapter 7.

c Enroth, Ronald M. *Youth, Brainwashing, and the Extremist Cults.* Grand Rapids, Mich.: Zondervan, 1977. 218 pp.

Considers the range of sociological, psychological, and spiritual phenomena surrounding the emergence and growth of cults. Case histories of deprogramed excult members provide the data for summaries of enlistment and commitment procedures. The nonobjective view is that New Age cults are demonic.

c Erb, Frank O. *The Development of the Young People's Movement.* Chicago: University of Chicago Press, 1917. 122 pp.

Historical classic describing the development of Christian Endeavor, denominational youth societies, and chivalric groups and societies in the United States.

dt Erikson, Erik H., ed. *The Challenge of Youth.* New York: Anchor, 1965. 340 pp. (Originally published as *Youth: Change and Challenge.*)

Collection of essays (originally published as a special issue of *Daedalus*) by leading authorities on subjects such as the sources of developmental and other changes in young people, individual and social change, responsibility and leadership in youth, technology and legislation, and cross-generational relations. Includes essays on youth in Japan, France, and Russia, as well as the U.S.

dt Erikson, Erik H. *Identity: Youth and Crisis.* New York: W. W. Norton, 1968. 336 pp.

Identity confusion leading to identity crisis is described as a formative stage in the human life cycle, and central to historical and sociogenetic evolution. Emphasis is given to negative identity (images, individuals, and groups despise and wish to exterminate in self and others). Successful identity formation leads to more inclusive identities and personal transcendence.

dr Farel, Anita M. *Early Adolescence and Religion: A Status Study.* Carrboro, N.C.: Center for Early Adolescence, 1982. 45 pp.

A survey of research and writing on religion and the young adolescent, together with report of four successful religious programs for young adolescents.

d _____ . *Early Adolescence: What Parents Need to Know* Carrboro, N.C.: Center for Early Adolescence, 1982. 37 pp.

A handbook for families with adolescent children. Summarizes adolescent development and new ways families and adolescents communicate and relate, in order that parents and teens may anticipate adolescent and mid-life (parental) change to become mutually supportive.

r Fee, Joan L., Andrew Greeley, William McCready, and Teresa Sullivan. *Young Catholics in the United States and Canada.* New York: W. H. Sadlier, 1981. 256 pp.

Summary and analysis of research data extrapolated and applied to issues such as the religious experience of youth, relationship to the church and its organizations, socialization, religious imagery, influences on the religious life cycle, and religious and other attitudes.

cd Feeney, Stephanie. *Schools for Young Adolescents: Adapting the Early Childhood Model.* Carrboro, N.C.: Center for Early Adolescence, 1980. 39 pp.

Proposes the early childhood model of education as pedagogically and developmentally more appropriate for junior high schools than the existing senior high model.

r Flynn, Marcellin. *The Effectiveness of Catholic Schools.* Holmebush, N.S.W.: St. Paul, 1985. 409 pp.

This book is about Catholic schools and their effectiveness in serving the needs of Year 12 students, their parents, and teachers. Its aim is both exploratory and analytical, namely, to examine aspects of the development of Year 12 students—and to interpret these against a framework of certain key dimensions of Catholic schools.

dr Fowler, James W. *Stages of Faith: The Psychology of Human Development and the Quest for Meaning.* San Francisco, Calif.: Harper & Row, 1981. 332 pp.

Research on faith development over the life span. Adolescence is discussed frequently throughout; chapter 18 addresses the synthetic-conventional stage ascendant in adolescence.

ct Friedenberg, Edgar Z. *Coming of Age in America: Growth and Acquiescence.* New York: Vintage, 1967. 300 pp.

Research-related discussion of the influence of mass society's values on the school and its students. Contains six narratives about an imaginary school and analyzes and details student choices and responses, including verbatim responses. Assesses the community's notions of education and postulates an alternative, liberal education in the best and broadest sense.

ct _____ . *The Vanishing Adolescent.* New York: Dell, 1962. 144 pp.

Discusses the contention that the natural process of development, including the adolescent need for identity and self-definition, is being eroded by both society and the schools. Explores necessary and unique experiences of adolescence, and adult myths about teenagers.

g Fuhrmann, Barbara A. *Adolescence, Adolescents.* Boston: Little, Brown, 1986. 583 pp.

Textbook for courses in adolescent development, emphasizing scientific study, theory, and research about adolescence and the understanding of individual adolescents. Focuses on the contexts of youth, including the historical and developmental aspects of both normal and problematical adolescence. Religious development and education is considered in chapter 10.

r George H. Gallup International Institute. *The Religious Life of Young Americans: A Compendium of Surveys on the Spiritual Beliefs and Practices of Teenagers and Young Adults.* Princeton: Gallup, 1992. 84 pp.

An authoritative survey of American teenagers, young adults, and adults regarding their religious practices and beliefs. The survey provides up-to-the-minute data on these and offers youth workers a series of questions to use in their own attempts to keep abreast of youth's spiritual beliefs and practices.

r Gallup Organization, Inc. *The Religious Beliefs and Sexual Attitudes and Behavior of College Students.* Princeton: Gallup, 1989.

This is a report conducted for the Christian Broadcasting Network of representative college students and their particular religious beliefs and sexual attitudes and practices. This is an excellent survey of current data and is helpful for those who wish to continue to ascertain this sort of information in the future.

r Gilmore, Perry, and Allan A. Glatthorn, eds. *Children in and out of School: Ethnography and Education.* Washington, D. C.: Center for Applied Linguistics, 1982. 257 pp.

An ethnographic study of children and youth in schools, demonstrating the possibility of a currently much-used approach to anthropology.

cr *Giving Youth a Better Chance: Options for Education, Work and Service.* Carnegie Council on Policy Studies in Higher Education. San Francisco: Jossey-Bass, 1979. 345 pp.

Reports research studies on the education, work, and community involvement of U.S. youth, together with recommendations for improving education, employment, and service systems. Challenges prevalent view of youth as "outsiders."

rt Goethals, George W., and D. Klos. *Experiencing Youth: First-Person Accounts.* 2d ed. Boston: Little, Brown, 1976. 399 pp.

Presents first-person accounts to serve as subjective, personal data for analysis in the context of theory or empirical studies. The book is divided into three parts: cases dealing with autonomy, with identity, and with sexual intimacy. Each case has its own introduction, which summarizes some of the narrative and identifies one or more psychological issues raised by the case.

dr Goldman, Ronald P. *Readiness for Religion: A Basis for Developmental Religious Education.* New York: Seabury, 1970. 238 pp.

Part I deals with the psychological basis for religious development, the needs and limitations of children and adolescents, and research reports about emotional and cognitive development. Part II examines content and methodology for healthy development. Chapters 8 and 9 address adolescence specifically.

r _____ . *Religious Thinking from Childhood to Adolescence.* New York: Seabury, 1980. 276 pp.

Research-based study of the ability of British students, 6 to 17 years, to understand religious concepts such as Bible, God, Jesus, prayer, and the church. Considers development of religious thinking in the context of cognitive development. The final chapter presents implications for religious education.

ct Goodman, Paul. *Growing Up Absurd: Problems of Youth in the Organized Society.* New York: Vintage, 1962. 296 pp.

Young people are the products of "The Organized System," a cautious, competitive, game-playing, limited enterprise. That system and its mores are death to the human spirit. Rebellious and disaffected youth offer hope that the future may make sense.

d Gordon, Sol. *The Sexual Adolescent.* 2d ed. North Scituate, Mass.: Duxbury, 1979. 413 pp.

Written for professionals and parents who want to communicate with adolescents about sexuality. Research is based on what youth have said. Included is a series of suggestions for creative action addressed to adolescents, parents, educators, the community, and government.

cr Gribbon, Robert, and Nancy Van Scoyoc. *Let's Put Young People in their Place!* New York: Youth Ministries, The Episcopal Church, 1984.

This study was commissioned by the Episcopal Church through the Office of Youth Ministries; all the congregations are Episcopal. A summary of the findings, and a further description of the study and people involved, can be found in the primary document *Let's Put Young People in their Place!* for which *Case Studies* is a complement.

c Hargrove, Barbara, and Stephen D. Jones. *Reaching Youth Today: Heirs to the Whirlwind.* Valley Forge, Pa: Judson, 1983. 125 pp.

Describes and assesses the youth culture of today, contrasting it with that of preceding generations. Aimed at helping churches enable communication between generations and evaluate their own needs for youth ministry. A second section concentrates on nurture, socialization, and evangelism of youth.

crt Havighurst, Robert James, and Philip H. Dreyer, eds. *Youth.* Seventy-fourth Yearbook of the National Society of the Study of Education. Chicago: University of Chicago Press, 1975. 463 pp.

One of the most comprehensive collections of interdisciplinary research relating to youth.

d Hill, John P. *Understanding Early Adolescence: A Framework.* Carrboro, N.C.: Center for Early Adolescence, 1980. 52 pp.

Considers classic issues related to developmental tasks and changes young people work through in the environments that are part of their daily lives: families, school groups, peers, communities. Emphasis is on a framework which makes sense out of adolescence as a whole.

r Hyde, Kenneth E. *Religion in Childhood and Adolescence: Comprehensive Review of the Research.* Birmingham, Ala.: Religious Press, 1990. 528 pp.

Indeed, this is a comprehensive review of research on children and youth that covers just about all the empirical research on these age groups. If one wants to know about a certain topic, the extremely complete index and bibliography are very helpful. When one seeks to know what has been uncovered in youth and children's research, this is the book to turn to. It is not one for picking up and reading for "how to.. .."

d Jersild, Arthur T. *The Psychology of Adolescence.* New York: Macmillan, 1966.

A comprehensive text covering the adolescent's growth and behavior with valuable inquiry into the subject meaning of what is happening in their lives. The growth of the "self" is traced through the physical, mental, emotional, and social development with implications for education, vocation, and moral development.

crt Johnson, Mauritz, ed. *Toward Adolescence: The Middle School Years.* Seventy-ninth Yearbook of the National Society for the Study of Education. Chicago: University of Chicago Press, 1980. 338 pp.

A collection of essays focusing on interdisciplinary research relating to young adolescents, and implications for their education.

r Josephson Institute of Ethics. *The Ethics of American Youth: A Warning and Call to Action.* Marina del Rey, Calif.: 1990. 82 pp.

A startling report on the values and behaviors of the 18- to 30-year-olds in the United States. Its findings, widely reported in the U.S. press, raise serious questions concerning the efficacy of American teachings of ethics and justice to the youth.

dt Kagan, Jerome, and Robert Coles, eds. *Twelve to Sixteen: Early Adolescence.* New York: Norton, 1972, 356 pp.

A collection of essays by social scientists reflecting on topics such as physical maturation, social characteristics, political awareness, and social settings. Posits that early adolescence is a more complex period than conventionally conceived, and neglected as subject for scientific inquiry.

dt Kegan, J. Robert. *The Evolving Self: Problem and Process in Human Development.* Cambridge, Mass.: Harvard University Press, 1982. 318 pp.

Suggests moral meaning-making as the context in personality which is philosophically prior to and constitutive of the various polarities in ego or personality development theory. Describes five natural emergences of the self, understood in a helix of evolutionary truces. Influenced by Piaget. Adolescence is discussed in chapters 6 and 7.

ct Keniston, Kenneth. *The Uncommitted: Alienated Youth in American Society.* New York: Harcourt, Brace and World, 1965. 500 pp.

Two foci, "alienated youth" and "alienating society," are examined from the perspectives of depth psychology, history, and sociology. The alienation of young men (ones who reject the basic values of their culture) is described and reconstructed, then contrasted with ideological rebellion. The second section examines the tensions inherent in technological society.

c Kett, Joseph P. *Rites of Passage: Adolescence in America 1790 to the Present.* New York: Basic Books, 1977. 327 pp.

A historical overview of rites of passage, with general background content relating to society's current efforts to promote youth's passage to adulthood.

r Konopka, Gisela. *Young Girls: A Portrait of Adolescence.* Englewood Cliffs, N.J.: Prentice-Hall, 1976. 176 pp.

Report of research involving girls aged 12 to 18. Gives their views on marriage, education, sexuality, drugs, life goals, adults, friendship and loneliness, school, youth organizations, and political and social concerns. Includes verbatim interviews and excerpts from diaries and other writings by girls.

d Levine, Arthur. *When Dreams and Heroes Died: A Portrait of Today's College Student.* San Francisco: Jossey-Bass, 1980.

The quiescent college generation of the '70s stands contrasted to those of the turbulent '60s. They are full of paradoxes: liberal in life-style yet conservative in politics. Hopeful for their personal future yet despairing for the countries' future. Dr. Levine accurately paints the portrait of the student and prescribes the missing component in liberal education for this hopeful and hopeless generation.

d Likona, Thomas. *Raising Good Children: Helping Your Child Through the Stages of Moral Development.* New York: Bantam, 1983. 446 pp.

Describes six predictable stages of moral development (Kohlbergian) from preschool to adulthood. Aimed at parents, to help them teach children and youth to act on the basis of moral reasoning. Part III covers adolescence, and Part IV deals with adolescent concerns such as conflict, television, sex, and drug use and abuse.

cr Liebert, Robert M., Joyce N. Sprafkin, and Emily S. Davidson. *The Early Window: The Effects of Television on Children and Youth,* 2d ed. New York: Pergamon, 1982. 257 pp.

Details the effects of television exposure on the first 18 years of life. Interprets the role of television and explores political and social questions about television's influence on attitudes, development, and behavior. Accommodates most recent research, including reports on effects of prosocial and educational efforts.

c Lipsitz, Joan, ed. *Barriers: A New Look at the Needs of Young Adolescents.* New York: Ford Foundation, 1979. 70 pp.

Summary statement of the proceedings from six regional conferences focused on young adolescents and the question of how better to serve their needs. "Barriers" refers to underserviced areas, or the provision of services.

dr Lipsitz, Joan. *Growing up Forgotten: A Review of Research and Programs Concerning Early Adolescence.* New Brunswick, N.J.: Transaction Books, 1980. 267 pp.

A report reviewing research focused on the biological, socioemotional, and cognitive development of young adolescents. Also considers programs and services of social institutions, including the school, institutions for the disabled, the family, voluntary youth-serving agencies, and the juvenile justice system.

cd Littwin, Susan. *The Postponed Generation: Why American Youth Are Growing Up Later.* Morrow, 1986.

Relates to responsibilities. A resource for individual study and for group discussions among parents and young people, as well as good reading for young adults and parents of young adults. Especially helpful in understanding the postponed adulthood of many college graduates.

cr Lofquist, William A. *Discovering the Meaning of Prevention: A Practical Approach to Positive Change.* Tucson: Associates for Youth Development, 1983. 151 pp.

A theoretical model relating to promotion of psychosocial health in youth; grows out of years of research by the Associates staff.

d Manaster, Guy J. *Adolescent Development and the Life Tasks.* Boston: Allyn and Bacon, 1977.

The facts and ideas about adolescents that are assumed to be unchanging occupy the first half of the book: distinctiveness in terms of biological, cognitive, moral, sex-role, personality, and emotional development. An integration chapter separates the book, with the last half covering the primary life tasks: love, sex, work, school, friends, community, meaning, and religion.

c Mead, Margaret. *Culture and Commitment: The New Relations Between the Generations in the 1970s.* Rev. ed. New York: Columbia University Press, 1978. 200 pp.

Using studies of contemporary cultures Mead discusses the continuity of tradition within three kinds of culture: (1) postfigurative, in which children learn from their ancestors, (2) configurative, in which both children and adults learn from their peers, and (3) prefigurative, in which adults also learn from their children.

pr Meanages, Robert J. *Teaching-Learning Experiences for College Students and Other Adults: A Selected Annotated Bibliography.* The Center for the Teaching Professions, Northwestern University, 1985.

The selections herein are limited to those that address *instructional* functions of the teacher of adults. The bibliography will be of most value to those who plan, conduct, and evaluate teaching-learning experiences for adults.

rt Moriarty, Alice, and Povl W. Toussieng. *Adolescent Coping.* New York: Grune & Stratton, 1976. 220 pp.

Report of longitudinal research on coping patterns of normal midwestern U.S. adolescents. Includes coping with a changing world, changing attitudes, and beliefs. Based on the research, an updated theory of contemporary adolescent development is offered. Contradicts assumptions that youth in more conservative areas are unlike their coastal counterparts, or resistant to change.

d Mosher, Ralph L., ed. *Adolescents' Development and Education.* Berkeley, Calif.: McCutchan, 1979.

The psychological theories of development are introduced in the first half of the text. Particularly the aspects of adolescent growth in: intellectual, moral, ego, identity, vocational, and aesthetic parameters. The second half of the book justifies, defines, and illustrates their use to stimulate teenage growth by describing some practical programs that enhance growth.

dt Muuss, Rolf E. H., ed. *Adolescent Behavior and Society: A Book of Readings,* 3d ed. New York: Random House, 1980. 547 pp.

Provides an in-depth survey of contemporary perspectives on the psychosocial correlates of adolescence. Intended as an anthology for undergraduate courses in psychology, education, and sociology, the text includes readings on the nature and history of adolescence, development, social and cultural influences, and the adolescent subculture.

t Muuss, Rolf E. H. *Theories of Adolescence.* 4th ed. New York: Random House, 1982. 336 pp.

Historical and philosophical theories of development, emphasizing those aspects relating to adolescence. Analyzes current expressions of adolescent behavior.

r National Catholic Education Association. *Sharing the Faith: The Beliefs and Values of Catholic High School Teachers.* Washington, D.C.: National Catholic Education Association, 1985. 85 pp.

Early in 1984, a total of 1,062 full-time teachers from a national sample of 45 Catholic high schools responded to a 260-question survey about beliefs and values. This document describes the results of the survey and offers some analyses and speculation about the significance of the findings.

c National Council of Churches. *We Have This Ministry. ..* Two monographs. No. 1: "The Objective of Christian Education for Senior High Young People." New York: National Council of Churches, 1958. 44 pp. No. 2: "A View Toward Youth in the Church's Ministry." New York: National Council of Churches, 1964. 46 pp.

Two classic statements of the objectives and purposes of youth ministry.

r Nelson, John, and Catherine Nelson. *Mindsets for Adolescents: Religious and Otherwise.* Naugatuck, Conn.: Center for Youth Ministry Development, 1988. 60 pp.

This document presents a partial review of studies (books and articles from periodicals) on adolescents published from 1980 through 1987. The review was funded in part by the Lilly Endowment through the Youth Ministry and Theological Schools Project at Union Theological Seminary in Virginia.

cd Nelson, John, Thomas Groome, John Shea, Reynolds Eckstrom, Gloria Durka, and Marina Herrera. *Readings in Youth Ministry,* Vol. 1, *Foundations.* Compiled by J. Roberto. Washington, D. C.: National Federation for Catholic Youth Ministry, 1986.

Focuses on research and analysis that contribute to the development of foundations upon which to build a contemporary and comprehensive approach to youth ministry. The first three articles utilize psychological and developmental research to describe and analyze the adolescent journey. The second three articles focus on the broader context to adolescent development: youth culture, family, and society.

r Norman, Jane, and Myron W. Harris. *The Private Life of the American Teenager.* New York: Rawson, Wade, 1981. 311 pp.

Reportedly the largest survey ever done on adolescents (160,000 young people as participants). Reports how young people feel about their parents, themselves, friendship, sex, dating, drug use, and describes their hopes, fears, and dreams.

rt Offer, Daniel. *The Adolescent: A Psychological Self-Portrait.* New York: Basic Books, 1981. 195 pp.

A basic refutation of adolescence as a time of turmoil and despair. Reports an extensive research project. Analyzes current concepts of self and details adolescents' view of five aspects of the self: psychological, social, sexual, familial, and coping. Maintains that most other research has focused on abnormal populations.

r Offer, Daniel, Eric Ostrov, et al. *The Teenage World: Adolescents' Self-Image in Ten Countries.* New York: Plenum Medical, 1988. 270 pp.

A survey of almost 6,000 urban adolescents in ten countries that compares them with each other across five aspects of the self. The major finding is that urban adolescents, regardless of their culture and nation, are more alike than dissimilar.

d Oraker, James R., with Char Meredith. *Almost Grown: A Christian Guide for Parents of Teenagers.* New York: Harper & Row, 1982. 178 pp.

From biological, sociological, and spiritual perspectives, describes growth from ages ten to nineteen. Focuses on sexuality and related issues, maturation, and the adolescent in the family setting. Aimed at parents, the book offers specific guidelines for designing a Christian family, using New Testament concepts of community as a model.

d Parks, Sharon. *The Critical Years.* San Francisco: Harper & Row, 1986. 245 pp.

An excellent review of the developmental growth of college/university students. Parks, a former associate of James Fowler, brings a keen insight into the holistic development of college/university students. This is an excellent book for anyone who teaches or works with college/university students.

d Parrott, Les, III. *Helping the Struggling Adolescent: A Guide to Thirty Common Problems for Parents, Counselors, and Youth Workers.* Grand Rapids: Zondervan, 1993. 272 pp.

A basic resource for anyone who works with or is related to an adolescent. Biblical and psychological insights help readers to grasp the issues, know what to do, and when to refer adolescents for professional help.

dr Peel, Edwin A. *The Nature of Adolescent Judgment.* New York: John Wiley, 1971.

Research report detailing a chronological scheme of adolescent cognitive development based on young, middle, and late adolescents' answers to a number of judgment problems.

r Potvin, Raymond, Dean Hoge, and Hart Nelsen. *Religion and American Youth: with Emphasis on Catholic Adolescents and Young Adults.* Washington, D.C.: USCC, 1976. 62 pp.

Describes the religious situation of adolescents and young adults in the United States, with emphasis on Catholic youth. It outlines the parameters within which an apostolate to youth must be carried on and reviews the pertinent literature on religious attitudes, beliefs, and behavior of young people between the ages of 13 and 29.

r Princeton Religious Research Center. *Religion in America.* (Vol. 1–). Princeton: Gallup Intermedia, 1971–.

Annual report of statistics, attitudes, measures of religious involvement, identification, and participation, primarily although not solely from Gallup polling. The nature and depth of religious commitment is interpreted. The 1984 volume includes an extensive study of the religious world of teenagers. Report No. 236 (May 1985) surveys the years 1935–1985.

cd Rice, F. Philip. *The Adolescent: Development, Relationships, and Culture.* 3d ed. Boston: Allyn and Bacon, 1981. 596 pp.

A textbook on adolescence, including its contemporary context, theories of adolescence, development, and behavior. Primarily from a psychological perspective, but incorporating sociological, anthropological, and educational perspectives. Includes reference to contemporary research studies.

d _____. *Morality and Youth: A Guide for Christian Parents.* Philadelphia: Westminster, 1980. 252 pp.

Biblical guidelines for understanding the process of moral development and influencing the formation of character and beliefs. Uses case studies to consider five crucial areas of ethical decision making.

cr Richardson, James T., Mary White Stewart, and Robert B. Simmonds, eds. *Organized Miracles: A Study of a Contemporary, Youth, Communal, Fundamentalist Organization.* New Brunswick, N.J.: Transaction Books, 1979. 368 pp.

Report of long-term research concerning a "new religious group," originating in the Jesus movement of the late 1960s. The group's history, demographics, and adaptation to change are analyzed, and the authors reflect on insights from their research methodology.

r Rosenweig, Susan. *Resources for Youth Workers and Program Planners.* Rev. ed. Carrboro, N.C.: Center for Early Adolescence, 1986. 40 pp.

An annotated bibliography of journal articles and books about early adolescence, programs, health, and racial, ethnic, and gender differences.

ct Roszak, Theodore. *The Making of a Counter Culture: Reflections on the Technocratic Society and its Youthful Opposition.* Garden City, N.Y.: Doubleday, 1969. 306 pp.

Assumes that the social and cultural changes of the '60s were the product of youth alienated from the parental generation, or of those who addressed themselves to the young. Examines the influence of this latter group and details their questioning of the conventional scientific world view/technocracy. Calls for the return to a magical or visionary world view as a source of human creativity and community.

c Rutter, Michael. *Changing Youth in a Changing Society: Patterns of Adolescent Development and Disorder.* Cambridge, Mass.: Harvard University Press, 1980. 233 pp.

Reviews adolescent psychosocial disorders. Presents effects of heredity, childhood, family, school, peer group, religion, media, and the urban environment on development of a model of adolescence. Asserts that concern about youth is ill-founded and that problems are self-correcting. Notes real problem areas and proposes solutions.

ct Scanlon, John, ed. *The Turbulent Years.* Academy for Educational Development, 1980. 247 pp.

An interdisciplinary report on the life cycle in years 14 to 24. Explores demographics, music, and political events of the generation. Effects of drugs, homosexuality, cults, crime, and biomedical advances; and Third World perspectives are identified.

r Schultze, Quentin, Roy M. Anker, et al. *Dancing in the Dark.* Grand Rapids, Mich.: Eerdmans, 1991. 348 pp.

A serious study of electronic mass media and youth culture in the United States. Particular attention focuses upon MTV. This very helpful sociological critique is worth reading for youth workers both in the U.S. and anywhere the electronic media are present or will be.

r Search Institute. *Young Adolescents and Their Parents.* Search Institute, Minneapolis: 1984. 51 pp.

Here are the results of a survey of 8,000 5th- through 9th-grade adolescents with 10,000 of their parents. The parents and adolescents each answered one of two questionnaires, each with over three hundred items. Charts and graphics which report the results are easy to read and interpret. The report ends with a helpful summary of the major themes and recommendations.

dt Shelton, Charles M. *Adolescent Spirituality: Pastoral Ministry for High School and College Youth.* Chicago: Loyola University Press, 1983. 336 pp.

Integrates counseling and developmental psychology, pastoral theology, and spirituality, in an overview of adolescent spiritual growth and religious problems. Applies developmental perspectives to areas such as sexuality, social consciousness, family problems, problems with God, and the church. Includes adolescent questions and related counseling strategies.

c Snyder, Ross. *Young People and Their Culture.* Nashville: Abingdon, 1969. 221 pp.

A classic consideration of the relationship of youth and culture.

r Sorenson, Robert C. *Adolescent Sexuality in Contemporary America: Personal Values and Sexual Behavior, Ages Thirteen to Nineteen.* New York: World Press, 1973. 549 pp.

Report of a research project conducted through self-administered and confidential questionnaires, plus tape-recorded interviews. Contains research methodology and statistical data as well as conclusions related to the influence of values and attitudes on sexual behavior, and the relation of behavior to social change.

c Steinberg, Lawrence D. *Understanding Families with Young Adolescents.* Carrboro, N.C.: Center for Early Adolescence, 1980. 30 pp.

An examination using the categories of systems thinking of the developmental changes in the family lifecycle as children and parents progress through two periods of marked change and growth: early adolescence and early middle age. The critical bibliographic essay summarizes recent research from other perspectives.

r Strommen, Merton P., and A. Irene Strommen. *Five Cries of Parents.* San Francisco: Harper & Row, 1985. 212 pp.

Describes five primary concerns in family life (understanding self and adolescent, achieving close family life, developing moral purpose and behavior, making faith central, finding help in crises). Offers guidelines in meeting these concerns. Focuses on adolescence.

r Strommen, Merton P. *Five Cries of Youth.* New York: Harper & Row, 1974. 155 pp.

Research report on values, beliefs, and opinions of over 7,000 U.S. church youth. Strommen contends that such data are important, and should inform an effective youth ministry. The five cries or clusters of opinion are self-hatred, psychological orphans, social protests, prejudice, and joy.

r Sussman, Alan. *The Rights of Young People: The Basic ACLU Guide to a Young Person's Rights.* New York: Avon, 1977. 251 pp.

Concise guide to the legal rights and obligations of young people in the United States. Covers topics such as driving, hitchhiking, drugs and alcohol, employment, police actions, rape, pornography, abuse and neglect, and adoption.

c Tyler, Ralph W., ed. *From Youth to Constructive Adult Life: The Role of the Public School.* Berkeley, Calif.: McCuchan, 1978. 195 pp.

Considers educational issues involved in young people making the transition from adolescence to adulthood (or not having such an opportunity). Examines problems young people face and suggests how schools may help, with some program reports.

c Van den Huevel, Albert H., ed. *The New Creation and the New Generation: A Forum for Youth Workers.* New York: Friendship Press, 1965.

A forum examining church youth work from the perspectives of sociology, psychology, theology, biblical study, and culture. Contains a brief critical history of youth work by the editor. Other authors speak from Asian and European, as well as American backgrounds.

c Van Der Bent, Ans J. *From Generation to Generation: The Story of Youth in the World Council of Churches.* Geneva: World Council of Churches, 1986. 135 pp.

An interpretative survey of ecumenical youth work from 1925 to the early 1980s, primarily with reference to the World Council of Churches.

cr Vergote, Antoine, and Tamayo Alvaro. *The Parental Figures and the Representation of God: A Psychological and Cross-Cultural Study.* New York: Mouton, 1980. 255 pp.

Examines the symbolic meaning and functions of parental figures, especially what the mother-father polarity means for child and adult, and the ways God is presented and represented in terms of maternal and paternal characteristics. The connection between the parental relationship and the belief relationship is explored across cultural, psychological, and faith-stance lines.

d Wilcox, Mary M. *Developmental Journey: A Guide to the Development of Logical and Moral Reasoning and Social Perspective.* Nashville: Abingdon, 1979. 286 pp.

Suggests that the processes of developing a value system and of decision making are part of a developmental journey founded on logical reasoning (Piaget), moral reasoning (Kohlberg), and faith development (Fowler). Two chapters are devoted to adolescent development, and three chapters apply the author's theory in practical settings, such as youth ministry.

c Yankelovich, D. *New Rules: Searching for Self-Fulfillment in a World Tuned Upside Down.* New York: Random House, 1981. 278 pp.

Describes the effect of changing American values (a loosened attachment to the ethic of self-denial and deferred gratification) in a time when the economy is no longer abundant and expanding. Interprets young American's views in relation to both self-fulfillment and commitment.

r Zelnik, Melvin, John F. Kanter, and Kathleen Ford. *Sex and Pregnancy in Adolescence.* Beverly Hills: Sage, 1981. 272 pp.

Report of research projects on adolescent female sexuality and fertility control, especially in regard to choices and sequences of alternatives. A profile of respondents is expanded to a chapter on the world of the teenager; religion is addressed briefly.

r Zuck, Roy B., and Gene A. Getz. *Christian Youth—An In-Depth Study.* Chicago: Moody, 1968. 192 pp.

An important early study of youth in conservative youth groups.

Part II: Youth Ministry

CODING

a Approaches to youth ministry
g General
o Organization and leadership manuals
p Program planning
r Program resources

---

r Adebonojo, Mary. *Free to Choose: Youth Program Resource from the Black Experience.* Valley Forge, Pa.: Judson, 1980. 144 pp.

Designed to help youth learn, worship, and experience the Christian faith in their own cultural contexts. Includes session plans, long-term projects, retreat outlines, simulation games, and craft work. Topics include decision making, faith, community, justice, values, identity, and unemployment.

p Ambrose, Dub. *Ministry to Families with Teenagers.* Loveland, Colo.: Group Books, 1988.

A basic approach to ministering to adolescents and their whole families.

pr Arterburn, Stephen, and Jim Burns. *Drug-Proof Your Kids.* Pomona, Calif: Focus on the Family, 1989.

A guide for parents and youth workers in the crucial area of drugs and how to prevent and intervene in the areas of drugs and alcohol.

pr Bailey, Betty Jane, and J. Martin. *Youth Plan Worship.* New York: Pilgrim, 1987. 214 pp.

This is a six-session course on worship for youth, an interpretation of worship, guides for planning, and resources.

r Bannerman, Glenn, and Robert Fokhema. *Guide for Recreation Leaders.* Atlanta: John Knox, 1975. 127 pp.

Theory of recreation and description of activities for all ages and settings. Most chapters relate directly to recreation, games, fellowship, and other activities with and for church youth.

r Bell, Martin. *The Way of the Wolf: The Gospel in New Images.* New York: Seabury, 1970. 127 pp.

Parables, stories, poems, songs on themes such as love, forgiveness, acceptance, salvation, and commitment.

r _____ . *Return of the Wolf.* New York: Seabury, 1983. 125 pp.
Stories, poems, and songs on gospel themes.

g Benson, Dennis C., and Bill Wolfe. *The Basic Encyclopedia for Youth Ministry.* Loveland, Colo.: Group Books, 1981. 348 pp.

Contains an index, which groups entries under topics such as youth culture, adults and youth ministry, media. Each entry is followed by a resource list, and cross-references to related entries.

pr Benson, Marilyn, and Dennis Benson, compilers. *Hard Times Catalog for Youth Ministry.* Loveland, Colo.: Group Books, 1982. 288 pp.

A collection of program ideas for learning, fellowship, outreach, and worship. Entries are cross-referenced, and planning help is included.

op Benson, Peter L., and Dorothy L. Williams. *Determining Needs in Your Youth Ministry.* Loveland, Colo.: Group Books, 1987.

Shows youth workers how to determine needs of youth. Provides research questions to ask and shows how to score the responses. Questions cover a breadth of areas; analyses and helps are extremely useful. One does not have to be a social scientist to use this resource.

g Benson, Warren S., and Mark H. Senter, III, eds. *The Complete Book of Youth Ministry.* Chicago: Moody, 1987. 518 pp.

A comprehensive selection of readings related to understanding and development of youth ministry. Essays range from theology and history of youth ministry, to leadership, principles, and strategies.

ap Berkowitz, Irving, ed. *Adolescents Grow in Groups: Experiences in Adolescent Group Psychotherapy.* New York: Brunner/ Mazel. 1972.

Thirty professionals of the three major disciplines—psychiatrist, psychologist, and social worker—describe examples of experiences in small group settings. A guide for group work with youth.

220

o   Bertolini, Dewey M. *Back to the Heart of Youth Work.* Wheaton, Ill.: Victor, 1989. 210 pp.

    Seeks to provide a balanced approach to youth ministry that starts with the spiritual development of youth workers and then moves to philosophy and programs. Twenty pages of sample program materials fill out the appendices.

r   Billups, Ann. *Discussion Starters for Youth Groups.* Valley Forge, Pa.: Judson, Series One, 1966, 224 pp. Series Two, 1969, 256 pp. Series Three, 1976, 224 pp.

    Each kit contains all needed materials for twenty discussion programs for a youth group.

op   Bimler, Rich. *77 Ways of Involving Youth in the Church.* St. Louis: Concordia, 1977. 64 pp.

    A source book on youth involvement in the parish. Includes strategies, and evaluation, planning, and organizational material.

r   Bingham, Mindy, Judy Edmondson, and Sandy Stryker. *Challenges: A Young Man's Journal for Self-Awareness and Personal Planning.* Santa Barbara, Calif.: Advocacy, 1984. 240 pp.

    A workbook-style journal with art and commentary essays dealing with attitude formation, financial aid for school, values assessment, goal setting, skills identification, career planning, future visions.

r   _____ . *Choices: A Teen Woman's Journal for Self-Awareness and Personal Planning.* Santa Barbara, Calif.: Advocacy, 1987. 240 pp.

    A workbook-style journal with art and commentary essays dealing with attitude formation, goal setting, nontraditional careers, decision making, future visions, being a healthy adult.

g   Black, Wesley. *An Introduction to Youth Ministry.* Nashville: Broadman, 1991. 242 pp.

    An excellent introductory text on philosophy of youth ministry from within the Southern Baptist tradition. The emphasis on shared ministry is vital.

r   Blume, Judy. *Are You There, God? It's Me, Margaret.* New York: Dell, 1980. 149 pp.

    Faced with the difficulties of growing up and choosing a religion, a twelve-year-old girl talks over her problems with her own private God.

o   Borthwick, Paul. *Organizing Your Youth Ministry.* Grand Rapids, Mich.: Zondervan, 1987.

    Helps youth workers get themselves and especially their youth programs organized.

p   _____ . *Youth and Missions.* Wheaton, Ill.: Victor, 1988. 160 pp.

Provides psychological, developmental, and theological insight into youth involvement in service and mission along with practical how to's.

o _____. *Feeding Your Forgotten Soul.* Grand Rapids, Mich.: Zondervan, 1990. 181 pp.

Youth workers need first to keep their own spiritual selves growing. Borthwick helps to focus intentional actions on this area that is often neglected in the hurried, action-filled lives of youth workers.

o Bowman, Locke. *How to Teach Senior Highs.* Philadelphia: Westminster, 1963. 191 pp.

Emphasizes engagement in rigorous thinking and inquiry. Course outlines as well as various methodologies are included. Stresses learning as well as teaching.

ao Brown, Carolyn C. *Youth Ministries: Thinking Big with Small Groups.* Nashville: Abingdon, 1984. 96 pp.

Youth ministry for groups of ten or less. Deals with ministry issues, programing, and evaluation.

r Brown, John. *Worship Celebrations for Youth.* 2d ed. Valley Forge, Pa.: Judson, 1984. 64 pp.

Resources for twenty worship celebrations or devotions for youth in a variety of settings, throughout the church's year and the calendar year. Includes readings, prayers, dramas, activities, poetry, and other material which may be copied and distributed to participants. Aside from suggested hymns and recordings, all needed material is included.

pr Burns, Jim. *Handling Your Hormones: The Straight Scoop on Love and Sexuality.* Eugene, Ore.: Harvest House, 1986. Rev. ed.

A practical, useful, and very helpful approach to sex education for youth and for those working with youth.

a _____. *The Youth Builder.* Eugene, Ore: Harvest House, 1988. 325 pp.

The twenty-five chapters are crammed with very practical, helpful, and on-target information in almost every conceivable area of youth ministry, including some areas not usually found in many books. This is a "how to book" by a well-seasoned veteran of youth ministry. Includes three chapters of examples and resources.

pr Burns, Marilyn. *I Am Not a Short Adult!: Getting Good at Being a Kid.* Boston: Little, Brown, 1977. 125 pp.

Deals with various aspects of childhood: family, school, money, legal rights, TV and movies, body language. Addressed to older children or young adolescents, suggesting how to make the most of childhood. Includes reflection and discussion activities.

a Burns, Ridge. *Create in Me a Youth Ministry.* Wheaton, Ill.: Victor, 1986. 203 pp.

A personal account of the lessons a youth minister found in the early stages of his ministry. Focus is upon the life of the youth worker and not on programs, etc. Ministry starts in the person, not in the program, and this book helps to focus there.

pr Cagle, Bob. *Youth Ministry Camping.* Loveland, Colo.: Group Books, 1983. 350 pp.

Almost every conceivable topic on youth camping is covered in this double-columned book; it is very helpful and encyclopedic.

o Campbell, Sheila. *Youth Ministries with Senior Highs.* Nashville: Board of Discipleship, United Methodist Church, 1971. 61 pp.

A United Methodist youth fellowship manual which examines the various tasks of youth ministry (leadership, organization, program building, teaching, and counseling).

pr Campolo, Tony. *Ideas for Social Action.* Grand Rapids, Mich.: Zondervan, 1983. 162 pp.

Foundations for youth in ministry and many practical ideas for how to carry out those projects.

pr _____. *Growing Up in America.* Grand Rapids, Mich.: Zondervan, 1989. 217 pp.

Looks sociologically at youth in the United States with a focus on attacking middle-class values and the need to work with urban youth. Many good sociopsychological insights along with an activist intervention into urban issues.

ao Carroll, John L., and Keith L. Ignatius. *Youth Ministry: Sunday, Monday, and Every Day.* Valley Forge, Pa.: Judson, 1972. 62 pp.

Sees youth ministry not as a once-a-week, part-time effort, but as a high priority within the total ministry of the church. Stresses involvement of youth in planning of youth ministry as well as its practice. Emphasizes leadership and organization.

o Christie, Les. *How to Recruit and Train Volunteers.* Grand Rapids: Zondervan, 1987. 202 pp.

Provides basic information and practical "how-to's" in the devlopment of adult youth workers.

o _____. *Unsung Heroes.* Grand Rapids, Mich.: Zondervan, 1987. 202 pp.

Lays the ground work for understanding the need for co-workers in youth ministry, including both adults and youth. Provides plenty of practical helps.

r Clapp, Steve. *Repairing Christian Lifestyles.* 2d ed. Champaign, Ill.: C-4 Resources, 1984. 174 pp.

Kit: Books, audiocassette, packet. Resources for a 16-session program of journal writing and personal spiritual discipline. Contains manual for youth with same title as kit.

a Clapp, Steve, and Jerry O. Cook. *Youth Workers' Handbook.* (C-4 Resources, P. O. Box 27, Siudell, IL 63876), 1981.

Frustrated by the problems that so many volunteer youth workers seemed to experience, the authors set to work to provide a basic, practical, and readable handbook for teaching purposes. Every aspect from media to evangelism, from fund raising to lock-ins—it's all here.

pr Clark, Chap. *Youth Specialities Handbook for Great Camps and Retreats.* Grand Rapids, Mich.: Zondervan, 1990. 191 pp.

A basic how-to book on camps and retreats, including forty-one pages of resources.

op Cole, Charles E. *Alternate Lifestyles: Youth Ministry.* Notebook VIII. Seabury, 1974. 95 pp.

Designed to help adults and youth plan for an effective youth ministry at the local church level. A collection of issue-related articles with suggested ways of digging further into the issue. Common themes are alternatives and variations in areas such as marriage, sexuality, Christian life-style, culture, work, protest, family.

ao Coleman, Bill, and Patty Coleman. *Parish Youth Ministry: A Manual for Beginners in the Art.* West Mystic, Conn.: Twenty-Third Publ., 1977. 120 pp.

Manual covers organization and philosophy of youth ministry, program models, leadership training, and support resources. Catholic perspective.

op Corbett, Jan. *Creative Youth Leadership for Adults Who Work with Youth.* Valley Forge, Pa.: Judson, 1977. 128 pp.

Leadership skills for both the new and the experienced leader/teacher of youth. Includes program ideas.

ap Corbett, Janice M., and Curtis E. Johnson. *It's Happening with Youth.* New York: Harper & Row, 1972. 176 pp.

Describes 14 forms of youth ministry in and near the church: communities, political action groups, services for youth; includes program ideas.

r Dausey, Gary, ed. *The Youth Leader's Source Book.* Grand Rapids, Mich.: Zondervan, 1983.

Twenty-four youth workers share successes and failures within the very practical format of this handbook of ideas and insights. This is not a theory of youth ministry, but a carefully chosen collection of principles, outlines, charts, forms, and step-by-step plans covering: program building helps, insights into the agencies for ministry, and plans for activities with a purpose.

apr Cromer, William R. *Casebook for Youth Ministry.* Nashville, Tenn.: Broadman, 1991. 160 pp.

Provides both an understanding of case studies and their use along with twelve cases that cover basic areas of youth ministry. Useful for discussions with youth workers and parents and for knowing how to write one's own case studies.

r Davitz, Joel, and Lois Davitz. *How to Live (Almost) Happily with a Teenager.* Minneapolis: Winston, 1982. 261 pp.

Straightforward guidelines and advice for rational parenting in issue areas such as responsibility, privacy, relationships, and limits. Focuses on parental attitudes, especially tolerance and trust, and the importance of listening.

or Dielmann, Dale, comp. *The Go Book.* Grand Rapids, Mich.: Baker, 1982. 55 pp.

Basic resources for those working with youth in ministry-service projects.

pr Dockrey, Karen. *Youth Workers and Parents.* Wheaton, Ill.: Victor, 1990. 143 pp.

A guide for involving youth and their parents in guided discussion in nine critical areas of youth life.

ap Doherty, Mary. *Electives for Revitalizing High School Religion.* Staten Island, N.Y.: Alba House, 1972. 256 pp.

A collection of books and guides for curriculum development. Contains school-based alternatives and electives or mini-electives for religious education. Assumes a Catholic high school setting.

r Dorman, Gayle, Dick Geldorf, and Bill Scarborough. *Living with 10-to-15-Year-Olds: A Parent Education Curriculum.* Carrboro, N.C.: Center for Early Adolescence, UNCCH, 1982.

A kit containing resources for a comprehensive curriculum to be used with parents.

r Estrada, Christelle L. *Telling Stories Like Jesus Did: Creative Parables for Teachers.* San Jose, Calif.: Resource Publications, Inc., 1987. 92 pp.

A resource giving guidance for the use of parables in teaching various age groups, including youth.

ao Evans, David. *Shaping the Church's Ministry with Youth.* Rev. ed. Valley Forge, Pa.: Judson, 1977. 125 pp.

Aimed at pastors, church educators, and others who work with youth in the local church. Raises questions about historical assumptions concerning youth ministry, and proposes a way of thinking about and involving young people as a part of the people of God, in the gathered faith community and in the world.

ao Fackre, Gabriel, and Jan Chartier. *Youth Ministry: The Gospel and the People.* Valley Forge, Pa.: Judson, 1979. 135 pp.

The first section focuses on implications of the Gospel message for youth and ways that leaders can share their faith with young people. The second section concentrates on identity and

225

esteem issues for young people, and the importance of an environment of love and care in the church.

o Feldmeyer, Dean. *Beating Burnout in Youth Ministry*. Loveland, Colo.: Group Books, 1989. 143 pp.

Seeks to help youth workers get and stay organized in order to insure the likelihood of successful youth ministry.

r Fletcher, Judy, ed. *Much Ado About Something*. Atlanta: Materials Distribution Service, PCUS, 1977. 80 pp.

An information packet and guidelines for further study about independent Christian youth movements and the church.

ar Fletcher, Kenneth R., et al. *Extend: Youth Reaching Youth*. Minneapolis: Augsburg, 1974. 112 pp.

A group interaction plan for training young people in peer ministry (as well as ministries to other ages). Ten training sessions are included, focusing on understanding the needs of others, handling conflict, and reaching out in friendship.

r Fluegelman, Andrew, ed. *The New Games Book*. Garden City, N.J.: Dolphin Books/ Doubleday, 1976.

Provides noncompetitive games that are fun.

ao Fox, Zeni, Marisa Guerin, Brian Reynolds, and John Roberto. *Leadership for Youth Ministry*. Winona, Minn.: St. Mary's, 1984. 165 pp.

Organized in three sections: an overview of leadership theory and its implications for youth leaders; descriptions and distinctions in the leadership roles in youth ministry; and "how-to" chapters on recruiting, training, and supporting youth leaders. Contains practical worksheets.

or Friedman, Alfred, and George Beschner. *Treatment Services for Adolescent Substance Abusers*. Rockville, Md.: U.S. Department of Health and Human Services, 1985. 242 pp.

Highlights and integrates what is currently known about adolescent substance abusers, their drug and drug-related problems, the programs that serve them, and the treatment methods and approaches that have proven most effective. It is intended to serve as a guide for those who are currently involved or who plan to become involved in the treatment of adolescent substance abusers.

r Gieschen, David, ed. *Five Weekend Conferences for Youth*. Philadelphia: Parish Life, 1976. 80 pp.

Teaching/leadership plans for conferences on topics such as doubt, career choice, death, the global community, and the person, work, and lordship of Jesus Christ.

a Gilbert, W. Kent, ed. *Confirmation and Education*. Philadelphia: Fortress Yearbook, 1969. 222 pp.

Collection of articles on Lutheran confirmation education, its purpose, history, and various forms.

or Ginott, Haim G. *Between Parent and Teenager.* New York: Avon, 1971. 256 pp.

> Aimed at parents of teenagers. Gives advice and offers skills for handling small and large crises and events, and for anticipating and dealing with growth and change.

ao Gobbel, A. Roger, Gertrude G. Gobbel, and Thomas E. Ridenhour, Jr. *Helping Youth Interpret the Bible: A Teaching Resource.* Atlanta: John Knox, 1984. 208 pp.

> Presents a model of or approach to interpreting the Bible, centered around major developmental tasks which confront adolescents. The book is designed to help youth engage biblical texts, and illustrates the theory proposed.

op Graendorf, Werner C., and Lloyd Mattson, eds. *An Introduction to Christian Camping.* Chicago: Moody, 1979.

> Thirteen writers have contributed to this basic textbook on camping as a form of ministry and community. Four divisions introduce (1) the subject, through camping forms and history; (2) the program, with principles and components of a successful camping ministry; (3) the camper, through building a staff and the nature of counseling, and; (4) the operations requiring organization, management, and facilities.

op Hall, Robert T. *Moral Education: A Handbook for Teachers.* Minneapolis: Winston, 1979. 209 pp.

> Insights and practical strategies for helping adolescents become more caring, thoughtful, responsible persons. Contrasts hard-line vs. soft-line approaches to moral education and proposes a middle way composed of five strategies: awareness, debate, rationale, concept, and game. Applies this middle way to five units for the classroom (justice, property, honesty, integrity, and relationships).

r Harbin, E. O. *The New Fun Encyclopedia.* Nashville: Abingdon, 1985.

> A compiliation of games, etc., for youth ministry.

ag Harris, Maria. *Portrait of Youth Ministry.* New York: Paulist, 1981. 225 pp.

> Considers youth ministry in terms of who/what young people are (and are not) , and critical agenda items for youth ministry in each of the five traditional ecclesial areas of ministry. Includes tested study and practice activities for exploring issues at depth. Stresses the need for common language and adequate theory for youth ministry.

ar Hebeisen, Ardyth. *Peer Program for Youth.* Minneapolis: Augsburg, 1973. 112 pp.

> A group interaction plan for developing self-esteem, self-understanding, and communication skills.

ao Holderness, Ginny Ward. *The Exuberant Years: A Guide for Junior High Leaders.* Atlanta: John Knox, 1976. 215 pp.

Guidance on preparing for, planning, and developing a complete youth ministry program for junior highs. Includes 11 minicourses and help for developing courses of activity and study. A collection of methods is included.

ao ———. *Youth Ministry: The New Team Approach.* Atlanta: John Knox, 1981. 143 pp.

A leadership model for youth ministry which uses teams for planning and program leadership; intended to involve all youth in the total life of the congregation.

a Holmes, Urban T. *Confirmation: The Celebration of Maturity in Christ.* New York: Seabury, 1975. 98 pp.

Reconsideration of confirmation and the appropriate age, proposed changes in Christian initiation rites, and the theology of a maturity rite.

r Hutterian Brethren, ed. *A Straight Word to Kids and Parents: Help for Teen Problems.* Rifton, N.Y.: Plough, 1987. 153 pp.

Useful in individual study, group discussions, and topical presentations. Touches on most major issues—T.V., drugs, alcohol, dating, pregnancy and abortion, depression and suicide, crime, homosexuality, cults, help, and hope. Gives facts, research findings, personal experience, and a help list for each chapter.

g Irving, Roy G., and Roy B. Zuck, eds. *Youth and the Church: A Survey of the Church's Ministry to Youth.* Chicago: Moody, 1974. 442 pp.

A series of essays on youth, their development, and the planning and developing of a youth ministry program. This book will be of help to adult leaders, especially in more conservative churches.

ao Jesuit Secondary Education Association. *Companions in the Ministry of Teaching.* New York: Jesuit Secondary Education Association (JSEA), 1986.

The purpose of the Companions in the Ministry of Teaching Project is to help a Jesuit secondary school design a Companions in the Ministry of Teaching Program for the religious development of its faculty. It is an attempt to gather, develop, and distribute a variety of resources and services that each school is free to adopt and adapt as it designs its own program.

ao Jones, Jeffrey D., and Kenneth C. Potts. *Organizing a Youth Ministry to Fit Your Needs.* Valley Forge, Pa.: Judson, 1983. 61 pp.

A guide to planning and organization of a youth ministry program. Includes examples, case histories, questionnaires, and procedures. Evaluates three approaches: meeting-centered, event-centered, individual-centered, with guidelines for choosing appropriate combinations. Stresses importance of a statement of purpose and sound organization.

ao   Jones, Nathan. *Sharing the Old, Old Story: Educational Ministry in the Black Community.* Winona, Minn.: St. Mary's, 1982. 113 pp.

      A catechist training program for ministers working in black communities. Develops principles for communicating the Christian faith, drawing on the history, culture, spirituality, and religious ethics of black people in the United States.

ao   Jones, Stephen D. *Faith Shaping: Nurturing the Faith Journey of Youth.* Rev. ed. Valley Forge, Pa.: Judson, 1988. 144 pp.

      Affirms that young people claim and develop their own faith but that the church and families as well as other adults have specific faith shaping or nurturing roles to play. Anecdotal in style, and written from perspective of a pastor, describes dual approaches of "nearness" and "directness" in nurture and intentional socialization. Contains tested program resources.

o   Keefauver, Larry. *Starting a Youth Ministry.* Loveland, Colo.: Group Books, 1984. 80 pp.

      Practical helps for getting a youth ministry program underway.

o   Kerr, John, ed. *Teaching Grades Seven Through Ten: A Handbook.* Philadelphia: Parish Life Press (LCA Catechetical Series), 1979.

      Deals with communicating doctrine to youth, taking into account difficulties of early adolescents in thinking abstractly. Concludes with methodology for confirmation and other classes.

gr   Kesler, Jay, ed. *Parents and Teenagers.* Wheaton, Ill.: Victor, 1984. 693 pp.

      An encyclopedic volume containing over 300 articles by various youth and adult education workers giving practical advice on parenting of adolescents.

r   Kilgore, Lois. *Eight Special Studies for Senior Highs.* Scottsdale, Ariz.: National Teacher Education Project, 1976. 169 pp.

      Learning centers (ten to fifteen per concept) for use in examining eight concepts: happiness, fear, tradition, obedience, sin, forgiveness, justice, and faith.

pr   Klaus, Tom. *Healing Hidden Wounds: Ministering to Teenagers from Alcoholic Families.* Loveland, Colo.: Group Books, 1989. 201 pp.

      Helps youth workers be effective in dealing with youth whose parents are alcoholics. Gives basic understanding of youth and their situation and many approaches to helping in the healing processes.

ar   Kohler, Mary C. *Young People Learning to Care: Making a Difference Through Youth Participation.* New York: Seabury, 1983. 121 pp.

      Describes the principles of youth participation in over 30,000 programs nationwide. Encourages the recognition of adolescents and their energy as a largely untapped resource for caring and making a positive difference.

pr Liesch, Barry. *People In the Presence of God.* Grand Rapids, Mich.: Zondervan, 1988. 352 pp.

Provides a biblical foundation for worship along with many aspects of worship within the church and its manifold ministries, applicable to youth.

r Litherland, Janet. *The Clown Ministry Handbook.* Downers Grove, Ill.: Meriwether, 1982. 78 pp.

A practical handbook on clown types, makeup, wardrobe, props, and performance for in-church activities and outreach ministry.

ao Little, Sara. *Youth, World and Church.* Richmond, Va.: John Knox, 1968. 201 pp.

Emphasizes the present, full membership of young people in the Christian community, and the importance of the nurturing preparation of youth for involvement in the church's mission and common discipleship.

r Logan, Ben, and Kate Moody, eds. *Television Awareness Training: The Viewer's Guide for Family and Community.* 2d ed. New York: Media Action Research Center, 1978. 280 pp.

How to choose and use television, how to watch it critically. Aims, strategies, worksheets. Useful with youth.

r Lohmann, Hartivig. *I Can Tell You Anything, God.* Philadelphia: Fortress, 1978. 63 pp.

A collection of prayers for young people.

ao Ludwig, Glenn E. *Building an Effective Youth Ministry.* Nashville: Abingdon, 1979. 125 pp.

Concentrates on theoretical and theological bases for establishing effective youth ministry. Stresses importance of careful planning and congregational support and care. Gives practical help for all aspects of planning and building youth ministry.

pr Lynn, David, and Mike Yaconelli. *Teaching the Truth About Sex.* Grand Rapids, Mich.: Zondervan, 1990. 125 pp.

A twelve-session curriculum that helps youth workers teach a biblical perspective on sex and sexuality.

r McCoy, Kathleen. *Coping with Teenage Depression: A Parent's Guide.* New York: New American Library, 1982. 331 pp.

Aimed at parents. Indicates how depression may be recognized, what causes it, and how crisis situations may be resolved. Practical advice on communication with troubled young people.

pr McNabb, Bill, and Steven Mabry. *Teaching the Bible Creatively.* Grand Rapids, Mich.: Zondervan, 1990. 208 pp.

Covers basic principles of teaching the Bible, with concrete illustrations.

ao Martinson, Roland D. *Effective Youth Ministry: A Congregational Approach.* Minneapolis: Augsburg, 1988. 156 pp.

Presents an approach to youth ministry best categorized as "congregational." This book offers a theological structure along with specific suggestions for programs.

r   Miller, Donald, Graydon F. Snyder, and Robert W. Neff. *Using Biblical Simulations.* 2 vol. Valley Forge, Pa.: Judson, 1973–75.

Instructions for reenacting events from the Bible. Includes guides for subsequent discussion by participants and observers.

ar   Moore, Joseph, and James P. Emswiler. *Handbook for Peer Ministry.* New York: Paulist, 1982. 99 pp.

Theory and programing for a system of peer ministry for young people in school or parish settings. Relates peer ministry to developmental theories.

g   Murphy, Elly, Marisa Guerin, and John Roberto, eds. *Hope for the Decade: A Look at the Issues Facing Catholic Youth Ministry.* Washington, D.C.: National Catholic Youth Organization Federation, 1980. 260 pp.

Report of a national symposium on Catholic youth ministry in the 1980s. Contains research papers, issues papers, models for youth ministry, and assessment tools.

pr   Murray, Stephen, and Randy Smith. *Divorce Recovery for Teenagers.* Grand Rapids, Mich.: Zondervan, 1990. 155 pp.

Helps youth workers cope with the increasing number of teenagers from divorced families. Shows how to provide a workshop that can give further assistance.

a   Myers, William. *Black and White Styles of Youth Ministry.* New York: Pilgrim, 1991. 202 pp.

Combines sociological and theological insight to describe youth ministry in two differing racial settings along with reflection on the theoretical underpinnings of each approach.

ao   ————. *Theological Themes of Youth Ministry.* New York: Pilgrim, 1987.

A constructive approach in a theologically based understanding of youth ministry.

g   National Federation for Catholic Youth Ministry. *The Challenge of Adolescent Catechesis: Maturing in Faith.* Washington, D.C.: National Federation for Catholic Youth Ministry, 1986. 21 pp.

English and Spanish versions of a working paper on the issue and urgency of adolescent catechesis. Includes sections on the foundations, aims, framework, process/activities, and leadership of youth ministry in a variety of Catholic settings.

pr   Nelson, C. Ellis. *Helping Teenagers Grow Morally.* Louisville: Westminster, 1992. 109 pp.

Emphasis is on the local congregation's influence on the moral development of adolescents.

r Ng, David. *Christian Answers to Life's Problems.* New York: Program Agency, United Presbyterian Church, U.S.A., 1981. 38 pp.

Brief, biblically based answers to religious questions, such as, "How can I know God?" "Is God active in the world?" "How can I receive salvation?" An evangelism booklet.

o _____. *Developing Leaders for Youth Ministry.* Valley Forge, Pa.: Judson, 1984.

A resource for leadership development growing out of the consultation reported in Wyckoff and Richter, *Religious Education Ministry with Youth.*

ao _____. *Youth in the Community of Disciples.* Valley Forge, Pa.: Judson, 1984. 79 pp.

Advocates rediscovering the central purpose of youth ministry: helping young people hear and respond to the call of Christ to discipleship, community, and service. Suggests that such a wholistic ministry is compatible with search for identity. Considers the roles and responsibilities of the church and adult leaders of youth.

apr Ng, Donald, ed. *Asian Pacific American Youth Ministry.* Valley Forge, Pa.: Judson, 1988. 160 pp.

Provides one of the first attempts to look at Pacific Asian youth ministries.

r Olson, G. Keith. *Counseling Teenagers: The Complete Christian Guide to Understanding and Helping Adolescents.* Loveland, Colo.: Group Books, 1984. 528 pp.

An overview of the issues faced as well as the knowledge and skills needed to do crisis and growth counseling with young people.

pr Parsons, Richard D. *Adolescents in Turmoil, Parents Under Stress: A Pastoral Ministry Primer.* New York: Integration Books, 1987. 145 pp.

Provides helpful directions in counseling adolescents through many of the crises facing contemporary youth.

ap Posterski, Donald C. *Friendship: A Window on Ministry to Youth.* Scarborough, Ont.: Project Teen Canada, 1986. 166 pp.

A proposal for a model of youth ministry arising out of the research of Project Teen Canada.

opr Reed, Bobbie, and Ed Reed. *Creative Bible Learning: Youth Grades 7–12.* Glendale, Calif.: International Center for Learning, a division of Gospel Light Publications, 1977.

Offers easy-to-follow guidelines for helping youth study and learn from God's Word. Also, the authors provide helpful information on the needs of youth, department organization, scheduling, planning a lesson, using Bible-learning methods, and more. Specific plans are suggested and various teaching methods are described.

r Reichter, Arlo, et al. *The Group Retreat Book.* Loveland, Colo.: Group Books, 1983. 400 pp.

Thirty-four retreat designs on a variety of themes for youth groups, plus a retreat planning guide.

pr Reimer, Sandy, and Larry Reimer. *The Retreat Handbook.* Wilton, Conn.: Morehourse-Barlow, 1987. 192 pp.

The book is a compilation of experiences and learnings which the authors have integrated during fifteen years of professional retreat experience. Chapter topics include: The All-Church Retreat, Youth-Group Retreats, The Small-Group Adult Retreat, and the Planning Retreats.

r *Respond.* 5 vol. Valley Forge, Pa.: Judson, 1971–1977.

Outlines programs, study sessions (both biblical and issue-related), and worship for senior high groups. Additional helps for leaders. Most needed resources included (dialogues, dramas, readings, data summaries).

ao Reynolds, Brian. *A Chance to Serve: Peer Minister's Handbook.* Winona, Minn.: St. Mary's, 1983. 75 pp.

A formation program that helps teenagers to become effective ministers to their peers. Two books are involved: a leader's manual for peer ministry and a peer minister's handbook.

ao Rice, Wayne. *Junior High Ministry: A Guidebook for the Leading and Teaching of Early Adolescence.* Grand Rapids, Mich.: Zondervan, 1978. 199 pp.

Describes development of early adolescents, including spiritual development. Considers junior high ministry and leadership in the local church. Approximately one-third of the book contains programing activities.

r Rice, Wayne, and Mike Yaconelli, eds. *Ideas.* El Cajon, Calif.: Youth Specialities, 1968–.

There are more than 50 volumes in this series, with publication continuing. Some earlier volumes have been combined and reprinted in a larger book. An index is available for volumes 1–40. Ideas for programs include crowd breakers, games, methods, special events, service projects, skits, fund raisers, camps, holiday events, and family activities. Also included are tips on publicity and help with leadership and planning.

r Rice, Wayne, and Mike Yaconelli. *Play It!* Grand Rapids, Mich.: Zondervan, 1990, revised.

Over 400 suggestions of games and other activities to play with adolescents culled from past editions of the *Ideas* library.

g Richards, Lawrence O. *Youth Ministry: Its Renewal in the Local Church.* Rev. ed. Grand Rapids, Mich.: Zondervan, 1985. 364 pp.

Describes the overall development of young people, and analyzes contemporary youth culture in order to suggest ways young people may be reached in the contemporary context.

From a sociological basis, argues that the teaching and learning of the Christian faith should be a part of the culture of youth.

opr Roadcup, David, ed. *Methods for Youth Ministry*. Cincinnati: Standard, 1986. 271 pp.

Provides the basics for organizing and planning methods for youth ministry programing in numerous venues.

a _____ . *Ministering to Youth*. Cincinnati: Standard, 1980.

The nature, program, method, and activities appropriate for the age-characteristics of youth are addressed by the contributors. The youth culture, personal life of the youth worker, and the main goals of ministry are defined. Specific disciplines are outlined and the problems of programing in the local church are reviewed. The age-level characteristics from preschool through senior high are assessed—with specific ministry suggestions, ranging from camping and choirs to puppets and socials.

apr Robbins, Duffy. *The Ministry of Nurture*. Grand Rapids, Mich.: Zondervan 1990. 237 pp.

Looks at youth ministry not as programs as much as basic spiritual nurture that surrounds youth throughout their everyday lives.

pr _____ . *Youth Ministry Nuts and Bolts*. Grand Rapids, Mich.: Zondervan, 1990. 270 pp.

Probably one of the most practical books for professional youth workers on how to get and stay organized, and how to work with others in the youth ministry.

aor Roberts, William D., Jr. *Initiation to Adulthood: An Ancient Rite of Passage in Contemporary Form*. New York: Pilgrim, 1982. 182 pp.

Describes need for a modern rite of passage to adulthood, the classical and historical rhythms and shapes of such rites (including scriptural and traditional models), and the relation of baptism to other Christian initiation rites. Program areas (society, sex, self, spirituality) impart entry-level knowledge of the techniques and mysteries of adulthood.

opr Roehlkepartain, Eugene C. *Youth Ministry in the City*. Loveland, Colo.: Group Books, 1989. 251 pp.

A comprehensive guide to the challenges and methods of youth ministry in an urban setting.

a Roehlkepartain, Jolene L. *Youth Ministry: Its Impact on Church Growth*. Loveland, Colo.: Group Books, 1989.

Shows that an effective youth ministry directly affects the growth of a local church.

ap Rowley, Bill. *Equipped to Care: Counseling Youth*. Wheaton, Ill.: Victor, 1990. 157 pp.

Provides basic help to youth workers in their counseling roles, including crisis intervention.

pr Schroeder, Donald B., comp. *Ideology: Creative Ideas for Younger Youth.* Atlanta: GAMB, Presbyterian Church U.S., 1979. 96 pp.

An anthology of 64 activities for younger youth. Each activity follows a standard outline: objectives, planning, steps, options, evaluation.

pr Schultz, Thom, and Joani. *Do It! Active Learning in Youth Ministry.* Loveland, Colo.: Group Books, 1989. 144 pp.

Lays out a reasonable rationale for active, experience-oriented learning particularly focusing on classroom experiences. Useful in achieving application of ideas for teaching the Bible with youth.

ao ———. *Involving Youth in Youth Ministry: A New Way to Help Kids Take Responsibility.* Loveland, Colo.: Thom Schultz Publications, 1987. 201 pp.

Provides the basics for getting and keeping adolescents involved in a youth-based ministry.

ag Senter, Mark. *The Coming Revolution in Youth Ministry.* Wheaton, Ill.: Victor, 1992. 216 pp.

Taking a historian's perspective first, this book looks at the history of youth ministry. Then a prophetic perspective is taken, looking to future models of youth ministry.

r Sheaves, David. *Early Adolescence: A Resource Directory.* Carrboro, N.C.: Center for Early Adolescence, 1981. 54 pp.

An interdisciplinary resource directory for professionals who work with young adolescents. Includes organizations, publications, and readings.

r Slaikeu, Karl. *Crisis Intervention: A Handbook for Practice and Research.* Boston: Allyn and Bacon, 1990. 519 pp.

A basic textbook that introduces crisis intervention, provides strategies, and examines various delivery systems. Although not written particularly for youth workers, it serves to provide a serious foundation for crisis intervention programs.

ao Sparkman, G. Temp, ed. *Knowing and Helping Youth.* Nashville: Broadman, 1977. 152 pp.

A collection of essays on adolescent development and life tasks, with application to counseling, leading, and involving youth in faith, life, and the community of faith.

r Sparks, Lee, ed. *The Youth Group How-To Books: 66 Practical Projects and Programs to Help You Build A Better Youth Group.* Loveland, Colo.: Group Books, 1981.

These projects and programs have been gleaned from the past seven years of Group, the interdenominational magazine for Christian youth groups. The ideas are designed to be easily plugged into local youth groups as is, or with adaptation. Categories include basic aspects of youth ministry, building community, creative retreats, worship and service ideas, using the arts, publicity and larger projects, group trips, and management assistance for leadership.

o Spots, Dwight, and David Veerman. *Reaching Out to Troubled Youth.* Wheaton, Ill.: Victor, 1987. 256 pp.

The focus is on the call to and ministry with troubled youth. Helpful guide to the many facets of understanding troubled youth and the various means and venues for working with them.

a Stevens, Doug. *Called to Care: Youth Ministry for the Church.* Grand Rapids, Mich.: Zondervan, 1985. 216 pp.

Establishes a biblical/theological basis as a unifying philosophy for youth ministry and applies that to adolescent developmental factors, the world/culture of youth, and a wholistic strategy for ministry. Possibly the best chapter available on incarnational youth ministry.

g Stone, J. David, ed. *The Complete Youth Ministries Handbook.* 2 vol. Nashville: Abingdon, 1979, 1981.

A collection of articles, emphasizing ideas and models, about youth ministry. A total-concept approach, includes practical help as well as inspirational chapters. Volume II is titled *Catching the Rainbow.*

a Stone, David. *Spiritual Growth in Youth Ministry: Practical Models to Help Your Young People (and You) Grow Closer to God.* Loveland, Colo.: Group Books, 1985.

The spiritual and relational needs of young people are first explored. Then the implications for the youth worker are outlined: disciplines and programs for growth. Finally, the spiritual growth of the group is addressed—through caring, Bible study, worship, prayer, meditation, retreats, spiritual and physical fitness, and a program for relational spiritual growth.

r Strandberg, Arlene B., and Dick Troup, eds. *Skits, Plays and Projects for Youth Ministries.* Tempe, Ariz.: Success With Youth Publications, 1975. 102 pp.

Skits worth talking about, plays with a purpose, and plays for special occasions, all with discussion suggestions, and two project areas: a drive-in learning center approach to the Christmas message, and puppetry.

pr *Strategies for Youth Programs: Junior High.* 3 vol. Philadelphia: Westminster/Geneva, 1978–82.

Articles, programs, and projects grouped around themes, and resources for program planning.

pr *Strategies for Youth Programs: Senior High.* 3 vol. Philadelphia: Westminster/Geneva, 1978–80.

Articles, programs, and projects grouped around themes, and resources for program planning.

o Sullivan, Ann. *How to Guide Youth.* Nashville: Convention, 1982. 220 pp.

> A manual and workbook for Baptist youth workers in all aspects of the church's life.

a Taylor, Bob R., comp. *The Work of the Minister of Youth.* Nashville: Convention, 1982. 110 pp.

> Looks at the youth minister from six perspectives and investigates the calling and job descriptions of minsters of youth.

pr Taylor, Jack R. *The Hallelujah Factor.* Nashville: Broadman, 1983. 184 pp.

> Provides a biblical foundation for worship and praise that the author sees is missing from many churches. Foci are on both corporate and personal praise; both are applicable to youth ministry.

cr "Tuning into Television," *Media and Values* (Summer/Fall 1987).

> Special issue on television and its affect on society. A summary of the value and power of television helpful as a discussion piece for youth and adult study groups.

r *United States Education in Human Sexuality for Christians: Guidelines for Discussion and Planning.* Washington, D.C.: USCC, 1981. 118 pp.

> Guidelines for the church's responsibility in supplementing and carrying forward sexuality education which begins in the home. Emphasizes Christian morality from a Catholic perspective. Aimed at educators and planners. Age-level characteristics and desirable emphases for youth appear in chapters 2 and 3.

ar Varenhorst, Barbara B. *Real Friends: Becoming the Friend You'd Like to Have.* New York: Harper & Row, 1983. 160 pp.

> Written to and for youth, this book is helpful in developing a peer counseling strategy in various settings.

pr Van Pelt, Rick. *Intensive Care.* Grand Rapids, Mich.: Zondervan, 1988.

> A basic introduction to the need for crisis intervention with youth with numerous helps for doing crisis intervention. A crash course in crisis counseling and the setting up of such a program in one's church.

p Veerman, David R. *Youth Evangelism.* Wheaton, Ill.: Victor, 1988. 214 pp.

> A basic and sane approach to doing youth evangelism for both youth and youth workers.

a _____. *Reaching Kids Before High School: A Guide to Junior High Ministry.* Wheaton, Ill.: Victor, 1990. 203pp.

> The often overlooked early adolescent age group comes into sharp focus. This is a book of basic principles and practical insights for working with these youth and their parents, and building a program to reach them.

opr Verkuyl, Gerrit, and Harold E. Garner. *Enriching Teen-age Worship.* Chicago: Moody, 1950. 192 pp.

A classic text on helping adolescents appreciate and plan worship experiences.

a Vincent, John J. *The Jesus Thing: An Experiment in Discipleship.* Nashville: Abingdon, 1973. 123 pp.

Describes communities of young people interested in doing the deeds of Jesus, but uninterested in the church for its own sake.

ao Warren, Michael. *A Future for Youth Catechesis.* New York: Paulist, 1975. 113 pp.

Addressed to volunteer catechists; aimed at helping them understand why and how to lead young people to faith. Describes models of youth catechesis and considers the role of the catechist.

a Warren, Michael. *Youth and the Future of the Church: Ministry with Youth and Young Adults.* New York: Seabury, 1982. 148 pp.

Focused around twin themes of spirituality and culture, the book proposes a wholistic youth ministry aimed at character and ideal development and empowerment, rather than simply activity programing.

ao ———. *Youth, Gospel, Liberation.* San Francisco: Harper & Row, 1987. 138 pp.

An analysis of the impact on youth of social structures and forces. Moving from history through work with a Youth for Peace team toward a projection for the future, Warren offers a working document for the present situation.

ao Warren, Michael, ed. *Readings and Resources in Youth Ministry.* Winona, Minn.: St. Mary's, 1987. 254 pp.

In part, this is a reissue of pertinent material from two earlier Warren texts: *Youth Ministry: A Book of Readings,* and *Resources for Youth Ministry.* In part it also presents new material and the author's own recent reflections on such phenomena as social reality and such issues as social justice.

r Watts, Richard G. *Straight Talk About Death with Young People.* Philadelphia: Westminster, 1975. 92 pp.

Describes experiences in discussion groups with young adolescents which isolated their questions, concerns, and fears about death. Aimed at answering the questions and meeting the concerns of young people.

pr Webber, Robert E. *Worship Is a Verb.* Waco, Tex.: Word, 1985. 224 pp.

Focuses on the adoration and worship of Christ with biblical foundations for doing so and with practical helps to actually accomplish it.

pr Winn, Albert Curry. *You and Your Lifework.* Chicago: Science Research Associates, 1963. 90 pp.

    A study book to help young people make decisions about their lifework, and to see the relation between their faith and their jobs. References dated, but a classic approach to understanding youth's relation to vocation.

a Woods, Ray, ed. *New Covenant Community: A Model for Ministry with Youth in the United Presbyterian Church, USA.* Philadelphia: Geneva, 1977. 81 pp.

    Describes a model for doing ministry with youth in congregations and a structured fellowship program called "Fellowship of the Carpenter."

ag Wyckoff, D. Campbell, and Don Richter, eds. *Religious Education Ministry with Youth.* Birmingham, Ala.: Religious Education Press, 1982. 257 pp.

    Report of a Lilly project aimed at recommitment of churches to youth ministry. Contains a survey of findings about youth and youth work in the church, and perspective papers lifting up essential elements for the future of youth ministry. Systematic reflection links together the papers and outcomes and future directions of the work.

aopr Yaconelli, Mike and Jim Burns. *High School Ministry.* Grand Rapids, Mich.: Zondervan, 1986. 301 pp.

    A general and helpful overview of youth ministry with middle adolescents.

ag Zuck, Roy B., and Warren S. Benson, eds. *Youth Education in the Church.* Chicago: Moody, 1978. 478 pp.

    A mature presentation of evangelical youth ministry by notable teachers, practitioners, and leaders of youth.

JOURNALS

Group: The Youth Ministries Magazine, Box 202, Mt. Morris, IL 60154.

Youthworker: The Contemporary Journal of Youth Ministry, Youth Specialties, Inc., 1224 Greenfield Drive, El Cajon, CA 92021.

Youthworker Update, Youth Specialities, Inc., 1224 Greenfield Drive, El Cajon, CA 92021.

Various denominations also publish journals and newsletters for youth workers. Likewise, various publishers of youth curricular materials also publish youth worker catalogues and, sometimes, newsletters.

Notes

Chapter Three: The Youth Worker

1. William Myers, *Theological Themes of Youth Ministry* (New York: Pilgrim, 1987), 35–37.
2. *Youthworker Update* (June 1988): 1.
3. *Group* (March 1990): 9.
4. *Journal of Early Adolescence* (Fall 1986), as reported in *Youthworker Update* (May 1987): 3.
5. *Youthletter* (October 1984): 75.
6. Elisabeth Elliot, *Shadow of the Almighty: The Life & Testament of Jim Elliot* (New York: Harper & Brothers, 1958), 247.
7. Disequilibration is that sense of inner dissonance or imbalance that causes a person to seek for resolution of an internal conflict between what is already known and some new data and/or experience that does not fit the old. Disequilibration is the inner motivation for a learner to accommodate new data and experiences into personal, internal categories. By so doing, a learner moves from disequilibration to equilibration, from dissonance to a harmonious balance, from conflict to resolution. The desire to turn disequilibration into equilibration is what causes learning to occur.
8. Warren Bennis, *On Becoming a Leader* (Reading, Mass.: Addison-Wesley, 1989), 45–46.
9. *Campus Life Leader's Guide* (February 1985).

Chapter Four: Teaching Youth

1. Jean Piaget, *The Psychology of Education and the Psychology of the Child* (New York: Viking, 1971), 145.

Chapter Five: Worship

1. Gerrit Verkuyl, *Enriching Teen-Age Worship* (Chicago: Moody, 1950), 28–30.
2. For the youth worker who may not know what various colors mean, the following is a brief explanation, along with the appropriate seasons for the use of each color: (1) Red means loyalty, zeal, Pentecost; it can be used year-round if no color change is made. (2) White is for joy, victory in Christ, Christmastime and Eastertime, Days of Epiphany and Trinity Sunday, baptism, weddings, communion. (3) Green stands for life and growth; Kingdomtime (the time near Advent) and undesignated times when following Epiphany (the coming of the Magi and Jesus' first revelation to the Gentiles) and Pentecost. (4) Purple is for humility and penitence; preparatory season of Advent and Lent. (5) Black is for mourning, Good Friday,

funerals; church called to humiliation and prayer. (6) Maroon is used when only one color is available.

Chapter Six: Fellowship

1. Wick Broomall, "Fellowship," in Everett Harrison, ed., *Dictionary of Theology* (Grand Rapids, Mich.: Baker, 1960), 218–19.
2. Dietrich Bonhoeffer, *Life Together* (New York: Harper, 1954), 21.
3. Ibid., 25.

Chapter Seven: Expression

1. Roy B. Zuck, *Success Tips for Youth Leaders* (Wheaton, Ill.: Scripture Press, 1966), 5.
2. Personal letter.
3. Ibid.
4. Ibid.

Chapter Eight: Leadership Development

1. Bernard M. Bass, *Stogdill's Handbook of Leadership* (New York: Free Press, 1981), 72.
2. I am indebted to Jay A. Conger's thoughts in his book *The Charismatic Leader* (San Francisco: Jossey-Bass, 1989) for some of these characteristics. However, their expression here is my own.

Chapter Ten: Camp and Retreats

1. *Guiding Principles for Christian Camping* (Chicago: National Sunday School Association, Camp Commission, 1962), 27–28.

Index